WHERE MOTLEY IS WORN

TRANSNATIONAL IRISH LITERATURES

WHERE MOTLEY IS WORN

TRANSNATIONAL IRISH LITERATURES

Amanda Tucker and **Moira E. Casey**
EDITORS

CORK
cup
UNIVERSITY
PRESS

Published in 2014 by
Cork University Press
Youngline Industrial Estate
Pouladuff Road, Togher
Cork, Ireland

British Library Cataloguing in Publication Data
A CIP catalogue record for this book is available from the British Library.

ISBN: 978-1-78205-100-8

Printed and bound by CPI Group (UK) Ltd, Croydon, CR0 4YY

CONTENTS

National and transnational Irish literatures

AMANDA TUCKER and MOIRA CASEY

Yeats's poems have had a curious reincarnation as the titles of other authors' works, Chinua Achebe's powerful novel *Things Fall Apart* being the most notable example. We too are borrowing from Yeats: 'where motley is worn' comes from a lesser-known line of 'Easter 1916'. Of the many great poets and poems that Ireland has produced, perhaps none has a firmer position in the Irish canon than Yeats's 'Easter 1916'. The poem's canonical status cannot just be credited to Yeats's aesthetic powers, but also to its subject matter: the Easter Rising was a formative event in establishing Irish independence and continues to hold a prominent place in the Irish cultural narrative. For us, however, 'motley' is a symbol of the complexities and contradictions of transnational Irish literature. The image suggests both fragmentation and amalgamation: a diversity of traditions, beliefs, and values can be united through national feeling—that is, 'wherever green is worn'. Motley thus represents a rich tapestry of different cultures and traditions that the Irish-born—be they in Dublin or Dubai—and non-Irish born alike help to invent and re-invent. Though it might be overlooked, the motley element has been present in Irish culture for some time, rather than belonging solely to the contemporary moment.

In this collection, we use the phrase 'transnational Irish literature' to denote writing that places Irish identity in dialogue with other cultural, national, or ethnic affiliations. Transnational Irish literature is invested in the multiple points of identification and belonging that result from a writer's commitment to Ireland, to other countries, and to the world at large. A transnational approach can complement and supplement our understanding of 'national literature', a concept that by definition is limiting. National literature necessitates the creation of borders, so that the principles and preoccupations of Irish literature are distinguished from those of other countries. In this way, national canons effectively reduce the complexities of national life and, over time, can become prescriptive as to what defines a country's chief characteristics and values. Consequently, national literature places national culture in an oddly timeless and ahistorical state: since national literature becomes something like a collective unconscious for the people occupying the nation, it often assumes an affixed, changeless quality. Paul Gilroy, for instance, notes that 'the defense of communal interests has often mobilised the fantasy of a frozen culture, of arrested cultural development. Particularity can be maintained and communal interests protected if they are fixed in their most authentic and glorious postures of resistance. This understandable but inadequate response … reduces cultural traditions to the simple process of invariant repetition'.[1] As a result, authors and literary works that do not meet already established criteria—let alone those that directly challenge traditional understandings of national life—are either neglected or regarded with suspicion.

The mid-twentieth-century author Kate O'Brien provides a useful example of how selections of an author's work become absorbed into or ejected from the Irish canon. O'Brien was one of the first Irish writers to pay sustained attention to lesbian and queer sexuality, and her most important work is probably her last and best novel, *As Music and Splendour*, which follows two young Irish girls who become opera singers in Rome. This novel follows a trajectory that was well-established in her earlier novels: an Irish female protagonist leaves Ireland in order to pursue emotional, intellectual, and sexual freedom abroad. Despite this recurring trope, O'Brien remains best known as the author of *The Land of Spices*, one of her few novels to take place in Ireland and which itself is frequently called a female version of *Portrait of the Artist as a Young Man*. In this manner, Ireland's literary canon almost seems to reproduce itself.

In this collection, we want to move away from the idea of Irish literature as a nation-centred literature. In Ireland, this nation-centred focus has often established a close relationship between literature and politics. From the birth of the Irish-language *aisling* tradition in the eighteenth century to the Young Ireland movement in the 1840s and the Northern Ireland Irish Literary Renaissance in the 1960s, Ireland's literary movements have been intertwined with its political agendas. In particular, Irish literature during the first part of the twentieth century became nearly inextricably linked to cultural politics; John Wilson Foster argues that the Irish Literary Revival 'developed a synthetic and triumphantly eloquent cultural nationalism; it formulated a definition not only of Irish literature but of Irish culture and Irish nationalism'.[2] We do not aim to remove the political impetus of Irish literature; rather, we want to re-orient the political beyond the nation. Through a transnational framework—that is, through sustained attention to the social, cultural, and political relationships that those with ties to Ireland have formed beyond national borders—we want to uncover the longstanding history of Irish multiculturalism and hybridity that has been neglected in traditional canon formation. We also hope to show

how the notion of national literature in Ireland (and at its heart, the white Gaelic monolith) have created inequities for those who have Irish affiliations but do not fit into this traditional model—inequities that are revealed in Irish literature and have real-world counterparts in Ireland.

One advantage of a transnational approach is that it allows us to compare and connect issues that we tend to divide along national/global lines. In Irish Studies, for instance, we find it helpful to think about multiculturalism (typically conceived within the nation) in connection with diaspora (usually conceived as outside or beyond national borders). Irish multiculturalism and the Irish diaspora are both issues of growing public interest and academic inquiry over the last two decades, and the ideologies that surround them provide a fitting example of the kinds of complexities that a transnational approach can illuminate. On the one hand, the Irish diaspora has significantly widened the geographical parameters of Irish culture; however, it has also served to function as a sort of de-territorialised nationalism—especially in its popular incarnations. As Floya Anthias has argued, 'the concept of diaspora, whilst focusing on transnational processes and commonalities, does so by deploying a version of 'ethnicity' which privileges the point of origin in constructing identity and solidarity'.[3] First, diaspora often reinforces the idea of belonging based upon blood ties and heredity—so that an eighth-generation Irish-American belongs but an Afro-Irish migrant living in Dublin does not. Moreover, the Irish diaspora in particular has served as what Breda Gray calls 'a reassuring site of cultural preservation'.[4] Indeed, we might question how the Irish diaspora became part of public consciousness through media like President Mary Robinson's political speeches and the erection of Famine memorials in the 1990s—almost exactly as inward migration during the Celtic Tiger was making Ireland more diverse. It is through such re-direction of geopolitical affiliations that, as Martin Mac An Ghaill has argued, 'the Republic of Ireland seems to have found it relatively easy to move from a closed to an open, global economy, while maintaining a closed society'.[5] In this way, diaspora allows Ireland to be global in theory and insular in practice.

A similar double bind is reflected in Ireland's relationship to multiculturalism. On the one hand, the country seemed to embrace multiculturalism during the Celtic Tiger. But the widely accepted version of Irish multiculturalism focuses more on global consumption than interpersonal engagement, with migrants being viewed as 'factors of production rather than as human beings with rich and vibrant cultural resources who could contribute not only to the globalised Irish economy but to the development of a cosmopolitan Irish society'.[6] Through facile celebrations of clothing and cooking, people can pretend to be cosmopolitan and multicultural without ever having to think about structural inequalities based on race, ethnicity, and nationality. Moreover, these superficial invocations of multiculturalism tend to ignore previous failures of Irish multiculturalism. In the early twentieth century, for instance, Jewish migration in Limerick ended in ethnic-based violence.[7] Travellers, despite their long history in Ireland, have faced widespread discrimination and harassment: 'State responses to Travellers continue to be characterised by monoculturalism and to be dominated by ideological goals of assimilation notwithstanding the emergence of a new discourse of inclusion and integration'.[8] Based on this history, Bryan Fanning and Ronit Lentin have been particularly adamant that Irish multiculturalism has been nothing more than a shallow tolerance of cross-cultural difference. A transnational approach reveals the parallel shortcomings of diaspora and multiculturalism as theory versus practice. It can also provide an avenue through which to explore a more genuine cross-cultural engagement: for instance, instead of looking at Irish emigrants as part of a victimised diaspora, we might instead consider how they participated in the multicultures of their adopted homelands.

Yet there seems to be some interest in transnational Ireland in the wake of the 2008 global recession. Since the economic collapse, Irish citizens seem to have become less interested in even shallow versions of multiculturalism or social integration, and Irish migrants themselves often serve as scapegoats for the economic downturn. Polls and surveys show that Irish-born citizens feel that immigrants are taking 'their' jobs and should go back to their countries of origin—which suggests that returning to an 'authentic and glorious posture' of Irish nationalism will somehow restore the country's economic prosperity.[9] We oppose this viewpoint and argue that transnationalism will continue to be central to Irish culture for the foreseeable future. Data from the 2011 census finds that seventeen per cent of people currently living in Ireland were not born there, a dramatic increase from the 2006 census statistics.[10] Moreover, the formation of various support networks and institutions—such as Dublin's Centre for Creative Practices and the Northern Ireland Community of Refugees and Asylum Seekers, to name just two—has made it impossible to dismiss contemporary Irish migration as a transient issue.

Indeed, we believe that the global recession forces us to pay more attention to the cultural, political, and ethical dynamics of Irish transnationalism. In 2006, Ronit Lentin and Robbie McVeigh argued that racism had become institutionalised in contemporary Irish society; they assert that the 2004 Citizenship Referendum marked Ireland's transition from a racial state, in which '"race" and "nation" are defined in terms of each other', to a racist state, in which 'the totalising control over the individual is enforced by the state in its efforts to render the population under its jurisdiction racially coherent'.[11] After the 2008 economic downturn, suspicion and outright hostility towards Irish migrants increased. While the UK and Australia approve ninety per cent of citizenship applications, the Irish government approves little more than half.[12] Asylum seekers have not fared any better: in 2007, ten per cent of refugees were granted asylum; in 2010, only 1.5 per cent of refugees were. (For comparison's sake, the average rate in the European Union is twenty-seven per cent.)[13] Racism has also become more pervasive and explicit. In particular, black Africans in all forms of community life are especially vulnerable to harassment and violence; yet seventy-six per cent will not report their experiences for fear of retribution or of weakening their chances at permanent residency.[14] Regardless of Ireland's economic status, race and migration—key areas in a transnational approach—will continue to be significant not only as academic issues but as social justice concerns. While Fanning, Lentin, and other scholars working in the social sciences have examined the complexities and contradictions surrounding migration both in and out of Ireland, less progress in this area has been made in Irish literary studies than one might wish. It is crucial that such work be done, for writing has played an undeniably integral role in constructing an Irish national consciousness, both at home and abroad. Given the overwhelming success of Irish writers in the literary arena, academic institutions outside of Ireland often focus their attention on literary giants like Yeats or Joyce, thereby reinforcing the need for scholars who can teach canonical figures. A transnational methodology is therefore necessary in order to re-conceptualise Irish literary studies.

Although it is a thriving area of research across multiple disciplines, transnational studies is more often characterised by debate rather than by consensus. What we propose to do here is to outline the major issues and controversies in the field in order to contextualise our own transnational approach. One of the key issues at stake is how transnationalism is related to, and yet distinct from, globalisation. The two terms are often used together, and transnationalism is most commonly understood as the cultural counterpart of the economic forces of globalisation. Scholars within globalisation studies are often assumed to prioritise an exclusively materialist view: after all, one of the first uses of the term was to describe the practices of international businesses and corporations. Transnational studies scholars, on the other hand, are seen as employing approaches from cultural studies in order to focus on multidirectional flows of cultures and social networks. This essentialising dichotomy is of course problematic, given that economic concerns cannot easily be separated from cultural ones. Cultural elements, including identities and values, are not simply abstract ideas or feelings; they are goods that can be bought and sold across borders. And 'authentic and glorious postures' tend to sell very well: as Sean Kay comments, 'Irishness' is a high-value commodity across global brands—I would buy it as a (very) long-term investment'.[15] Because of the interrelationship of culture and commodities, the delineation between globalisation/economics and transnationalism/culture studies seems unproductive.

If the subject matter of transnational studies and globalisation studies cannot be precisely divided, what does separate the former from the latter? For Nadje Ali-Ali and Khalid Koser, transnationalism's focus on the interplay between the nation and the world distinguishes it from globalisation: 'Whereas global processes are often de-centered from specific national territories, transnational processes are anchored in but also transcend one or more nation-states'.[16] For some critics, the persistence of the nation-state within such processes has been seen as problematic. Ulf Hannerz has criticised what he sees as the ironic tendency of transnationalism to draw attention to the continued significance of the national.[17] Certainly the notion of a collection of essays focusing on transnational *Irish* literature would seem to pull us back, time and again, to Irish national identity. But as other scholars working in transnational studies have shown, the dynamic between the nation and the world expands national affiliations and re-conceptualises national identities. Inderpal Grewal, one of the leading figures of transnational feminism, asserts that 'nationalism itself has proved to be protean and mobile, providing identities and affiliations to mobile as well as settled subjects'.[18] Because cultural and political nationalism—protean though they may be—have been such major issues in Irish literature, we feel that transnationalism, as opposed to globalisation, will be particularly productive in Irish Studies. Indeed, a transnational approach allows us to see how Irish nationalism was formed alongside commitments to other nationalist or imperialist causes, like the Boer War or the Indian Independence Movement.[19] Despite the prominence of an inwardly focused nationalism in Ireland, these types of commitments beyond the native shore indicate a broader, more global outlook.

Moreover, the ability of Irish historical figures like Arthur Griffith, Roger Casement, and John Mitchel to assume multiple national affiliations hinges on imaginative reach. There has been recent interest, across multiple fields, in how increased interconnectivity occurs not simply through physical movement but also through creative endeavours. Scholars working in globalisation and transnational studies have repeatedly emphasised the importance of the imagination in constructing global cultures. In his groundbreaking work, *Modernity at Large*, Arjun Appadurai builds upon Benedict Anderson's notion of imagined national communities to posit that, given the widespread technological advances in recent years, people can envision multiple possible lives that they can inhabit to a much greater extent—creating an increasing number of crosscultural and transcultural affiliations.[20] Moreover, Grewal deploys the concept of transnational connectivities to show how these connectivities not only 'enable communication across boundaries and borders', but also shape people's identities and affiliations.[21] For Grewal, the communication fostered by these connectivities impacts subjects who may never physically cross borders but who are nonetheless shaped by the imaginative processes of transnationalism. Kwame Anthony Appiah similarly emphasises the role of creative works in forging transnational connections, asserting that 'conversations across boundaries of identity—whether national, religious, or something else—begin with the sort of imaginative engagement you get when you read a novel or watch a movie or attend to a work of art that speaks to some place other than your own'.[22]

This idea of transnationalism as an imaginative and creative practice has opened up transnational studies to those working in the humanities. Peter Hitchcock has argued for the centrality of the humanities, and in particular, literary studies, within transnationalism, and he laments that 'as long as culture engages in imaginative processes, the marginalisation of the literary or its reduction to sociological method seriously underestimates the value of the literary for knowledge'.[23] In his emphasis on creativity, Hitchcock insists that transnational studies should involve not only quantitative but also qualitative analysis—including the close and careful examination of literary works. Literary texts not only serve as representations of transnational subjects and themes related to cross-border movements, networks, and affiliations; they become transnational connectivities themselves. In *Globalization and Literature*, Suman Gupta puts Hitchcock's theories into practice by examining the narrative performance of Richard Powers' novel, *Plowing the Dark*, about the creation of a virtual reality simulator. After close reading a passage from the novel, Gupta outlines how literature offers a different perspective of globalisation. His insights are worth repeating at length:

> Mediations take place through a descriptive language that is not transparent but curiously opaque, drawing attention to itself. Within the carefully crafted descriptions, clearly visualizable metaphors and barely visualizable technical abstractions are negotiated …
>
> Language is used to perform and convey something about the intellectual scope and aesthetic simulation of ideas of globalisation. This language is not as precise and systematic as the scholarly language in which globalisation is usually discussed. And what is conveyed of globalisation is not quite as well-ordered as academic texts about globalisation—it is impressionistic. Yet what is conveyed is suggestive. The quotation of Powers's novel could be thought of as a snap-shot literary apprehension of globalisation.[24]

From Gupta's perspective, the close and careful analysis of literary texts allows us to see the multi-faceted processes of globalisation. Literary works like Powers' novel represent globalisation through 'impress-ionistic' means that emphasise the aesthetic and the personal; as such, they offer a perspective different from quantitative research. Gupta never privileges literary studies' relationship to globalisation at the expense of other disciplines, but he does demonstrate how the humanities might play a crucial role in understanding global circulations. Through an investigation of the ways in which writing embodies and portrays transnational experiences, literary studies can offer a new dimension to globalisation and transnational studies; in particular they can offer insight into the lived experiences of individuals confronting these phenomena.

Disciplinary differences don't simply produce diverse perspectives; they offer alternate understandings of what and where transnationalism is. In the social sciences, transnationalism is distinguished from globalisation because the former is seen solely as a contemporary phenomenon. Transnational studies scholars working in sociology, such as Alejandro Portes and Nina Schiller, agree that increased access to technological advancements like electronic communications and inexpensive airfares and the increasingly global circulation of capital distinguish the present era from earlier epochs. Schiller, one of the first to use the term 'transmigrant' in order to highlight the differences between contemporary migrants and their ancestors, argues that these factors 'maintain or construct anew transnational interconnections that differ in their intensity and significance from the home ties maintained by past migrations'.[25] The emphasis on transnationalism as a contemporary phenomenon relies on concrete and material circumstances; however, this notion of transnationalism differs markedly from most conceptions of globalisation. For instance in his seminal work on the global field, Roland Robertson begins his outline of globalisation in the early fifteenth century.[26] Of course, even those who acknowledge the long history of globalisation tend to agree with David Held, who admits that the present day is 'distinguished by some unique organisational features, creating a world in which the extensive reach of human relations and networks is matched by its relative high intensity, high velocity and high impact propensity across many facets of social life'.[27]

To a large extent, this distinction between globalisation and transnationalism depends in part on discipline: while those working in the social sciences seem divided over the issue, scholars in the humanities (and in particular, those working in literary studies) generally take a longer view of transnationalism. A quick glance through the MLA International Bibliography uncovers essays on transnationalism during the Middle Ages, in the work of Shakespeare, and in the eighteenth-century novel. Perhaps what is most compelling about this longer approach is that it historicises transnationalism. As Grewal argues in *Transnational America*, 'gender, race, and nationalism are produced by contemporary culture in a transnational framework that is linked to earlier histories of colonisation'.[28] Like Grewal, we agree that there is no way to talk about transnationalism in the contemporary moment without engaging transnational histories. Transnational studies in the humanities provide a framework to view the increasingly interconnected nature of the world, but it also acts as an umbrella term that allows us to see the nuances and ambivalences of cross-cultural contact that do not fit into the traditional practices of colonialism and diaspora.

THE TRANSNATIONAL TURN IN IRISH STUDIES

A historical approach to transnationalism allows us to see how the discipline of Irish Studies has changed and how these changes fit with larger developments in academia, especially Western academia. Paul Jay has drawn a parallel between the broadening of methodological approaches—including the widening of the literary canon—over the last several decades and the increasingly diverse faculty in higher education. According to Jay, the rise of theoretical approaches such as feminist studies, postcolonial studies, and transnational studies 'was the predictable effect of dramatic demographic changes produced by social justice movements that began in the streets and ended in the courts'.[29] At its core, a transnational methodology requires the recognition of the structural inequalities that global flows create and in which they participate. From their initial groundbreaking work on transnational feminism, Grewal and Caren Kaplan insist on this political dimension. For Grewal and Kaplan, transnational feminism 'signals attention to uneven and dissimilar circuits of culture and capital' and enables 'the links between patriarchies, colonialisms, racisms and other forms of domination [to] become more apparent and available for critique or appropriation'.[30] Grewal and Kaplan further argue that transnational studies help us to explain 'the asymmetries of the globalisation process'.[31] Thus transnational studies shares in common with other interdisciplinary areas such as gender and sexuality studies and race and ethnic studies, a desire to examine the objectives and the often unspoken political agendas of academic fields of study.

A historically expansive definition of transnationalism has the potential to help us become conscious of how Irish Studies as an academic field has directly or indirectly embraced certain ideologies about the Irish nation and Irish affiliations. In its earliest formation, Irish Studies as an academic discipline focused on a very narrow group of Irish writers who had won international fame and were not only of Irish origin but whose literary works had a direct connection to Ireland. Even well-known writers like Beckett or Wilde were not often considered to be under the purview of Irish Studies because their material was not 'Irish' enough. Of course, since then, these authors have been reclaimed into an Irish literary canon in works like *Beckett: The Irish Dimension* or *Oscar Wilde: The Importance of Being Irish*. As these titles indicate, criticism in this vein makes a direct connection to a writer's greatness and his national origins; this scholarship thus conforms to a nation-centred approach to Irish literature and culture.

But by and large, it is the scholars within Irish Studies who pursue this agenda. To this day, many members of associations like the American Conference for Irish Studies trace their scholarly interests to their own Irish-American ancestry. This mindset creates problems of belonging for those who decide to pursue this academic field for reasons other than biological affiliation: Cheryl Herr, for example, describes herself as 'someone who is not of Irish extraction and who has often been made to feel uncomfortable for my lack of "a real reason" to study Ireland'. She decries the centrality of Irish identity and identification within scholarship and academic enterprises around Ireland, asking when will 'phantasmal authenticity finally emerge from the Celtic twilight and allow the light of day to disperse its hold on Irish Studies?'[32] Herr's insightful essay raises provocative questions about the relationship between personal identity and academic interest and how the former may (or may not) shape the latter. Continued questions of authenticity will perhaps always be a point of debate in Irish Studies or indeed, any 'area' studies.

In the ten years since Herr's essay was published, there *have* been developments and changes within the field that reflect not only an increasing interest in social justice but also its own demographic shifts. One of the most prominent has been the changing dynamic of gender. As larger numbers of women join the ranks of faculty in higher education, Irish Studies has transformed from a primarily male-dominated field to one with an increased and increasing percentage of female scholars; subsequently, issues of gender have become a more sustained area of scholarly investigation. The controversy over the exclusion of female authors in the *Field Day Anthology*—and ultimately, the addition of Volumes IV and V, which focus solely on women's writing—provides the most celebrated example of this development, and over the last two decades, a considerable body of scholarship about gender and sexuality in Irish culture has been produced.[33]

But when compared to other fields, this emphasis on gender within

Irish Studies seems rather belated. This is not to criticise the scholarship itself, which is vital and exciting, but rather to suggest that Irish Studies as a field of study has been curiously resistant to new approaches and areas of inquiry. The same can be said of the transnational turn in Irish Studies. In particular, while many other disciplines seem to have made the transition from a focus on postcolonialism to globalisation (which would still encompass colonial interrelations), Irish Studies seems to be reluctant to relinquish its postcolonial focus. One consequence of associating itself with postcolonial focus is that Irish studies has been able to ignore the racial privilege that 'white' races like the Irish are accorded but that is denied to colonial subjects from Africa or the Caribbean. Yet as Steve Garner so cogently argues in *Race and the Irish Experience*, race has been a central concept in Irish national identity and belonging.[34] Postcolonial approaches to Irish Studies have at times ignored the ways in which cross-colonial comparisons of Ireland with other racialised groups have benefitted the Irish. Suzanna Chan points out, for instance, that 'so long as the Negrito, Hottentot and Aboriginal were configured as the lowermost rung on the ladder of racial development, they could underscore the Irish as "white"'.[35] Yet it is only relatively recently that race has become a serious and sustained topic of discussion in Irish Studies. Transnationalism allows us to explore the relational and situated nature of racialised identity, particularly as it intersects with nationality.

To be clear, there have been efforts to widen the parameters of Irish Studies since its formation. Several decades after the American Conference for Irish Studies (ACIS) was founded, the Irish Studies Association of Australia and New Zealand (ISAANZ), the Society for Irish Latin American Studies (SILAS), and the Japan branch of the International Association for the Study of Irish Literatures (IASIL) were brought into being. Also, within the past several years, the conference themes as well as individual panels at the meetings of IASIL, ACIS, and the European Federation of Irish Centres and Studies (EFACIS) have repeatedly emphasised the field's global connections.[36] Individual scholars have also worked to move beyond a nation-centred focus. One of the most important developments has been the arrival of the interdisciplinary journal, *Translocations: The Irish Race, Migration and Social Transformation Review*, which published its first issue in 2006, and individual scholars like John Brannigan, Gerardine Meaney, and Pilar Villar Argaiz have made important contributions to the study of race and migration in Irish literature.[37]

In the public and political spheres, it has become common to establish Ireland's position in past and present global networks. During the time of mass inward migration to Ireland, politicians and bureaucrats frequently cited Ireland's large diaspora as proof of the country's receptiveness to multiculturalism. Former Minister of Integration, Conor Lenihan, for instance, commented that 'there's an emotional sense of understanding about what immigrants are going through because of our experience as immigrants'.[38] Prominent Irish cultural commentators and critics express a similar desire. In *The Irish Writer and the World*, Kiberd stresses the need for reinterpretation of the Irish canon in multicultural terms and he argues that 'it is time to imagine just how the son of a Brazilian worker in a midlands meat factory might read *Gulliver's Travels* or how the daughter of Nigerian immigrants might respond to *Dancing at Lughnasa*'.[39] While this remark indicates that Irish immigrants can relate to the Irish canon, it still privileges traditional Irish authors, rather than allowing new voices into the canon: Irish migrants can be readers, but not writers.

At times, public declarations like these seem little more than hollow attempts at political correctness rather than any genuine desire to change the nation-centred Gaelic monolith that still lies at the heart of Irish culture. Indeed, elsewhere Kiberd seems deliberately to privilege the Irish experience over the non-Irish-born migrants. Rather than simply pointing to exile as a common thread between Irish citizens and Irish immigrants, Kiberd somewhat bizarrely depicts exile as though it were a competition that the Irish have already won. He claims that 'if the migrant is a sign of the modern, then the Irish were modern earlier than most peoples, enduring the fate of uprooting, of learning a new language, of leaving a Neolithic civilization and settling into modern conurbations'.[40] Through its neglect of global social networks, this statement curiously individualises, even personifies, the nation: migration becomes a tool to delineate central and peripheral nations, the winners and losers of history. As this example attests, the historical development of Irish Studies cannot be read as moving from a relatively closed to an open field. Nor can we subscribe to a progressive view of Irish culture that sees the country as dramatically transforming from insularity to highly globalised multiculturalism, for such a reading overlooks important complexities and contradictions in the past and present Irish culture, as the essays in this collection attest. Indeed, one of the distinct advantages of a transnational approach is its ability to uncover the multiple and the messy versions of Irish literary culture that lie beneath the surface of a national literature.

TRANSNATIONAL IRISH LITERATURE

We conclude by demonstrating what a transnational approach to Irish literature might look like and, in particular, how reading past and present Irish literary texts alongside one another offers a more nuanced understanding of both. As stated above, we understand globalisation and transnationalism to be long-standing historical phenomena rather than being rooted in a contemporary moment. At the same time, we want to be sensitive to the particular nature of contemporary globalisation. As such, we begin with a contemporary example of transnational Irish literature, Roddy Doyle's *The Deportees*, which will lead us into an example from an earlier era. *The Deportees* is undoubtedly the most famous work in contemporary Irish multiculturalism. Although Doyle has enjoyed critical and commercial success as a novelist for over two decades, his reputation has changed in recent years. Due to his monthly contributions to *Metro Éireann*—collected in *The Deportees* (2007)—and his adaptation of *The Playboy of the Western World* (co-written with Bisi Adigun, founder of the Dublin-based African theatre company, Arambe), Doyle has become well-known as a writer and advocate for twenty-first-century Irish multiculturalism. Doyle's work, particularly the penultimate story in *The Deportees*, 'Home to Harlem', illustrates the promise and the pitfalls of the transnational turn in Irish Studies. Through its content, the story suggests how race and nationality alter according to geopolitical location: in other words, if culture travels, as James Clifford has argued, then so too do race and nation. These transformations occur on a collective as well as an individual level, and for Ireland, the migration and multi-culturalism in countries like America and Britain—countries that have become the home of Irish emigrants—have provided a lens through which to view Ireland's own diversity. As a material product, *The Deportees* reveals how racial and national privilege continues to shape discourse about cultural difference in Ireland.

'Home from Harlem' departs from the earlier stories in meaningful ways. Roughly half the stories feature a white, Irish-born protagonist while half feature an Irish migrant. The main character of 'Home to Harlem' crosses this divide; Declan is a mixed-race, Irish-born college student. This story is also the only one to take place outside of Ireland; as one can tell from the title, the story takes place in New York, where Declan is spending a semester abroad. Declan's academic objective is no less than to rewrite the master narrative of Irish literary history. While other literary scholars have investigated how Irish writers influenced the Harlem Renaissance, Declan wants to reverse this trajectory by proving that black American writers inspired Irish authors: 'Declan would prove that Harlem had kick-started Ireland's best writing of the twentieth-century—or at least some of it. And, if he couldn't do it, he'd cheat; he'd make it up. Yeats had died clutching his copy of *The New Negro*. Beckett never went to the jacks without *The Souls of Black Folk* under his arm'.[41] Humorous though this imagery may be, Declan's quest illustrates the political dimension to transnational studies: it not only works against conventional how-the-Irish-saved-civilisation readings; it also works against the type of scholarship that upholds white privilege by emphasising black artists' debt to white writers. Of course, it also links African American and Irish culture only through oppression — literally excrement and death.

Declan's thesis is intimately related to his quest for a better understanding of his own identity; while he is in New York, he searches for his African American grandfather, a WWII soldier with whom his grandmother had a brief relationship. Like many of the black writers he reads, Declan feels himself to be both an insider in Ireland—where he was born and has lived his entire life—and an outsider because he is black. Indeed, Declan's psychological state is perhaps best described in *The Souls of Black Folk*, in which Du Bois's theorises the notion of a double consciousness: a black American 'ever feels his twoness—an American, a Negro; two souls, two thoughts, two unreconciled strivings; two warring ideals in one dark body, whose dogged strength alone keeps it from being torn asunder'.[42] Once he is outside of Ireland, however, some of this tension dissolves, and in America, Declan has more freedom of choice regarding his affiliations. (Back home, Declan's mother always advocated for Declan to 'choose' to be white, since he has a lighter skin tone than hers.) In New York, his Irishness seems to mark him as different more than his blackness does. Declan dances in and out of Irishness, metaphorically wearing the green when he wishes. He accepts and even exploits his nationality one minute and resists it the next: though he hates the plastic paddy nature of Irish American identity, Declan cheerfully wears an Ireland hat and drinks Guinness to attract the attention of an American girl he likes. Geopolitical location clearly affects not only which ethnic or racial affiliation that Declan privileges, but also how he performs that identity.

What Declan ultimately desires, beyond academic achievement or female companionship, is an identity that feels less 'problematic' than being both black and Irish: at one point, he quotes Du Bois's question, 'How does it feel to be a problem?' Declan's questions about identity are further fuelled by his descent into history—both his own, as he attempts to find his grandfather, and America's vexed history with immigration and race. The narrative structure of 'Home to Harlem' allows readers to see the links between the struggles of a contemporary Irish-born man and the migrants from earlier periods and other cultures. For instance, Doyle intercuts a scene in which Declan interviews his potential grandfather with Declan's visit to Ellis Island, to show how the personal and the historical worlds of transnational movements are intertwined. In Declan's view, his national identity is at odds with his ethnicity, but the reader is led to consider how national identity itself has shifted and transformed through migration and change. Declan's personal feelings of dislocation eventually lead him to his thesis topic: he decides to study what it means to be Irish as represented in Irish literature, but he also wants to compare that notion of national identity to the Harlem Renaissance writers, who questioned what American national identity meant to them. Through Declan, Doyle is clearly poking fun at the notion of influence as well as the master narrative of Joycean and Yeatsian contributions to literature. He also calls for literary scholarship that will highlight inequalities of race, gender, and class and critically interrogate canons and their ideological underpinnings.

Although 'Home to Harlem' examines social and cultural issues clearly related to contemporary Ireland, its preoccupations have clear antecedents in earlier transnational Irish literature. Indeed, many of the rhetorical strategies and literary devices that Doyle uses in 'Home to Harlem' can be found in Goldsmith's *The Citizen of the World* (1762). As an Irish author writing a first-person narrative as a racialised other, Goldsmith utilises a similarly double-voiced perspective: *The Citizen of the World* offers his observations about English culture through the filter of Lien Chi, a visitor from China. In the eighteenth-century, writing from the perspective of an Asian narrator was an established trend—Montesquieu's *Persian Letters* (1721) being the most notable example —and can be viewed as symptomatic of European desire for Chinoiserie in all forms. Masquerading as Lien Chi also allows Goldsmith to critique various elements of English culture, ranging from gender relations to literary trends to foreign politics. And as James Watt asserts, Goldsmith 'uses Lien Chi here to voice a more explicitly ethical anti-imperialism'. In Letter VII, for instance, he tells a story about the kingdom of Lao in order to interpret colonialism as a purely avaricious and commercial move. Linking this history to present-day Europe, he admonishes that 'when a trading nation begins to act the conqueror, it is then perfectly undone'.[43] David Parker and others have pointed out that, in voicing these kinds of critiques through Lien Chi, Goldsmith also implies his own marginalised status as an Irishman in London. We might go so far as to suggest that the tentative connection between Ireland and Asia suggested here anticipates similar moves made by both Irish and Indian nationalists in the early twentieth century.[44]

In addition to suggesting this type of alliance, Goldsmith's double-voiced perspective, like Doyle's, also allows us to better appreciate the performative nature of racialised identity. On several occasions, Lien Chi is asked to essentially perform the role of exotic Other and refuses to do so, much to the dismay of his English hosts. In Letter IV, he recounts his visit to an unnamed 'lady of distinction', who praises the 'outlandish cut of his face' and the 'exotic cut of his forehead' while expressing a 'violent passion to see him eat' (pp. 13–14). Notably, these effusive comments come only *after* she has mistaken Lien Chi for an Englishman. She is later disappointed, not only because Lien Chi does not eat with chopsticks, but also because he refuses to confirm her own knowledge about China. Called upon to verify the various Chinoiserie around his host's abode, he instead gracefully points out her mistaken assumptions about Eastern culture. For instance, she asks him to praise her vast collection of 'Chinese' jars for being the proper shade of 'pea-green'. Lien Chi assumes that they are filled with tea, but his host assures him that they are 'empty and useless', as she insists is Chinese custom. Indeed, upon learning he is Chinese, she asks him for a 'pretty souvenir' from China, 'something one does not know what to do with' (p. 14). This scene clearly critiques how English society superficially commodifies Eastern culture. Yet the upper-class woman's attitude demonstrates that representations of culture are at times more powerful than realities: she is not interested in any genuine engagement with Lien Chi; she simply wants him to authenticate her own cosmopolitanism. In this way, Goldsmith demonstrates that what passes for cross-cultural exchange can often be shallow and one-sided.

Yet Lien Chi isn't a shining example of cosmopolitanism either. While Goldsmith uses the persona of Lien Chi to criticise England's superficial and consumptive understandings of the East, he also displays a lack of understanding of Chinese culture. For instance, at one point he refers to the 'Rajas' who attend upon the Chinese emperor. Moreover, throughout the letters, Goldmsith seems to purposefully drop the persona of Lien Chi in order to poke fun at Chinese customs. In the first letter, he pityingly describes Englishwomen as 'deprived of the allurements of feet no bigger than their thumbs'—a description that someone who valued small feet as a marker of beauty would not use. Moreover, because this description comes in the first letter, it sets up from the beginning for English readers a familiar perspective from which to view China. That this particular passage also mentions black teeth is unsurprising; in this way, it conforms to what Arjun Appadurai calls 'metonymic freezing', an ethnographic gaze that reduces an anthropological subject to one specific cultural aspect.[45] Beyond exoticising China, Goldsmith reinforces eighteenth-century Orientalism: at one point, Lien Chi refers to 'the Asiatic husband, who is justly jealous, because he knows himself to be impotent' (p. 52), and in another, he depicts the Chinese emperor as a tyrannical despot who seizes Lein Chi's land and family upon hearing of his travels to England. Here we can see the groundwork being laid for European imperialism in the East; China is portrayed as an emasculated, liberty-deprived nation in need of being saved from itself.

As this brief reading of *The Citizen of the World* shows, Goldsmith's transnationalism is complicated and contradictory. Yet its limitations also provide a way for us to approach more contemporary forms of Irish transnational literature: the double-voiced nature of Doyle's story shares some problematics with *The Citizen of the World*. While Declan feels something akin to writers like Du Bois and Claude McKay (to whom the story's title obviously refers), he lacks an understanding of contemporary racial politics in America, as a conversation with his African American thesis advisor demonstrates:

> It's hard being Irish, he tells the Professor. It's not like it is here.
>
> She does the over-the-glasses tick.

> You're not any less American, he tells her, because your people didn't come over on the fuckin' *Mayflower*.
>
> *My people*, she tells him,—came over on a *fucking* slave ship.
>
> There, he says. Exactly. And you're still American. (p. 212)

As Henry Louis Gates, Jr., Eric Sundquist, and others have argued, African American culture has, to a very large extent, defined American culture.[46] However, what Declan misses here is that black Americans are often seen as 'less' than white Americans, as the recent shootings of Trayvon Martin and Jordan Davis attest.[47] Like Goldsmith's Lien Chi, Declan misinterprets key elements in his adopted country.

Goldsmith's focus on consumption and the material contexts of transnationalism is also illuminating in thinking about how Doyle's *The Deportees* has been received in Irish culture. In particular, we might question Doyle's status as the poster child for Irish multiculturalism as well. Why does a white, Irish-born man assume that privilege rather than the multitude of Irish migrant creative writers? First of all, Doyle seems to have fewer problems publishing his work than other writers working in this area; certainly, *The Deportees* is the most easily accessible and therefore most well-known literary text on Irish multiculturalism. Moreover, the content of his stories presents an idealised, idyllic version of multiculturalism: their popularity resides in the fact that they ease cultural anxieties surrounding recent inward migration and its perceived threat to national culture.[48]

'Home to Harlem' ends with Declan safely ensconced in New York for the foreseeable future; his semester abroad may have ended, but his work on his thesis has just begun. As such, the one character in the story collection who is *both* Irish *and* a racial other leaves the country. This is not to deny Doyle's genuine desire to work with Irish multiculturalism; indeed, he seems to be one of the few writers who consider multiculturalism and social integration to be the responsibility of the Irish-born rather than a burden solely for the new Irish. Merely, we want to point out that Doyle's position as a spokesperson for Irish multiculturalism rests upon his own status as a white, Irish-born man. Although important work in contemporary multiculturalism has been recognised through things like the *Metro Éireann* Media and Multicultural Awards (MAMA), ironically, overseas, there is considerably less awareness about these contributions.[49] Like Declan, we would like to open up possibilities for cross-cultural comparisons, highlight the multidirectional influences of Irish writers and Irish-influenced writers, and continue the substantial work of liberating both Irish Studies and popular perceptions of Ireland from its nation-centred focus. We hope that with this book, we can not only imagine new transnational readings of Irish canonical writings but also bring to the fore some less canonical works that might be reclaimed in the interest of Irish transnational literature. We believe that the essays that follow do both.

The following essays are ordered in reverse chronological order. In 'To adapt or not to adapt', Bisi Adigun, a theatre director and playwright as well as a theatre scholar, discusses his personal and professional experiences with Arambe Productions, the Dublin-based African theatre group he founded in 2003. Best known for co-writing the 2007 adaptation of *The Playboy of the Western World*, Adigun explains how much of his success is based upon his development of an intercultural perspective, which for him involves being able to 'imbibe Irish artistic sensibilities without losing my Yoruba cultural identity'. For Adigun, adapting plays from one cultural context to another becomes a metaphor for the cross-cultural affiliations that migrants cultivate in their adopted countries. Theatre adaptation therefore creates a space not to passively reflect but to actively engage with a diverse, transnational Ireland.

In 'Greengos: Irish constructions of Latin American before and after the Celtic Tiger', Mary McGlynn traces the development of contemporary transnationalism as represented in Irish fiction that depicts Latin American characters. She argues that this turn to Latin America 'reveal[s] a sense of instability within a contemporary Irish society undergoing class reorganisation'. While 1990s' novels by Joseph O'Connor, Colum McCann and other Irish writers utilise the Americas as a setting and include Latin American characters, they still focus predominantly on Irish identity—thus exhibiting what McGlynn terms a 'postcolonial egoism'. Later novels by O'Connor and McCann give greater voice and agency to their Latin American characters. Nationality in a transnational setting becomes a way to speak about class and social mobility—both in Ireland and in the Americas.

Abigail Palko focuses on another contemporary Irish novel, Kate McCafferty's *Testimony of an Irish Slave Girl*, in 'Triangulating identity: An Afro-Irish Caribbean Act of Union', but her interests focus more on race and religion rather than class. Palko looks at how this work of historical fiction explores the transnational Irish past in order to comment on the contemporary transnational Irish present. Through the relationship of its Irish protagonist to African revolt (particularly her marriage to Quashey, a fellow slave), *Testimony of an Irish Slave Girl* attempts to narrativise interracial solidarity and imagine how multicultural integration might be achieved. Palko considers both the historical setting of the novel and its contemporary context; in doing so, she argues that the novel attempts to 'offer a direction out of the racial tensions affecting contemporary Ireland', while simultaneously problematising the possibility of true interracial solidarity.

In Ed Madden's essay, 'Transnationalism, sexuality, and Irish gay poetry: Frank McGuinness, Cathal Ó Searcaigh, Padraig Rooney', he demonstrates how sexuality is an important critical lens for transnational literary analysis and argues that 'Irish gay poetry is almost inevitably transcultural in reference and transnational in scope'. Madden contextualises his analysis of these contemporary poets with a brief overview of the transnationalism of the Irish gay rights movement, demonstrating that queer identity in Ireland has repeatedly been depicted as both indigenous *and* alien to Ireland. The three emblematic figures on which he focuses his analysis embody this transnational conflict and represent themes of alienation, mobility and escape: the resident alien, the migrant flâneur, and the escape artist. Through the deployment of these figures, McGuinness, Ó Searcaigh, and Rooney depict what Madden refers to as the 'translocational influences and impulses of Irish queer culture'.

Gender and sexuality are also central issues in Kelli Maloy's "Home with a queasy nudge": Transnationalism and Irish identity in Julia O'Faolain's *Three Lovers*'. Sally Tyndal, the novel's protagonist, is an Irish postgraduate student at the Sorbonne who imagines Parisian life will provide her with the cosmopolitan identity she craves. Sally particularly desires to free herself from the rigid expectations of Irish Catholic womanhood and actively pursues romantic attachment and sexual experience that counter the prescribed purity of State and Church. As such, she co-opts and sexualises the Algerian Revolution, in which her lover Mesli is a participant. But as Maloy argues, Irish identity in the novel 'resists cultural hybridity, compelling transnational subjects to replicate prescribed identities as Irish expatriates or to return to Ireland'. Ultimately Sally can only build a transient and superficial cosmopolitan identity for herself and reaffirms Ireland's cultural narratives about womanhood by becoming a Kathleen Ní Houlihan figure at the novel's end.

Amanda Tucker's 'Becoming *contrahecho*: An Irish-Irelander in Argentina' moves us to the late nineteenth century, when race was an integral part of nation-building projects in Ireland and other countries. Tucker explores the early writings of the Irish nationalist figure William Bulfin, who emigrated in the 1880s to Argentina as 'white' European immigrants were being recruited to counteract the influence of the country's indigenous and *mestizo* populations. Bulfin wrote dozens of stories about the *mestizo* figure of the gaucho, based on his brief but significant experience working on a cattle ranch in the Pampas. His collection, *Tales of the Pampas*, showcases stories that parallel the gaucho with the Irish Catholic as the true embodiments of their respective nations alongside tales that suggest the inherent racial and cultural superiority of the Irish-Argentine community over Argentine natives. Bulfin thus demonstrates the difficulty of developing a cross-cultural orientation in an age of ethno-nationalism. In *Tales of the Pampas*, his attempt to integrate wildly different racial and national ideologies into a cohesive whole results in a type of multicultural schizophrenia, in which his genuine desires to engage with cultural difference are thwarted by his own ethno-racial assumptions.

The final three essays in the collection focus on earlier nineteenth-century manifestations of transnational Irish literature and thus offer tantalising possibilities for the further historicising of transnationalism within the field of Irish Studies. In 'The politics of comparison: Romance at the edges of Europe', Katarzyna Bartoszyńska challenges the dominance of both British and Irish literary traditions as the primary means of under-standing text produced within the Irish nation. Situating the nineteenth- century Irish novel alongside contemporaneous Polish fiction, she argues that the marginalised political positions of both countries in the nineteenth century gird our assumptions about their relationship to the development of the novel. Rather than reading Irish and Polish novels as uncritically cleaving to romance, Bartozyńska problematises the dichotomy between realism and romanticism, satire, and sincerity. This transnational comparison of the Irish and Polish traditions in relation to one another thus allows us to see what complexities lie underneath the hegemonic narrative of this genre's development.

Sonja Lawrenson turns to a canonical text within Irish national literature—Maria Edgeworth's *Essay on Irish Bulls*. Edgeworth, like later Anglo-Irish writers such as Oscar Wilde and Samuel Beckett, has been 'reclaimed' as an Irish author. However, in 'Imperial interrelations in *Essay on Irish Bulls*', Lawrenson insists that Edgeworth's representation of the Irish and Ireland's relationship with England both must be placed within a wider transnational framework, particularly that of the growing British empire: in her words, the collection 'deals precisely with the question of Ireland's global economic and political networks, and, in particular, Irish interconnections with an increasingly global British Empire'. Lawrenson reads against the common interpretation of the didactic tale, 'Little Dominick', in order to show how, through what she terms a comic cosmopolitanism, Edgeworth elides any ethnic or national typecasting and instead insists upon the destabilising influences of transnational connections.

In the closing essay, 'Subverting the waves of global capital', Andrew Kincaid demonstrates how transnationalism intersects with oceanic studies. Investigating the trope of piracy in Irish maritime literature written in the aftermath of the Act of Union, Kincaid notes that fictional piracy flourishes as it diminishes in reality, and he asserts that piracy is a fluid and transnational concept through which these novels address pressing concerns of post-Union Irish life: the erosion of indigenous economic exchange, the disruption of Irish families due to emigration and dislocation, the ramifications of cultural and linguistic inheritance, and the constant threat of violence and suspicion of outsiders. In the novels that he explores, piracy functions as a transnational discourse in several ways: as a euphemism for Jacobitism; as a means to maintain pre-modern economies of local scale; as a way to unite transatlantic smugglers; and as a way of protecting Celtic clan structures.

The essays in this collection cannot, of course, encompass the entirety of a transnational literary methodology. Nor do they cover the enormous historical and geographical range of transnational Irish literature. Nonetheless, the work included in this volume represents the significance of a transnational approach to Irish literature and culture. When taken together, these essays allow us to rethink literary history—both by examining marginalised Irish writing, and by carefully uncovering the cosmopolitan dimension of canonical writers like Maria Edgeworth. The discussions of Irish literature also take into account how race, gender, sexuality, and class shape the Irish transnational experience. Rather than offering a master narrative of transnationalism in Irish literature, we hope that this volume sparks conversation and debates that will allow us to continue to negotiate the boundaries of national and transnational Irish literature.

To adapt or not to adapt: The question of originality in a Nigerian rewrite of an Irish classic

BISI ADIGUN

No personal originality is enough to make a rich work unique unless it has also the characteristic of a particular [time] and locality and the life that is in it.

J.M. Synge[1]

Growing up in western Nigeria as kids, we learnt a lot of lessons of life by listening to moon-lit stories about the exploits of various animals. It is no surprise, therefore, that on many occasions, I have had to draw inspiration from animals in an attempt to comprehend certain obstacles that I have been confronted with as an adult. The chameleon's survival depends on its ability to change colour at will, enabling it to blend in with any environment. And by being less noticeable, the chameleon can easily protect itself from its predators and at the same time hunt its prey more effectively. As a scientist has put it, 'The more ways a single adaptation helps an animal to survive, the better it is.'[2]

In the course of researching for this paper, an interesting article entitled 'Are We Still Evolving?' caught my attention:

> The environment is always changing on the planet and living things in order to survive must adapt to these changes. This adaptation is what made the fish to come out of water and evolve into amphibians. In other words, if a living thing wants to survive, it must adapt itself to the changing environment. Change is part of nature.[3]

The word 'adapt' is one that we use regularly and casually without recognising that it is inextricably linked to our evolution and survival. 'To survive', according to Charles Darwin, 'human must adapt'. In other words, to adapt is to be human and to be human is to adapt. Shakespeare would not have been far from the mark therefore if he had written, 'to adapt or not to adapt? that is the question', by virtue of the fact that to be and continue being human one must learn how to adapt. But, if adaptation is essential for all humans, even when they are in their countries of origin, it is unarguably the most important strategy at the disposal of any immigrant who wants to survive the emotional, psychological or cultural stress of being a foreigner. 'Adapting to a new and unfamiliar culture is more than survival', as Young Yun Kim has noted in her book, *Becoming Intercultural*. 'It is a life-changing journey. It is a process of 'becoming'—personal reinvention, transformation, growth, reaching out beyond the boundaries of our own existence.'[4]

I am originally from the Yoruba nation of Western Nigeria. After graduating with a Bachelor of Arts degree in Dramatic Arts from Obafemi Awolowo University, Ile Ife in 1990, I worked as a radio presenter for a year for my National Youth Service Corps (NYSC) before subsequently joining Swift Studios, an independent television company. I worked there for approximately two years as a production executive, and in 1993 an opportunity arose for me to travel to Britain to supervise an animated television commercial. After completing the project, I decided to extend my stay for a year in order to spend some more time in Europe to broaden my horizons. I became an immigrant, in the same way the fish, in the passage quoted earlier, evolved out of water on to dry land and became an amphibian.

Having worked as a performing artist—musician, storyteller, actor, workshop facilitator—and adapted to the cold, cosmopolitan and regimental London life for three years, I suddenly and, dare I say, unexpectedly found myself in a much more laid back, community-oriented and 'mono-cultural' Ireland in 1996. My arrival on Irish shores, however, coincided with the birth of the Celtic cub: the period when Ireland began to experience an unprecedented economic boom. As Luke Gibbons has pointed out, Ireland was regarded in a 1988 edition of *The Economist* as 'The Poorest of the Rich', but in a 2004 survey conducted by the same magazine, Ireland emerged as 'the best place to live on earth'.[5] This latter survey is a testament to the dramatic fashion in which Ireland had transformed, within a decade, from a country with emigrants in every part of the world into a magnet for immigrants from various parts of the world. An estimated 250,000 migrants arrived in Ireland between 1995 and 2000. These included Africans, Americans, Eastern and Western Europeans, and Asians as well as returned Irish emigrants. Within five years, Ireland had metamorphosed from an ostensibly homogenous society into a diverse multicultural society. And so did the imagination of the custodians of Irish culture.

Armed with a degree in dramatic arts and professional experience both in the television industry and performing arts, I was one of the many migrants who ended up on the shores of the Emerald Isle in the mid-1990s in pursuit of a better life. Being a black theatre artist in a predominantly white society such as Ireland of the mid-1990s, it goes without saying that I stood out like a sore thumb. Whilst it was impossible to change my skin colour to blend in with my new environment as the chameleon would do, I quickly learnt how to adapt emotionally, mentally, psychologically and, more importantly, culturally, to my new society. I was fully aware that in order for me to be relevant or, shall I say, in order to be creatively productive and be able to survive as a theatre artist, I must imbibe Irish artistic sensibilities without losing my Yoruba cultural identity. In other words, the challenge was to become transnational by imagining ideas that Irish people, despite my Nigerianness, would not regard solely as exoticised Africanness and which African people would not perceive as purely a parody of Irishness. That was when the question, 'to adapt or not to adapt?' began to rear its head.

In this paper, I want to problematise, within the framework of transculturalism, the concept of playwriting as we know it. From my perspective as a playwright, I want to argue that adapting Irish plays, from a non-Irish perspective, rather than writing brand new ones, is not only an original and challenging initiative, it is also an epitome of transnational literature. To support these assertions, I discuss briefly my reinterpretation of Jimmy Murphy's *The Kings of the Kilburn High Road* and, in greater detail, my adaptation, with Irish novelist Roddy Doyle, of the Irish classic, *The Playboy of the Western World*, originally written by J.M. Synge.

I saw *The Kings* in 2000 in the company of my Irish wife, whom I had recently married, and my niece from Nigeria. No one in the audience at that time could ever have imagined that within a decade it would be feasible for black actors to play the quintessential Irish parts in the play. 'Multiculturalism', with all its shortcomings,[6] was the buzzword and multicultural events[7] became the fad. And as expected, artists and theatre artists in particular were at the forefront of representing a multicultural Ireland. Theatre productions began to have an 'Other', best amplified by a black person, in them. I could not have chosen a better time to arrive in Ireland. Between 1997 and 2003, I was involved on a yearly basis in a stage production of a play that required a black performer. Without any doubt, I enjoyed every part I played in all of the productions in which I partook and I am thankful for the opportunity to tread the Irish boards as regularly as I did. However, looking at these projects collectively with the benefit of hindsight, one would notice the one-dimensional way in which the 'Other' was consistently portrayed. If you see a black character on stage, he or she is more than likely a pathetic outsider or a victim of institutional racism who lacks agency to do anything about it him/herself. I recall, for instance, how emotionally draining it was for me playing nightly for two weeks, the part of Paul, the Nigerian asylum seeker in Eithne Mc Guinness's play, *Limbo*, when it had its premiere in 2000. The play revolves around Paul as he patiently awaits the outcome of his refugee application. Though it has been a long and tedious wait, Paul remains hopeful, affable and a very likeable character until the end when he becomes a knife-wielding emotional wreck as a result of his asylum application being turned down.[8] In the end Paul has no choice but to give up and go underground to lead the life of an illegal immigrant. Similarly, Fishamble Theatre's 2002 production of *The Buddhist of Castleknock* begins with the arrival of Rai, a black British girl who is in Ireland for the first time hoping to enjoy a pleasant and quiet Christmas with her Irish boyfriend and his family, the O'Sullivans. But no sooner has she arrived than she realises that her liberal views are regarded as wayward in the O'Sullivan's household. As the cultural gap widens unabated, Rai decides to go for a walk in a nearby park to give her boyfriend and his family some breathing space. But while at the park, Rai is set upon due to her skin colour. In the end, she has no choice but to return, on her own to London, bruised and battered.[9]

This pattern of ensuring the 'Others' disintegrate or get sent packing with their tails between their legs was not peculiar only to stage drama. In the Irish film, *When Brendan Met Trudy* (2000), written by Irish writer Roddy Doyle, for instance, there is an asylum seeker from Nigeria named Edgar. Throughout the film, Edgar is portrayed as the life of every party he attends and he is a very personable character, but shortly before the credits roll, he is arrested on the charge of being an illegal immigrant; we see him in handcuffs, like a criminal, walking towards the camera as he is led into a waiting police van in preparation for his eventual deportation to Nigeria.[10] And in the television drama, *Black Day at Blackrock* (2001), Irish writer-director, Gerard Stembridge, depicts how the members of the fictional village of Blackrock are divided in their deliberation upon hearing the news that a number of asylum seekers have been dispersed from Dublin to come and live among them. In this two-part drama series, the only time we actually catch a glimpse of the asylum seekers is the sequence shortly before the end. They arrive on a bus and leave immediately thereafter for God knows where, as it has been decided at the culmination of the series of meetings held before their arrival that asylum seekers are not welcome in Blackrock village.

After a long time, *Fair City*, the popular Irish TV soap, began to run a story of an African family known as the Udenzes in September 2005. But after about five months of showing how the Udenzes are struggling to integrate in Carrickstown, they have no choice but to return to London, albeit without Gabriel Udenze.[11] The story of the Udenzes comes to an end when Gabriel Udenze meets the most tragic and brutal death at the hands of arsonists who set the home of the Udenzes on fire on the basis of their skin colour. As a dramatist, I am aware that all of these fictional representations that I have cited here were inspired by reality, but it would be wrong to conclude that all African immigrants who arrived in Ireland in the mid-1990s onwards were asylum seekers. Similarly, not every black person in Ireland has suffered a racial attack.[12] By presenting and re-presenting multicultural Ireland thusly, these cultural offerings, rather than challenging stereotypes, were actually unwittingly reinforcing them.

Patrick Lonergan also observed this disturbing pattern in his review of Donal O'Kelly's *The Cambria*:[13]

> The problem of racism is rarely analysed or treated with any complexity on the Irish stage—instead, it's usually just a lever in a melodramatic plot. The genuinely racist are punished, the ignorant learn a lesson and order is restored as we have seen in *Done up like a Kipper*, *Guess Who's Coming for the Dinner*, *Hurl*, *The Buddhist of Castleknock*.[14]

Jose Lanters also made an observation of how Irish theatre was representing diversity and her view was articulated thusly: 'As far as representing, let alone celebrating, diversity, Irish theatre has not been very successful, probably for the simple reason that until recently, Ireland was not very diverse.'[15] From reading these two critical observations, it became clear to me as a theatre artist that Irish theatre *ain't* doing what it says on the tin: it *ain't* representing diversity as it should and it *ain't* challenging racism as it could. Change, therefore, was imperative. My conclusion was that Irish theatre itself needed to experience diversity for it to be in a position to successfully represent and celebrate diversity. That was the rationale behind the founding in 2003 of Arambe Productions, Ireland's first African theatre company.[16] 'The purpose of art and science', as Augusto Boal has affirmed, 'is to correct the faults of nature using the suggestions of nature itself'.[17] I recall that the very first time I was in the theatre was at the age of nine when I saw *The Gods Are Not To Blame*, a Nigerian adaptation of Sophocles' *Oedipus Rex* written, directed and narrated by Ola Rotimi. Peppered with proverbs, mime, songs, local wits, dance and music, *The Gods* tells the tragic story of Odewale, the King of Kutuje who in the end has to gouge out his eyes and becomes a pariah after coming to the realisation that he has not only married his own mother, he is also the murderer of the former king. As young as I was, I felt the cathartic feelings of pity and fear for Odewale; I laughed, I cried and I was taken by the spectacle of the production. It was that day that I made up my mind that when I grew up I wanted to be like Ola Rotimi.[18] In fact, it was this childhood experience that made me more resolute to pursue theatre instead of law, considered then by my parents as a much more prestigious and lucrative profession. And having worked as a dramatist and a theatre director for over twenty years now, I am in complete agreement with Peter Brook's argument that: '… what a book cannot convey, what a philosopher cannot truly explain, can be brought into our understanding through theatre, translating the untranslatable is its role.'[19]

So while I was fully aware of my responsibility as the founder and artistic director of Arambe to create theatre aimed at translating the untranslatable, the challenge for me was how to be transnational by sourcing and presenting plays that would appeal simultaneously to both Irish and African audiences, year in, year out. My problem was compounded by the fact that whenever I came across a good African play I thought the company could produce, the question instinctively sprang to mind: how will it resonate with my Irish audience? And when a good Irish play came my way, I asked: what will my fellow African brothers and sisters make of this? It was a dilemma for which I found a solution by adapting like a chameleon. I must explain what I mean.

Having managed to adapt to Irish society culturally and psychologically, it never occurred to me that my decision to set up a theatre company would necessitate another process of adaptation that I would term: 'inter-dramaturgical adaptation'. By aiming to ensure that whatever theatre I created resonated with both Irish and African audiences, I was displaying all the symptoms of an immigrant who was increasingly becoming intercultural and a theatre maker who was thinking transnationally.[20] I was not aware of this at the time, however, until I came across Young Yun Kim's book, *Becoming Intercultural*. Kim, a Korean immigrant in America, offers an insightful analysis of how a determined and perceptive immigrant can turn the hardship and trauma of being an immigrant into an advantage. According to Kim, 'the process of crossing cultures challenges the very basis of who we are as cultural beings. It offers opportunities for new learning and growth'. She continues,

> Being 'uprooted' from our home brings us understanding not only of people and their culture in our new environment, but of ourselves and our home culture ... Despite, or rather because of, the hardship and ambivalence we undergo when we cross cultures, we gradually find ourselves uniquely privileged to define ourselves and others anew with clarity and insight that we could not have cultivated without leaving home.[21]

Thus, it is as a result of trying to adapt and survive as a 'non-national' theatre practitioner in Ireland that I have learnt how to occupy that unique and privileged in-between space of Irishness and Yorubaness. And it as a result of this interculturality, or more pertinently trans-nationality, that, as a dramatist, I have worked more on adaptations than writing original plays. In fact, I have since come to the conclusion that there is more originality in adapting Irish plays from a Nigerian perspective than writing brand new plays altogether.

'For some people, adaptation suggests no more than one playwright taking another playwright's play and modifying it', writes Nigerian playwright and theatre scholar, Ahmed Yerima. Yerima contends, however, that 'adaptation' in playwriting goes beyond that. As he puts it, 'There are playwrighting principles to be considered; there are rules and end results which emerge as new drafts of the old play.' Thus in Yerima's view, adaptation is 'when playwrights make suitable, plays already written, for new surroundings or audience, for a greater appeal'.[22] Irish playwright, Thomas Kilroy, echoes the same sentiments when he remarks that 'The first thing to be said about adaptation, no matter how faithful it is to the original is, that it and the original are always two very different, distinct works, sometimes profoundly so'.[23] While I am in agreement with both Yerima and Kilroy's idea of what adapting a play is, I beg to disagree with the inference in the title of the latter's article that one can only adapt the work of a dead author. Jimmy Murphy, the author of *The Kings of the Kilburn High Road*, for instance, is well and alive. In fact, without Murphy's encouragement and support, I would not have been able to reinterpret his play when I did.

When I saw *The Kings* in 2000, I immediately thought the Irish characters in the play could be any group of immigrants from anywhere in the world. To my mind, the play skilfully captures the universality of the immigrant experience so well that I thought it could be employed to shed light on the seemingly incomprehensible phenomenon of inward migration that Ireland began to experience with the birth of the Celtic cub. It was towards this end that I began to present a ten-minute excerpt of the play with African actors at various conferences and events. I recall that on one occasion during a question-and-answer session that followed one such presentation, a woman refused to accept that the characters that my actors played are Irish men in London. Thus, I had inadvertently defamiliarised the familiar in my effort to use the familiar to elucidate the unfamiliar. At another event, a man said to me: 'Listen here to me: you people are coming here, taking our jobs, our women and our houses. Now you are doing our play, don't you have a play of your own?' It is true that there were a number of Nigerian plays that I could have presented excerpts from, but would any of them have had a similar resonance with my audience? I was a Nigerian immigrant in an island that was rapidly diversifying and I believe if I wanted to be heard, understood and be able to effect change, I must become transnational.

For the Dublin Fringe Festival of 2006, my company, Arambe Productions, presented *The Kings of the Kilburn High Road* in its entirety with black actors. Several reviewers remarked on the play's cultural impact, as Matthew Spangler points out: 'As a homily on the broad issue of immigration to Ireland, the performance functioned as both social critique and cultural intervention. First, as social critique, it targeted the Irish state's response to immigration in particular as well as race relations in contemporary Ireland in general.'[24] Ruth Kennedy in the *Irish Theatre Magazine*'s review asserts that 'The actors capture the loneliness and self delusion of the emigrants so well that, for a while at least, the audience is colour blind, focusing only on the story.'[25] Both Spangler and Kennedy recognise how Arambe used adaptation to highlight the chameleon nature of the play. It is hardly surprising, therefore, that the production was the highlight of the conference on 'Race and Immigration in the New Ireland' held at the University of Notre Dame's Keough-Naughton Institute in October 2007. Whilst Arambe was in Notre Dame University with the production of *The Kings*, the new version of *The Playboy of the*

Western World, which I wrote with Irish novelist, Roddy Doyle, was causing riotous laughter nightly at the Abbey Theatre at that year's Dublin Theatre Festival, then celebrating its fifthieth anniversary.

What really drew me to *The Playboy* was how Synge masterfully uses the idea of an outsider to critique the 'shenanigans' of the insiders. As an immigrant in Ireland, I have always seen myself as an 'inside outsider' or an international 'blow in'. Why? Because on a daily basis, I get reminded that no matter how long I have lived in Ireland I will never belong. Thus, I take the Nigerian proverb, 'A mangrove tree may dwell in the river, that does not make it a crocodile', very seriously. I, however, believe that as an artist, I am at a vantage position; I am a perpetual denizen of a cultural in-between space, a fertile ground for the conceptualisation, germination and realisation of ideas that are transnational in scope, content and form.

I first saw a student production of *The Playboy of the Western World* in 1998, and in reading the text again shortly thereafter, it suddenly occurred to me that Christy is the archetypal refugee. Christy is, after all, on the run having ostensibly killed his father in County Kerry. In the play, he arrives in a shebeen in County Mayo seeking protection after having travelled on foot for days. The veracity of the 'crime' he has purportedly committed in Kerry is not important; what earns him bed and breakfast, the admiration of young and old women as well as the respect of men in Mayo, is how Christy tells the story of the crime. While it was in 1907 that *The Playboy* was first produced, in my view, it foreshadowed the role that storytelling has played in the asylum-seeking process in Ireland, which began in earnest from the mid-1990s onwards. An asylum seeker who has a convincing story of torture or brutality in his or her country of origin but no evidence whatsoever to back this story up might have a better chance of being granted refugee status than an asylum seeker who has scars of torture and abuse but cannot tell a compelling story to corroborate the evidence. It is thus to highlight the inherent absurdity in the requirements necessary for obtaining refugee status in Ireland that I thought it would be a good idea to rewrite, with a Nigerian Christy, Synge's *The Playboy of the Western World*. In other words, I wanted to create a new piece of work that will transcend Irish national borders by using the familiar story of Christy Mahon to entertain and at the same time elucidate the lengths to which most asylum seekers will go and why they are prepared to go to such lengths in order to obtain a refugee status.

Creating such a new transnational work requires reflection on the relationship between art and reality. As a theatre artist, I do find very instructive a number of maxims about how art can be used to shape reality. My favourite is Bertolt Brecht's 'Art is not a mirror to hold to a society but a hammer with which to shape it.' Wole Soyinka, the Nigerian Nobel laureate, has similarly remarked that 'a book is a hammer, a grenade to denote … to scatter the stagnant way of looking at life'.[26] I would argue, however, that too often in contemporary and rapidly diversifying Ireland, drama is viewed as a mirror rather than a hammer. And what makes it worse is that this mirror is available to only a select, like-minded few, and, as a result, the reflection is skewed in the sense that it is only one dominant view of reality that is reflected all of the time. Most, if not all theatre practitioners in Ireland—writers, directors, producers, designers, crew members—are invariably middle class, white Irish. Thus, one can argue that the theatre they make tends to be reflective of their singular and subjective views. But by becoming transcultural (or should I say inter-dramaturgical), any Irish theatre maker would realise that art is more of a hammer than a mirror. It was perhaps in an attempt to be transnational that Gavin Quinn, of Dublin-based Pan Pan Theatre, initiated the idea of the so-called Chinese *Playboy* in 2005. The adaptation, which was performed in mandarin with English surtitles, featuring an all-Chinese cast, had its premiere in Shanghai in China before it was presented in Dublin towards the end of 2005. In my view, the adaptation would have been more of a transnational innovation had the adaptation been initiated and written by a Chinese theatre practitioner in the same way that *The Playboy of West Indies* was initiated and authored by London based Trinidadian playwright, Mustapha Matura.

First produced at the Oxford Playhouse in 1984 before touring the UK (and subsequently the United States of America), Matura's adaptation is set in the rural town of Mayaro in Trinidad in the 1950s. This enables him to draw a number of parallels between rural Ireland at the turn of the twentieth century, in which Synge's original is set, and Trinidad of the 1950s. In Mustapha's adaptation, Christy Mahon is Ken and Pegeen is Peggy and Widow Quinn is known as Benin. In lieu of the potato field in which Christy labours before purportedly killing his dad, Ken works in the sugar cane field. According to a review in the *Daily Telegraph*, 'this riotous and generous show is almost as welcome as a holiday in the Caribbean' and in the words of Albert Williams who reviewed the Court Theatre's production of the play for Chicagoreader.com on 28 April 1988, the adaptation 'is an interesting experiment in cross-cultural transplantations'. In light of positive reviews such as this, one can argue that what makes *The Playboy of West Indies* so successful is the chameleon nature of the original.

We should bear in mind that Synge, an ingenious and controversial dramatist, also came into his own as a playwright when he abandoned what was familiar to him, including his middle-class background and his interest in French literature, and embraced the unfamiliar by travelling to the Aran Islands in Galway to live among the peasants of these islands. In a sense, one can argue that Synge was being transnational within one nation. It is worth adding that it was W.B. Yeats, one of the founding directors of the Abbey, Ireland's national theatre, who advised Synge to leave Paris and turn his back on French studies. 'Go to the Aran Islands', was Yeats's call to Synge. 'Live there as if you were one of the people themselves; express a life that has never found expression.'[27] Had Synge remained in Paris instead of heeding Yeats's advice, the former would have forever remained 'a minor poet and critic of French literature', as Patrick Murray has pointed out—and not the author of *The Playboy* and the other important plays in his canon.[28]

No playwright works in vacuum. A play is a microscopic representation of reality on stage. Without inspiration a playwright cannot write. It follows logically therefore that any play that is written is either a reaction to or a version (or a theft), as the case may be, of something that a playwright has heard, read, felt, seen—whether it is noted down somewhere or lodged in his subconscious. Shakespeare was the greatest and most successful dramatist of his time but he ain't a saint. 'Shakespeare didn't scruple to steal plots, dialogue, names and titles', writes Bill Bryson in his book, *Shakespeare*. 'To paraphrase Bernard Shaw', Bryson adds, 'Shakespeare was a wonderful storyteller of stories so long as someone else has told it first.'[29] The same thing goes for every playwright. The originality of being an artist and no less a playwright is to take notice of something that appears ordinary to everyone and re-present it in such an extraordinary way for everyone to take notice of it, comprehend it, and, if possible, be moved by it.

The originality of Synge as a playwright was to write *The Playboy*, by adapting a true life story of a man who had committed a crime but was shielded from the law by the natives. In his travelling memoir titled, *The Aran Islands*, Synge writes about the oldest man on the island who is fond of telling him anecdotes of things that have happened. 'He often tells me about a Connaught man who killed his father with a blow of a spade when he was in passion', Synge writes,

> and then he fled to this island and threw himself on the mercy of some of the natives with whom he was said to be related. They hid him in a hole—which the old man has shown me—kept him safe for weeks, though the police came searching for him, and he could hear their boots grinding on the stones over his head. In spite of a reward which was offered, the island was incorruptible, and after much trouble the man was safely shipped to America.[30]

Synge's analysis of the above story in the context of the ontology of the peasants of the Aran Islands is very instructive here. In his words,

> The impulse to protect the criminal is universal in the west. It seems partly due to the association between justice and the hated English jurisdiction, but more directly to the primitive feeling of these people, who are never criminals yet always capable of crime, that a man will not do wrong unless he is under the influence of a passion which is responsible as a storm on the sea. If a man has killed his father and is already sick and broken, with remorse, they can see no reason why he should be dragged away and be killed by the law. [31]

It was pure serendipity therefore that a week after we (Doyle and I) began the process of adapting *The Playboy*, I came across an online newspaper report of a Nigerian man who had killed his sixty-five-year-old mother with a pestle because she had refused to let her son sell the family land and use the proceeds to travel abroad. [32] I doubt if I would have been able to come up with the idea of a pestle to replace Synge's loy had it not been for that single divine intervention—others will regard it as a sublime invention. The icing on the cake for us was phonetically, 'pestle' can be mistaken for 'pistol'. So, aside from changing the mother to father for the purpose of our version, it is this real life story as I read it online that inspired the following lines between publican Michael, his two henchmen Jimmy and Philly, his daughter Pegeen and Christopher in our modern version of *The Playboy*. This is the point in the play—just after Christopher has told them the news of the killing of his father back in Nigeria—where they are trying to find out how and with what weapon

Christopher did the 'heroic' deed before fleeing to Ireland:

MICHAEL: Was it a knife or something? Did you stab the poor man?

CHRISTOPHER (*Scandalised*): Do you take me for a slaughter boy?

JIMMY: So, did you strangle him, or what?

CHRISTOPHER: I knocked him down with a pestle.

PHILLY: A pistol?

PEGEEN: You said you didn't shoot him.

CHISTOPHER: Yes. I didn't shoot him. I hit him on the head with a pestle.

MICHAEL: What the fuck is a pestle?[33]

It is thus in the same way that Synge adapted, for the stage, a true life event that we also represented a real life event to adapt his play.

'On the stage one must have reality, and one must have joy' writes Synge in his Preface to *The Playboy*,[34] 'that is why the intellectual modern drama has failed'. In his view, 'people have grown sick of the false joy of the musical comedy that has been given them in place of the rich joy found only in what is superb and wild in reality'. And with regard to the richness of his language, Synge admits that: 'In writing *The Playboy of the Western World*, as in my other plays, I have used one or two words only that I have not heard among the country people of Ireland'; it is against this backdrop that Synge has contended that 'All art is a collaboration'. His view, as he further articulates it is that 'In a good play every speech should be as fully flavoured as a nut or apple, and such speeches cannot be written by anyone who works among people who have shut their lips on poetry'. Pegeen's last line in Synge's masterpiece goes, 'Oh my grief, I've lost him surely, I have lost the only playboy of the western world'. This is perhaps the most famous ending of any play ever written in the western world.

But lest we forget, those words were written over a hundred years ago and in Ireland surely we don't talk like that any more. It would be crass therefore to have our Pegeen, a west Dublin girl in a twenty-first-century, diverse, post-Celtic-tiger Ireland, where drug dealing and gangland-killing are a regular occurrence, say: 'Oh my grief, I have lost him surely'. So we thought of the word that anyone is not supposed to use at any time but which everyone uses every time and we came up with: 'Fuck off' to end our rewrite. As Synge himself has said 'in countries where the imagination of the people, and the language they use, is rich and living, it is possible for a writer to be rich and copious in his words'. So I want to argue that it is in the same way that Synge had collaborated with the islanders of the Aran Islands to write the original *Playboy* that Doyle and I collaborated with one another as well as the residents of Dublin city, in which we live, to rewrite the new *Playboy*. Conceptually, the process can best be described as collaborative osmosis: an epitome of transnationalism.

Theoretically, it is like turning Patrice Pavis' hourglass intercultural model[35] on its head to blur the line between what he refers to as the 'source culture' and the 'target culture'. So in this hourglass model, both the foreign culture and the target culture become indistinguishable. What he terms the 'cultural product', which for the purpose of my argument here, is the rewrite of *The Playboy*, becomes neither this nor that or, if you prefer, both this and that. And that is perhaps why Melissa Sihra has referred to the so-called Adigun/Doyle rewrite of *The Playboy* as both intercultural and intracultural.[36] In a mixed-up place such as Ireland, it is important for a discerning playwright to shake things up a bit. The nose, according to the wisdom of the Yoruba people, cannot smell itself. A close-knit society such as Ireland, as any other I would argue, needs the perspective of the 'Other' for self-development. That, in my view, is the role of Christy Mahon in *The Playboy* when it was staged in 1907 and no less the role of Christopher Malomo when our rewrite was staged in 2007. That, in my view, is how the art of drama can make that which is seemingly impossible, plausible by hammering home the message that there is beauty in diversity.

Aristophanes, the great Greek comedian once said that 'a playwright must not be only an entertainer but a teacher of morals'. Theatre must be 'an agent of social or political intervention' in this our age of globalisation or should we say 'transnationalism' not to merely be, as Brian Singleton has argued, 'a performative tool of reflection'.[37] In my view, as a Nigerian playwright living in Ireland, there is no better way for me to reflect reality, represent the 'Other' from another perspective, and at the same time, help hammer things into shape in an increasingly diverse Ireland, than to use the familiar to illuminate the seemingly alien. There are a lot of myths and negative perceptions about immigrants and asylum seekers in modern Ireland. Had I written new plays to explore these issues, in all likelihood, they would have been pigeonholed as didactic, preachy. Furthermore, it is doubtful that the stage lights at the Abbey Theatre would have shone on any of them, no matter how well written they might have been. So, I felt the best way to diversify Irish theatre and ultimately contribute in a meaningful and effective way to the important discourses of identity, interculturality, and diversity in Ireland is to mix things up for real. To show a fictional world in which audience's expectations of what is, what ought to be and what can be are played with, queried and overturned, to paraphrase the theatre scholar and critic, Karen Fricker.[38] It was with this in mind that I initiated, facilitated and participated in the rewrite of the most known of Irish plays and, mind you, I did not do it on my own, but with a well-known Irish writer. It is 'chameleonic', I agree, but you will agree with me that it is an original and a much more creative way of being and surviving as a Nigerian/Irish playwright.

The two plays that I have discussed were originally written by two extraordinarily gifted Irish playwrights, but they have resonated with me in a way they can never resonate with an Irish person, by virtue of the fact that as a Nigerian immigrant living in Ireland, I have learnt how to become transnational.[39] It was out of the necessity to make these deep and strong transcultural resonances accessible to the public, that I could not help but initiate their re-writes. To create, one must adapt and to adapt one must be creative. So if to adapt or not to adapt is the question, the answer for me will once again be to adapt, because to adapt an Irish play, for me as a Nigerian playwright, is akin to writing a brand new play. 'Have you seen Bisi's new play?' does not have the same ring to it as 'Did you hear what Bisi has done to Friel's *Philadelphia Here I Come*?'[40] In my view, Ireland's present can best be represented by re-imagining her past; and perhaps (and it is only perhaps) we can re-create a future in which everyone has a prominent role to play in making this wonderful island the best place to live on earth, for one and all regardless of their colour, creed or inclination.

‘Greengos’: Irish constructions of Latin America before and after the Celtic Tiger

MARY McGLYNN

'Compare mio.[1] How many bambinos have yeh got that are goin' to school ...', says Bertie, a minor Roddy Doyle character, as he works to unload stolen calculators he acquired from 'a gringo tha' we all know an' think he's a fuckin' eejit'.[2] Providing moments of comic relief, Bertie appears as a mate of Jimmy Sr.'s in *The Snapper* and *The Van*, one of the lads down the pub. His Barrytown pidgin of Northside Dublin, Italian, and Spanish melds local language with an appropriation of foreignness—Italo-Spanglish animates Bertie's persona as part Mafioso, part 'Cowboy', both as a western cowpoke and in the less American sense of the word, a risk-taker doing things by the seat of his pants.[3] The few foreign words he knows would seem to come via exposure to television and film, to characters with exotic, dramatic lives that give colour to his scrounging and deal-making. The interpolations/corruptions thus provide a way for Bertie to expand the confines of his class and neighbourhood.

An analysis of such Spanish interpolations in English-language texts offers a possible means to test the proposition that constructions of ethnicity function in part as redirected discussions of class. Yet the exotic does not merely dangle the prospect of escape from economic realities; rather, Spanish in *The Barrytown Trilogy* functions both as a recognition of the limits of any single language and as an international common cultural idiom, a means of participating in a global popular culture. Bertie accesses Latin flavour via television and movies, the stereotypical nature of his appropriations a reminder that the production and circulation of these images remains shaped and dominated by metropolitan cultural producers. Substantial critical attention has been dedicated to the problems of these depictions, a worthwhile effort that nevertheless retains the primacy of the imperial centre. As Elizabeth Butler Cullingford points out at the outset of her study *Ireland's Others*, 'numerous critics have dissected the stereotypes of Irishness'[4] generated in British and American texts in particular; she proposes 'reversing a critical practice that has been central to Irish Studies'[5] by looking at how non-Irish Others are constructed in Irish texts. This article will extend her innovation beyond a reversal of a binary opposition of cultural coloniser and colonised. Examining Irish texts with Latin American subjects and settings will reveal how one postcolonial people portrays another in triangulation with imperial centres, exploring what motivates this interaction between provincials, whom Edward Said has called 'cultural contestants'.[6]

Interactions among provincials shift as their respective cultural and economic fortunes shift. Since the early 1980s, Ireland has converted from an economy whose main export was labour to one whose relative prosperity enables greater consumerist participation in the global market, meaning that youth culture's interest in the world beyond Ireland's borders has transformed from emigration, job searches, and political activism to global tourism and consumption. (About a final transmogrification in the wake of the Irish economic crisis, more later.) This change of scope and increase in exposure would seem to reduce the likelihood of stereotype and cultural presumption—part of the reason Bertie is comical is that Doyle's readers, including those who share his class origins, can parse the various strains of his pan-Latin mash-up. Yet encounters with the 'Other' can also reinforce notions of difference and distinct national characteristics. As Michael Cronin notes, during the time Ireland has reacted to its own increasingly immigrant population, 'the notion of diversity ... something of a mantra of official pronouncements on multicultural Ireland, supposes that different groups possessed of different sets of ready-made attributes are juxtaposed in the shop window of contemporary Ireland and each group acting out its predefined cultural script contributes to the effervescent display of cultural diversity'. Though 'often seen as a way of countering nativist genealogical exclusiveness' such neoliberal multiculturalism rather 'tends to partake of the same logic'.[7] As I will argue below, there are certainly elements of this sort of shallow evocation of the Other present in Irish depictions of Hispanic characters, particularly before the economic collapse. But more than an easy essentialism, Irish cultural appropriations reveal a sense of instability within a contemporary Irish society undergoing class reorganisation. As Ireland ceased to export human capital and instead became a destination for migrants seeking a better life,[8] its citizens found themselves free from the economic anxieties of the preceding decades. In what follows, I trace structural and thematic similarities in a number of texts with Latin American settings and characters, examining their differences alongside the changing Irish racial and economic scene.

My study spans novels published in the fifteen years that saw the rise and fall of Ireland's 'boom' era of growth and prosperity. I contend that the earlier texts use their transnational present to critique what they depict as Ireland's conservative past. The later texts shift their settings into a historical past, simultaneously offering a fuller critique of their

Celtic Tiger present, configuring imaginings of a (very problematic and imaginary) social mobility perhaps unimaginable in the years just before the boom. In all the novels I investigate, Hispanic characters function as exemplars of alternative mindsets, but their strategic deployment in stories about the transnational and Ireland reduce (in varying degrees) their voice, their power, and their subjectivity.[9]

Curiously, although the first group of novels I consider take place largely in the Americas and are set in Ireland for no more than a chapter or two, Irishness, rather than any other identity, remains the most explored. Importantly, the formal features of these texts, most notably narrative focalisation, reinforce the centrality of Irish identity and a 'white' perspective on a perceived region of turmoil, primitivism, and postcolonial racial dynamics.

HEALING OTHERS

Joseph O'Connor's 1994 novel, *Desperadoes*, takes place entirely in the Nicaragua of the mid-1980s and focuses on the frictions within a fractured Irish family as they interact with locals and Americans. Frank Little and his estranged wife Eleanor travel to Nicaragua to claim the body of their son Johnny. Focalised primarily through Frank, an aging Dublin taxi driver, the novel, like all those I discuss from before the onset of the Irish financial crisis in 2007, structures itself around a journey. Franco Moretti has talked about the way that nineteenth-century novels set outside of Europe, what he calls 'colonial romances', diverge from the genre of the picaresque and other 'road' stories whose narratives enact the formation of the nation-state.[10] *Desperadoes* begins, like Moretti's colonial romances, at 'a port, a garrison, a trading station along the coast: one of those "rim" settlements', as the geography of colonialism calls them, from which European conquest began,[11] in this case, in Managua in 1985, amidst the violent efforts of the Contras to overpower the popular but increasingly authoritarian Sandinistas.[12] And indeed, the journey resembles that of Conrad's character Marlow as Frank and the wife he has been separated from arrive to recover the body of their son, Johnny, only to find at the morgue that he has been mistaken for another European man. The interaction of the estranged couple as they search to discover what has actually happened to their son is mediated by Johnny's bandmates, an American hippie couple, a blind man endowed with spiritual vision and extra soul, and a hard-rocking apolitical singer. As the story of the Little marriage unfolds alongside the journey further and further from a western sense of order, we reach several hearts of darkness: it is the seemingly placid Eleanor, not the volatile Frank, whose alcoholism and physical abuse led to their breakup, and Johnny is alive, with a pregnant girlfriend his bandmates scarcely knew existed, in jail for running drugs for the Contras to earn money for his fledgling family. Both stories end up opposite to expectation, and in an upending of the colonial narrative, Johnny refuses to be rescued, citing barbarity at home compared to the simplicity of life with his woman. While Johnny sees Nicaragua's simplicity healing his complicated Irish past, such belief in cultural difference is at odds with the text's own assumptions, which Shawn O'Hare encapsulates as 'take away the heat and humidity, and Nicaragua is Ireland: green fields, impressive mountains, an abundance of poor people struggling to make a living, and dependence on the agricultural past'.[13]

As O'Hare suggests, *Desperadoes* sketches an alliance between the downtrodden, revolution-beset artists of Nicaragua and Ireland, creating a series of (tenuous) analogies between citizens of both nations and figuring the expatriate American characters as (shallow, materialistic) foils. But the analogies seem to break down when O'Connor's frustration with Irish sexual politics romanticises the Nicaraguan characters, whose Catholicism and earthy sensuality promise healthy relationships; Johnny functions as provider for a traditional nuclear family. Though in reality divorce is more possible for Johnny's girlfriend than for his mother during the 1980s, the Sandinistas having passed many such 'pro-woman' reforms, the novel contrasts a simpler Nicaraguan existence with the complexities of life in Ireland, where gender stereotypes are no longer predictive and divorce, while not yet legal, exists de facto. Johnny's Irish-Nicaraguan child, a hybrid, offers the promise of a blend of both cultures. As an emblem of the future, a break with the trope of the dysfunctional Irish family, the child improves upon Irish psychology. At the same time, Nicaragua receives an infusion of Irish wit and capitalist know-how.

Joe Cleary has written about how a Romeo and Juliet-style 'romance-across-the-divide' in conflict-riven regions can function as a means of removing a story from the public sphere and instead making it entirely personal.[14] Michael G. Cronin detects something similar in recent novels using gay characters to signal Irish pluralism and modernity: national stories are rendered secondary to personal narratives. Reading in this vein, we can see the romance plots in *Desperadoes* as a way of making sense of large-scale cultural shifts by figuring them as changes in the lives of individuals, a paradoxical effort to return Irish characters to a simpler time by escaping Ireland's old, insular values.

Colum McCann's 1995 *Songdogs* similarly expresses deep uncertainty about Ireland's past but, much more than *Desperadoes*, it is ambivalent also about the capacity of an outside Other to provide solace or solution. The novel tells the story of an only child, Conor Lyons, now an adult, who returns for a week to his aged father's home in County Mayo after a trek across North America in search of clues to his Mexican-born mother's disappearance during his childhood. Focalised through the eyes of an early-1990s', backpack-toting Conor, the novel tracks the father's and son's stories in parallel. *Songdogs* repeatedly and compulsively engages with the past, with the repressive culture of Ireland in the 1930s that ejects Conor's father into the Spanish Civil War. Yet its recurrent, interpolated shifts into present tense secure narrative focalisation strictly in the present, in ways that privilege the contemporary over the historical. Conor's perspective, like the framing the elder Lyons does with his Leica, selects and shapes the story. Indeed, the novel's structure arises from the week Conor stays in Mayo with his father, each elliptical chapter title preceded by a day of the week. The father at age eleven had 'renamed himself Michael Lyons, a name that was common among many of the locals, a name that could have belonged to his own father'.[15] Such an act of self-generation immediately undercuts any notion of genealogical continuity as foundational to Irishness. This self-invented creature makes an odyssey across America, subsequently retraced by Conor himself, the latter journey a symbolic trip into the past. The novel indulges in multiple, recurrent reflections on the nature of time, emblematised early on by the elder Lyons' view that 'the law of the water' was 'bound to move things on' (p. 5). Conor's efforts to unearth the past are therefore cast as a fight against nature itself, as is photography, another recurrent motif, one which carries 'the possibility of freezing time' (p. 9).

Lyons embodies the essentialising of Mexican culture by outsiders, venturing to Mexico on the strength of his attraction to a photograph: 'no more than seventeen years old, in a billowy white linen skirt, flour on her hands ... my father took a picture of the Mexican holding the picture' (p. 29). Via the multiple levels of mediation here—a verbal description of a fantasy of a woman captured in a picture of a picture—

McCann emphasises the constructed nature of the desire for an exotic other. Failing to find that woman, Lyons journeys across Mexico with his camera, only welcome in the Mexican town where he meets his future wife, Juanita, after she 'invented some fabulous lie about how my father was related to John Riley, an Irishman who had commanded the San Patricio Battalion in the Mexican War' (p. 37), a fanciful fabrication that shows how imaginative projection can run both ways.

Juanita's choice to account for Lyons through this historical connection prefigures the way in which she herself is embalmed by the text as part of that past. By contrast, the narration links Lyons to movement, progress, the future. He does not want to stay in Mexico, which is portrayed as static: 'Every sight of a burro or a cart gave him a want for movement' (p. 52), whereas when the couple emigrate to the US, 'Mam looked backwards over the car-seat' (p. 78), gazing back at and becoming part of the timeless Mexican landscape. The use of the word *burro* here associates Spanish with the rustic type of movement too slow for Lyons' escape, and Juanita is made to embody a quintessentially postcolonial—and especially Irish—imaginary equation of woman with land. Thus the mother/nation is cast as antiquated, so while the novel's emotional sympathy lies with Juanita, its narrative direction favours Lyons, who appears in the narrative present.

Not that Mexico does not change—Conor finds that his parents' home has been torn down, for instance. But it remains inexplicable, unknown, as does Juanita. It is telling that we do not even learn Conor's mother's name until halfway through the book, when Cici, her soul mate, raises a glass in her honour. Juanita is not present for Cici's toast; her son stands in for her to hear the toast. Significantly, Juanita is the only major character who does not appear in the narrative present (even her own mother's body has a cameo role, as do other bit players from the scenes in Mexico). And her name is yielded to us only long after vivid descriptions of photographs of her naked body in provocative positions. McCann's text leaves Juanita's inner thoughts, feelings, and motives obscure; her disappearance is unexplained and her whereabouts entirely unknown.[16] As much as the novel works to critique the objectification of her body, it replicates such othering through its essentialising of her as dark, sensual, temperamental, and unfathomable.

Even the Native American character, Eliza, who is never heard to speak by the Wyoming white population, not only gets a voice but a role in the novel's present. Eliza helps to reconstruct the story of Juanita's past, a story Juanita herself has no hand in shaping. Rather, Juanita walks away from her son and family, never communicating again. McCann's choice to leave her story untold privileges the father-son relationship recuperated in the week Conor spends in Mayo, just as his choice to intersperse present-day first-person narration with stories of the past allows the former to overshadow the latter. Conor's own hybrid identity stages the present moment as the one resolving the transnational encounter; the objectifying lens of the father and the inscrutability of the mother are improved upon through their resolution in the person of their son. Like *Desperadoes*, then, *Songdogs* sees a blending of Irish and Latin American cultures in the contemporary era as a way to make sense of the foreign and heal the self, as an improvement upon past insularity, racism, and ignorance. The current generation casts itself as more capable of fixing, through its transnational mobility and tolerance, the mistakes of its forebears.

Such postcolonial egocentrism also motivates Emer Martin's *More Bread or I'll Appear*, a 1999 novel which passes briefly through the slums of Mexico City and has its ethereal climax on the beaches of Honduras, using Latin America to shed light upon the problems of Ireland. Its global erotic picaresque critiques Irish sterility and immobility via depictions of the wholesome, polymorphously perverse sexuality of non-Europeans and their liberated Irish lovers. The most liberated of all is Aisling, the oldest of five children of an ailing mother; it is the search for her that drives the plot and the continual relocations of Keelin, the youngest, dutifully traversing continents and conventional morality to follow Aisling's footsteps. Each successive section brings Keelin more closely upon Aisling's heels. Martin has explained in an interview that she designed the novel so that each section aped the 'paces and themes' of its setting: gritty McCourt-style realism in Ireland, *Bladerunner* postmodernism in Japan, lurid *Jerry Springer* scenarios in New York, and magical realism in Latin America, the basically linear progression of the novel marked by a few flashbacks and these context-based shifts in style.[17] The novel approaches its conclusion in scenes in a remote part of the Honduran coast, where Keelin finds not just Aisling (larger than life and pregnant) but also Fatima, Aisling's beloved, as well as Fatima's own lover, Sadao. This unconventional ménage lives an anti-materialist life meant to serve as a reproof to ownership claims upon property or upon the affections of another. The climax comes when Keelin awakes (from a dream or drunkenness or hallucination—the novel is intentionally indeterminate) to find that Fatima, Sadao, and Aisling herself have either vanished or were never there at all. The scene serves as explanation and resolution, as we come to learn that although the rest of the family believed them to be estranged, Aisling and her mother are actually in contact. The journey thus frees Keelin from the (misdirected) sense of obligation that had propelled her.

Reducing the Latin American Boom to a depiction of narrative uncertainty, and conflating South and Central America, Martin's novel can be seen to use its exotic beachfront setting as a means of 'healing' a character damaged by traditional Irish constructions of family and by the new, postmodern, de-centred whirl of a prosperous nation. In reflecting on 'Time and Place in Global Ireland', Michael Cronin outlines the traits of the SlaveMaster, a hybrid figure, both subject and object, whose appearance in Ireland coincides with Irish uncertainty. '[A] dominant paradigm in a liberal-democratic market economy', the SlaveMaster 'is consumer, the supreme master of choice, the active agent of destiny, the flattered subject of his or her multiplying desires. On the other hand, the citizen as producer is simply another object to be used, an eminently replaceable part of a process, a figure on a balance sheet, utterly subject to forces over which he or she has no control'.[18] Keelin's epiphany in Honduras figures her as both halves of Cronin's fractured citizen simultaneously, proclaiming her acceptance of this state as a triumph of the neoliberal individual.

Ironically, while the novel stages this breakthrough in Latin America and credits it to contact with the Other, its focalisation remains strictly through Keelin. Moreover, though the entire Honduras section of *More Bread* mocks Willy, an American hippie who has never learned Spanish and only feigns close connection with the natives, the novel itself emerges as analogous to him, as there are no Hondurans with speaking roles save a slight part for a border patrol agent seeking a bribe. Unlike *Songdogs* and *Desperadoes*, which offer Hispanic characters in relationships with normative Irish ones,[19] *More Bread* is a hallmark of the uncritical dimension of the Celtic Tiger years, thoughtless in its relation to the rest of the world and to Latin America in particular. Its narrative multiplicity resembles the multiculturalism of the characters—while there are shifts in style, there is no true blending into hybrids. The novel's stylistic shifts replicate entrenched attitudes about the regions in which such styles have their origins, and none ever changes Keelin's focalisation. In this way, the novel resembles the uninformed characters in *Desperadoes* and

Songdogs, not the more enlightened hybrids.

It is of course too easy a critical gesture to disdain Martin's novel, much less dismiss the more nuanced but still early transnational work of O'Connor and McCann, as naïve or inadequate. Yet all three texts are unidirectional in their appropriation of Latin America. Said notes that Romantic idealism held that 'Indian culture and religion ... could defeat the materialism and mechanism . . . of Occidental culture. And from this defeat would arise a new, revitalized Europe [. . .] [W]hat mattered was not Asia so much as Asia's use to modern Europe'.[20] In Said's sense, 1990s' novels focus on Latin America's use to Ireland, primarily as a healing force and means to critique Ireland's past. Yet beyond the focus on the fate of present-day Irish characters, *Desperadoes* and *Songdogs* paid attention to and gave dimension to Hispanic characters at a moment when the parochial attitudes of Doyle's Bertie were predominant. To a certain extent, their treatment of multiculturalism and transnationalism as projects that lay ahead of Ireland was accurate, but, significantly and perhaps counterintuitively, it is with the move into settings in the past that the treatment of Latino characters begins to address contemporary issues of class and transnational identity.

MATERIALISM, PAST AND PRESENT

Anne Enright's 2002 *The Pleasures of Eliza Lynch*, about the nineteenth-century Irish mistress of Paraguay's oppressive dictator Francisco Solano López, marks a turning point—not only is the protagonist an economic migrant herself, coming into contact with colonial wealth, but the encounter occurs in a third space, neither Ireland nor Paraguay, a recognition of the triangulated nature of transnationalism.[21] While the earlier texts worked to disavow their rootedness in an Irish past, this novel begins with a frank, aggressively blunt statement of origins: 'Francisco Solano López put his penis inside Eliza Lynch on a lovely spring day in Paris, in 1854'.[22] This sexual act will result in the pregnancy which leads, ultimately, to the novel's, and history's, tragic story of greed, ambition, and needless bloodshed.

A novel obsessed with numbers, counting, and accounting, *Eliza Lynch* opens with a chapter that counts the thrusts which constitute the first, fateful sexual encounter of 'Francisco López and Eliza Lynch, Il Mariscal and La Lincha, Paco and Liz' (p. 2). Starting with this multilingual assertion of the amorphous nature of identity, the early pages set forth the transnational nature of the episode with many references to the various languages framing their encounter. 'Francisco put his penis, *son pénis, su penis*, into the nameless part of Eliza Lynch. He put that thing, which is the same in English, French or Spanish, into a part of Eliza Lynch that is, in any language, obscene' (p. 3). In noting that penis is an exact cognate in all three languages while vagina is unspeakable, the novel suggests that gender dynamics overrule national or linguistic differences. At the same time, in taking the time to give us the translations, the text places all three languages on an equal plane, declining to conflate them as Bertie does. The focus becomes on the different pronouns, on the unnamed female anatomy, rather than on the similarities.

Enright's stylistic repetitions structure not just the formations of identity but also the meta-fictive self-consciousness permeating the novel's intense awareness of its constructed status, foregrounding the variety of possible modes of expression as well as the text's ultimate unreality: 'The clock on the mantel said midnight, or five o'clock. The clock on the mantel was stopped' (p. 2). Not all these statements can be true at once, yet each is offered in a declarative form. The conjunction 'or' is where we can locate the moment of artistic composition, the point at which we are told we are not being given facts but having a story spun for us. Another instance of metalepsis occurs a few pages later, during thrust number eight: '*Eight*: Who was counting? She was counting' (p. 6). This exchange, in which the narrator questions his/her own structural choice, leads to a further metafictive incident, as it turns out the narrator is counting thrusts while Eliza counts previous lovers. Combined with the self-reflexive meditations on time throughout the first chapter, this moment creates narrative instability as a comment on the difficulties of ever knowing history. In adding a formal dimension to this exploration of the problematics of historiography, Enright declines to locate indecipherability on a dark continent, instead tying it to the very nature of storytelling, and of language itself.

The novel presses its investigation of storytelling at the level of plot as well as form. While on a physical journey by boat up the river from Buenos Aires to Asunción, Eliza Lynch asks her maid, Francine, 'if she had any intimation, when she opened the door to him that evening, of the journey we were about to embark upon—because it is her journey too' (p. 104). The passage explicitly extends the metaphor of life as a journey here to the working-class character, seemingly another move to destabilise the normative historical narrative. Eliza's scepticism of such metaphors becomes clear a few pages later as we learn that this breathless question about fate is something Eliza performs rather than feels: 'such love holds for me no fascination. But it is nice, sometimes, to pretend. To heave a sigh and say, "When did it begin?"'(p. 106). The question leads to yet another round of speculation about the alternate paths history, any story, may take. Enright's insistent recursions to such reflections on the role of chance in a novel (which must, as a written text, be the victory of choice and selection over chance) obviate simple narratives of manifest destiny. In place of simplified versions of the 'discovery' of America and unidirectional colonisation, Enright foregrounds the role of story in history, critiquing the archetypal river journey from rim settlement to heart of darkness by destabilising all its terms and calling attention to the various racial, national, and gender identities that gird colonial narratives. Via her depiction of the impossibility of a unitary narrative for characters with complicated origins and multilingual identities, Enright imagines global political events as shaped by the intersection of the personal and the global. The novel highlights in particular the quotidian episodes which replace grand narratives of nation to reveal the transnational undercurrents of multiple migrations, characters without national identifications, and emergent hybridity. Thus the novel reflects upon not just storytelling but, as forecast by the opening chapter, on hybridity and mixing, calling the 'half-gunboat, half-packet' riverboat 'a mongrel ship' (p. 19). The boat, like its owner and its inhabitants, is both European and Latin American, modern and primitive.

Where earlier novels were anxious for modernity, either demonstrating that Ireland had moved forward or admonishing it for its inability to let go of the past, Enright's text expresses ambivalence about technological progress. Lopez's grand plans include the new boat that will transport them home—the *Tacuari* (the mongrel ship) as well as an arsenal and a railway line. 'Above all, there would be railways. Eliza could not imagine it, but Francisco's father never left Paraguay. Before him, the first dictator, Francia, never left his own bedroom. And now, here he was in Europe, meeting men by the hour, hiring them with a look' (p. 12). Paco measures progress on a graph of time and space, a sendup of Irish real estate developers. In setting this modernising impulse in the past and focalising it through the Paraguayan dictator, at the moment that Ireland's economic fortunes began to soar, Enright critiques contemporary development and challenges the division of the globe into first and third worlds.

The novel also disrupts linear progression via an episodic narration style which titles each chapter (always a rich food or luxury item) and then gives a date and place setting the narrative present. 'A Fish' in Paris, March, 1854 opens the book, and 'A Little Dog' in Edinburgh, 1873 closes it, European bookends to a story whose body takes place in South America. In between, the years jump forwards and back, a denial of progress or development or modernity underscored by the narrative's continual return to the becalmed river Parana up which Eliza and Lopez travel to Asunción. The motionless river is mirrored by the narrative immobility—immobility foreshadowed by the stopped clock in the opening scene. Combined with the relentless attention to the constructedness of any history, the absence of narrative momentum denies the logic of causation. Enright's novel thereby predicts that the much-lauded economic engine, the Celtic Tiger, which was rampant when Enright's novel appeared, was itself mythical, dependent as it was on the rhetoric of progress and development. In hindsight, certainly, it is easy to read the bubbles and speculation as castles built on nothing more than stories; Enright's portrait of materialist excess in the past not only critiqued its contemporary Irish manifestation but also, it seems, predicted its collapse.[23] It's just too bad ministers of finance do not look for lessons in experimental fiction.

For all its global capital prognostications, however, the novel's perspective does not depart entirely from those discussed above. On the one hand, *Eliza Lynch*'s formal edginess, which privileges the thematic over the realistic, compounds the novel's challenge to colonialist dreams of bringing civilisation and progress to dark corners of the globe. But especially given such destabilisation of narrative reliability via a kaleidoscope of perspectives and disruptions of temporal sequence, the absence of the narrative voices of any indigenous characters seems stylistically and thematically problematic.[24] Enright's narrative focalisers are both outsiders, paralleled via their redheadedness and complicated relationships with the British Empire. Eliza herself narrates in sections of first-person discourse, alternating with the equally personal third-person free indirect discourse of another European expatriate, the Scottish doctor Stewart. In both cases, the view of 'the natives' is constructed both by formal features of the narration and by the characters' reflections on national identity, the structural technique somewhat in tension with the novel's other challenges to conventional form.

The Paraguayan characters remain vague, with the partial exception of Lopez himself. The attention to excess in the novel links Eliza's greed to Lopez's, their twinned ambitions and acquisitive natures erasing the difference between the upper class of Paraguay and the cultural dominance of his imported doctors, engineers, and mistress. Stewart speculates that Eliza is 'the right kind' of Irish: 'her manners seemed bred, not learned' (p. 141). With such asides, the novel ultimately suggests that class matters more than national origin, and then, when Stewart is left a prisoner and the Brazilian victors allow Eliza to leave Paraguay ('she was followed by her trunks—every last one of them' [p. 229]), that money matters more than cultural capital. The new world becomes a place where inequality is not figured in conventional terms of class: Louis XVI and Marie Antoinette are replaced by a courtesan and the son of a dictator who are just as greedy and materialistic.

The setting in the past here serves to remind readers that migration is not new, nor is it always in the same directions. Yet as much as this text critiques Celtic Tiger materialism and points out that its excesses occur at the expense of less prosperous populations, its focalisations reinforce the centrality of the European perspective. It is not until the next wave of novels, to which we now turn, that the subaltern has a chance to speak. Not by coincidence, class dynamics, here emergent, next move to the forefront.

BRAVE OLD WORLD

Juanita remained a silent object in *Songdogs*, a retrograde status in comparison to Fernando Yunqué Marcano, the adolescent Puerto Rican photographer in *Let the Great World Spin*, himself in control of the camera and, albeit it temporarily and ultimately peripherally, the narrative. Like *Eliza Lynch*, the novel is set in an unrecoverable past, here New York City in 1974, in the week that Nixon resigns and Philippe Petit walks between the World Trade Towers on a tightrope. To offer a complex portrait of this moment in cultural and political history, McCann shifts narrative perspectives frequently, with each section bearing a distinct voice. Fernando's chapter opens with him on the subway, his ride offering an analogy to his creative power: 'At times he gets dizzy just anticipating the next corner. That speed. ... Control and oblivion. Sometimes it feels like he's the one driving'.[25] The fact that we do not learn his name until he imagines himself as a famous 'imagist' (p. 172), makes it seem to the reader as though he is the one driving his story as well.

This section's narration is in third-person free indirect discourse—what makes it novel is the absence of italics for the occasional Spanish word 'the sheer cojones of it' (p. 168), he says, the code shifting invisible on the page, his slang-filled, neologistic Spanglish the standard language in this section. The Spanish epithets Fernando is called by others are still italicised, marking them as foreign interpolations even when the word is identical: '*Pendejo*' he is called, soon afterward dismissing those who taunt him as 'Pendejos' (p. 169). Creative visually and linguistically (he invents the word 'stepfathersmack' [p. 169]), Fernando's efforts to speak come not through a spray paint scrawl (the graffiti movement offered a voice to many in New York in the 1970s) but in a sophisticated mediation of such tags for others—he photographs graffiti, framing it and presenting it to an audience who would not see it, or not see it as art, otherwise. In this, McCann depicts the boy not as a narrative subject (as Juanita was in *Songdogs*) but as an artist himself.[26] Like the aerialist Petit, to whom Fernando is linked via the use of third-person narration (the majority of the sections, those by major characters, are first person), the young photographer redefines beauty as something intimately linked to, even arising from, everyday places and events.

Fernando's brief section—the novel's shortest—ends when he realises the police are not about to give him a ticket for riding atop the subway with his camera, as he had feared, and he decides to follow them through the turnstiles at the Wall Street stop of the #5 train. The photograph he takes, of Petit high above on the wire, a plane flying by, appears between two later narratives, a copyright logo affixed to it. We do not witness his act of creation, only the product, a move by McCann that invests his character with autonomy beyond the bounds of the words on the page. Fernando's creative gesture presumably brings him the fame he craves, at the same time as his misapprehension about the police indicates how peripheral he is to the storyline—we hear no more about him. The photograph, art and journalism at once, tells the story of another, a simultaneous sidelining of the Hispanic character and a freeing of him from an objectifying gaze.

McCann has been clear that he sees *Let the Great World Spin* as a post-9/11 novel, with Petit's performance and a car crash on the same day serving as the twin axes around which the novel revolves, and the two characters who die in the collision on the FDR East River Drive are in turn figured as twin towers themselves. In a novel related to us by twelve narrators,[27] the characters who die, Corrigan and Jazzlyn, are narrative subjects—they do not speak outside of quotation marks, nor do they ever serve as focalisers in the text. As in *Songdogs*, there is a male, Irish focaliser who begins the novel—here, Corrigan's brother, Ciaran. Even though Ciaran's preeminence indicates the normative position of the young Irish male, his brother's total silence and his own displacement by the panoply of other voices suggest that the opening of the novel is a point of departure rather than a locus. Indeed, Corrigan's near-total illegibility makes him as much of a heart of darkness as any of the other unvoiced characters: Ciaran's misreads of him multiply, concluding at one point that he is a heroin addict, for instance, and the prostitutes for whom Corrigan cares never realise that he is a priest. It is no longer just the racialised Other who is inscrutable in the transnational novel; rather, Ciaran's inability to understand his brother shows how Other all humans are to one another.

In contrast to the time-travel of *Songdogs*, the novel is largely linear, taking place in 1974, with a few flashbacks (there is also a coda set in 2006). The choice to enclose the past chapters within their own era gives their narrators an authority not undercut by a more contemporary perspective. The moral comes, too explicitly, too heavily, on the novel's final page: we 'find in others the ongoing of ourselves' (p. 349). This overly elegant idea accounts for the presence of 'Roaring Seaward, and I Go', the coda which tells us the outcomes of various survivors in order to convey the ongoings of all the characters who have died; it also enforces a present lens on the past, filtering out the characters whose narratives, with hindsight, we can now see offered local colour or atmosphere to the nuclear events. Gone are all the Hispanic characters. We hear no more of Fernando, for instance, but more troublingly, neither do we know what becomes of Adelita, Corrigan's beloved, and her children. Adelita's national origin becomes muddy in the memory of the Irish character who knew her: 'From South America—I can't remember where, Columbia or Nicaragua' (p. 349). The conflation of Central and South America in Ciaran's mental map, along with the utter erasure of her actual country of origin, Guatemala, which gets replaced by nations viewed as sensationally violent, eliminates any 'ongoingness' for Adelita and renders New York as a black and white and cosmopolitan city, not noticeably Hispanic at all. Instead, Hispanic identity becomes something distant and hazy, associated with political upheaval and the drug trade. Like Juanita in *Songdogs*, Adelita is vanished and silent.

At the same time, unlike Juanita, Adelita does narrate a portion of the novel, and her ambivalent class status speaks to the complexities of identity, complexities that Ciaran's callous geography overrides. The fact that she narrates her own section invests her with the same immediacy as the other first-person narrators, Ciaran, Lara, Tillie, and the Kid. Not a nuyorican but a guatemalteca, Adelita comes to New York with dreams of becoming a doctor, an ambition which distinguishes her class status from that of the prostitutes or even Gloria, a college graduate whose working life is not foundational to her identity. In this, Adelita is a precursor to Jaslyn, Jazzlyn's daughter, who focalises the novel's final section, presenting a view of twenty-first-century America as a place with racist mindsets still intact but social mobility possible for certain smart strivers. Jaslyn has a degree from Yale and a not-for-profit job, a combination which signals her membership of a politically progressive meritocracy, the endpoint of the dreaming we see from Adelita and Fernando.

Despite the complexities that erase and silence Hispanic characters in the novel, its presentation of them also invests them with creativity and ambition. It is telling that Adelita's reproductions, her children, do not factor in the 2006 narrative, but Fernando's reproduction, the photograph, does: McCann does not quite trust his story to have an impact without a present-day coda, and the work of art and Jazzlyn's child together bring the past into the present. Their spinning world suggests both stasis and movement, acknowledging that while time does pass, memory and reproduction posit alternative endings: 'The intrusion of time and history. The collision point of stories. We wait for the explosion but it never occurs. The plane passes, the tightrope walker gets to the end of the wire. Things don't fall apart' (p. 325). As Jaslyn stares at the photograph taken the day her mother died, the picture clearly the one credited to Fernando earlier, her thoughts suggest a multitude of other stories, most poignantly the one in which other planes pass the towers—Jaslyn melds the world without a terrorist attack and the one in which her mother survives, undermining Yeats's widening gyres of history. The only part of her imaginary world that did happen is that Petit did get to the end of the wire; the real man separates here from his symbol of a risk gone horribly wrong. McCann chooses to set his final chapter on the eve of the Irish (and global) financial crisis, but its crippling recession maps another type of risk onto Petit's caper. The present, so long held at bay, surges vengefully here to topple Petit from the tightrope.

O'Connor's 2007 novel, *Redemption Falls*, relies upon a similar time structure and final twist beneath its multitude of archival records, narrative voices, and pre- and post-Civil War plotlines. The novel interweaves the stories of a Confederate drummer boy, Jeddo; an Irish revolutionary and Union soldier, O'Keefe; and a New York intellectual, Lucia, whose lives intertwine in a fictionalised Western territory much like Montana. Their tortured efforts to form a family intersect with the tangled stories of, among others, a burn victim who loves Lucia, Jeddo's illiterate older sister Eliza, a bandit who cares for her, and a freed black slave who keeps the house. We begin the journey with Eliza, an Irish focaliser, walking from Louisiana north and west in search of Jeddo, in the waning days of the Civil War, passing through a melange of other American voices, only to end in the 1930s with a hybridised voice of unknown paternity who has, via adoption, become of elevated socioeconomic status, looking back seventy years from a more recent past and offering a meaningful frame to what has come before.

O'Connor's novel, like McCann's, offers a sensual and intelligent Hispanic protagonista who furnishes fleeting comfort to a picturesque, idealistic, mission-driven, Irish-born man in the US, not allowed to survive his novel. Lucia-Cruz Rodriguez Y Ortega McClelland O'Keefe, whose very ungainly name attests to her hybridity, is given far more voice than Adelita; we read her poems, a short narrative, letters, and journal entries. We also receive first-person testimony about her life from our narrator/archivist; the omissions of details are presented not as the hidden fires of an exoticised other but as facts excised for the narrator's own 'private reasons'.[28]

Part of the hybridising O'Connor effects in American culture comes in the class status of Lucia's family, the McClellands, who are wealthy New Yorkers. Lucia embodies an idealised version of an America in which the Civil War acts as a predictor of the suffragette movement, multiculturalism, and massive social mobility. The novel is clear that both Lucia and O'Keefe are hybrids—her mother is Nicaraguan, of Castilian blood, her father a 'Republican' and 'skeptical Presbyterian'

(p. 146, p. 147). O'Keefe 'had Italian blood from his mother' (p. 146). Her willingness to marry O'Keefe, educated but not pedigreed, signals an acceptance of social mobility that the novel sees as emergent in the postwar years.

Indeed, the central narrative arc of the story traces the path of Jeddo Mooney, child of an Irish peasant and an unknown (perhaps Mexican) father, to a professorship emeritus and swanky Fifth Avenue address. Jeddo's progress stands in for the American Dream itself, and the mute subaltern emerges as the puppeteer manipulating all the strings in this massive, complex narrative dance. The novel's final emotional payoff comes in our realisation that abject poverty, premature exposure to the violence of war, and early lack of opportunity cannot stop the intelligence and pluck coursing through the immigrant's veins, that the intellectual elite is the same as the huddled masses, a moving conclusion which nonetheless may deliver a troubling ideological message to a Celtic Tiger readership looking for a social system suited to their new affluence. The repeated triumphs over adversity enacted in O'Keefe's dramatic escapes from first the noose and then Tasmania are replicated and reflected in Jeddo's flight from destitution. Both characters are cast as diamonds in the rough, possessing both the intellect and drive to make something of themselves. Their ascensions are not entirely parallel—O'Keefe is known for his rhetorical grace in public speaking, while Jeddo is speechless for much of the novel—but both men navigate the American class system in ways that make it seem permeable. I have written elsewhere about the way in which the US provides Irish writers with a model for an emergent middle-class identity;[29] here my interest is in the notion of meritocracy, and in the suggestion in *Redemption Falls* that upon the elimination of the inequities of slavery, the United States becomes the storied land of opportunity, freedom, and justice for all. Jeddo is cleared by a court of wrongdoing in O'Keefe's death and comes to New York. Availing himself of the exceptional prospects laid before him, he ascends to social respectability and acclaim, able to cast off entirely the unsightly identity he inhabited before. The novel's message is that class status is negotiable, and that a working-class identity is one to be discarded. Ascension within the class system is the responsibility of the individual, on whom the task of overcoming hardship rests. Professor (Emeritus) J. Daniel McClelland has Irish servants in his house whom he claims to find inefficient and perhaps corrupt; he is not seeking equality for all, just equality of opportunity.

At the height of the Celtic Tiger euphoria, there was enough money for everyone to enrich himself, and Ireland en masse disowned its own poorer past, embarrassed by its thrift and economy. An ethic of consumption prevailed, one critiqued by novels decrying materialism. (Eliza Lynch is not the only hyper-consumer: McCann's Ciaran is a model of Celtic Tiger prosperity, complaining about real estate prices in his million-euro house, a bit of an ass with his internet startup smugness; his marriage to Lara, an heiress, stands in nicely for the way American capital fuelled the Irish bubble.) Ironically, however, the novels under consideration here from the late phase of the boom offer the US as an alternative to such materialism via an embrace of the notion of meritocratic upward mobility. The erasure of the Hispanic characters in all three—via the lack of voice in *Eliza Lynch*, the absence of Adelita and her children in the 2006 part of *Let the Great World Spin*, and the fact that Lucia has no genetic offspring—acts as a trace of the unworkability of meritocracy, of the fact that it tends to work to replicate the ruling class. The rulers are no longer an Anglo-Irish aristocracy or a class of moneyed robber barons but rather a credentialled intellectual elite. The social mobility in which the current generation of Irish literary luminaries has placed its faith is as mythical as the cowboys, the old west, and the essentialised others held up by earlier generations.

To a certain extent, the early novels discussed here are accurate in treating multiculturalism and transnationalism as projects that lay ahead of Ireland—in the late 1980s and early 1990s, only six per cent of residents were immigrants, and the nation was exporting more people than were moving to it. By contrast, the number of foreign-born residents in Ireland in 2011 was seventeen per cent, near the number of foreign-born inhabitants in the US.[30] Throughout the Tiger years, Ireland was intensely conscious of its reversal of economic and migratory fortunes. However, at no time in Irish history has traffic with Hispanic nations been statistically significant to migration patterns; all of these factors make clear that attention to Latin American characters and settings serves some purpose other than the processing of geopolitical fact. If the first wave of texts seems rather to be exploring the status of other postcolonial migrants, the second group may use nationality as a means to talk about class. Only with increased consciousness of class as something as formative to identity as nation can Irish literature begin to depict the subjectivity of Hispanic characters.

If, as Franco Moretti argues, literature 'obtains consent' for certain ideological positions, helping a culture to reconcile itself to or feel soothed by and comfortable with its status quo, these novels, in evoking their Hispanic others only to whisk them offstage, offer provisional hope to a few lucky individuals but embrace too uncritically the notion of a classless America. The imaginative projections out of Ireland offer little solace during austerity.

Triangulating identity: The Afro-Irish Caribbean Act of Union in *Testimony of an Irish Slave Girl*[1]

ABBY PALKO

In *Testimony of an Irish Slave Girl*, Kate McCafferty uses the historical intersection of African slavery and Irish indentured servitude to reposition the Irish as global actors, rather than mere pawns, in the rise of the modern world. From the opening sentence of the novel's testimony, McCafferty's protagonist steadfastly articulates a bifurcated identity that is based both on an allegiance to her home country as well as to the family into which her African Muslim husband has welcomed her: 'They call me Cot Quashey now, or Quashey's Cot, but I was born Cot Daley, in the city of Galway, in the nation of Ireland'.[2] Kidnapped at age ten from Galway, Cot spends the rest of her life on Barbados, where she interacts with her fellow slaves, including those from Ireland and Africa; after bearing a daughter by the first African slave with whom she is bred, she ultimately marries Quashey, an African Muslim, and they have four children together (only one of whom lives to adulthood). Given both the cultural differences between them (the most significant of these is Quashey's religious practice of polygamy, which Cot cannot accept) and the structural impediments created by servitude on a plantation and exacerbated by their lack of a common language, their life together is obviously difficult, but they nevertheless develop an emotional bond. When Quashey plans a revolt with his fellow slaves and freed Irishmen, which he labels a jihad, Cot cannot bring herself to join, although she belatedly takes his cause after he is executed, having come to believe that it is truly her cause as well. Through the biography of Cot, McCafferty suggests that the interracial alliance driving historical cooperation between Irish and Africans in the Caribbean offers a direction out of the racial tensions affecting contemporary Ireland. The novel's ambiguous ending, however, highlights both the promise and the peril of the vision of Irish-African solidarity offered by McCafferty's novel.

Although it draws upon a number of generic forms, *Testimony of an Irish Slave Girl* is foremost historical fiction. McCafferty highlights this intent with her preface, which foregrounds the historical phenomenon of the trepanning of Irish men, women, and children for servitude in the Caribbean. McCafferty frames this political move as an economic issue, noting that 'the British Empire expanded its labor market through a statute which called for the conscription' of those unable to prove appropriate employment (p. vii), and explicitly connects it to the European practice of enslaving Africans for labour in the New World. McCafferty is not merely concerned with chronicling this historical event, however; implicitly she aims to initiate cross-cultural (both racial and religious) understanding. McCafferty draws together rhetorical strands from seventeenth-century slave narratives and contemporary neo-slave narratives,[3] and *Testimony* builds upon centuries-long literary connections between Irish and African-diasporic communities.[4] As Ireland grapples with the increase of African, particularly Nigerian, immigrants in the twenty-first century and tries to determine what this means for the definition of 'Irishness', efforts like McCafferty's have the potential to influence public perception of the categories of 'Irish' and 'other'.

Using the 'historically expansive definition of transnationalism' laid out by Tucker and Casey in this volume's introduction, reading *Testimony* through a transnational lens elucidates the '(unspoken) political agenda' and the 'ideologies about the Irish nation and Irish affiliations' that McCafferty pursues in her novel (to borrow their terms).[5] In her preface to the novel, McCafferty suggests a political agenda that parallels this critical approach. She implicitly claims a transnational framework for her novel through her careful efforts to delineate the ways that the Irish experience of Caribbean servitude compared with the African experience of Caribbean slavery, particularly by drawing on the work of prominent scholars of slavery like Orlando Patterson and Hilary Beckles. She argues, for example, that 'Irish indentured servants were referred to as "stock," were matched for forced breeding—indeed were designated as a sub-human species' (p. viii). She then positions her novel as reflective of Irish hybridity, describing it as Cot's 'imagined participation in one of the historically verifiable plans, undertaken jointly between Irish and African slaves, to overthrow the plantocracy of the island' (p. ix). McCafferty's engagement with the various relationships formed in the Caribbean by the Irish-born Cot, then, represent an attempt to creolise the Irish immigrant experience—or to use Tucker and Casey's term, to uncover the Irish motley in the Caribbean. McCafferty also attempts to substantiate a 'natural' link between Irish Catholic and African Muslim which can then be leveraged for a political alliance. She draws heavily on other 'naturalised' identities, most notably motherhood, to support this connection. While McCafferty suggests she is writing a new history of this alliance, however, the text ultimately undermines it through its troubling racial politics and ambiguous ending.

Because the text employs the literary conceit of recorded testimony, the actions and words of all characters from the plantations are filtered through Cot's words. Cot has been arrested for carrying weapons illegally for another uprising, and Peter Coote, an Englishman hired by the Governor to investigate the connection between the Africans and the Irish in this plot, records her testimony. This narrative structure enables McCafferty to present Irish racism as the sole provenance of Cot (among the various Irish characters in the novel) and to then record within her direct testimony the ways in which she overcame this flaw.[6] McCafferty thus suggests a particular trajectory of understanding the Irish as raced; the way in which it unfolds in the novel, however, overlooks crucial historical details, thereby oversimplifying the story. As historian Nini Rodgers explains, 'In the last resort the Irish did not make common cause with the slaves. Only the wildest of them in their wildest moments were driven to it. They were white and wished to exercise the advantage it conferred upon them.'[7] Because McCafferty imagines her protagonist as one of the 'wildest of them' and furthermore combines Cot's desperation with what I am calling a maternal romance, her depiction is anomalous of the reality.

The maternal romance that McCafferty creates in *Testimony* requires the invocation of maternal instinct to initiate intercultural (racial and/or religious) bonding. Tying her transnational project to motherhood in this manner, however, undermines the notions of salvific maternity that the novel posits, as we see in Cot's observations about the Caribbean landscape. When Cot describes the island, she argues that 'on this island, fertility becomes a monstrous thing' (pp. 31–2). She describes cut down plants that spring back over night, beautiful vines that choke trees to death, offering visions of 'things [that] brought the opposite of what they promised' (p. 32). The fecund vegetation that she describes here symbolises the unsettling experience of motherhood that awaits slave women: fertility as Cot knows it is the forced reproduction of European servant and African slave. The slave woman who gets pregnant does not experience motherhood as either a moment of family bonding or a path to agency; rather, she births further chattel for her owner, as Cot will recount multiple times. Slave children are presented in *Testimony* as mixed-race and the offspring of forced couplings, and as a result, the novel undercuts the alliance McCafferty posits and projects problematic attitudes about the construction of racial differences. Given the context in which the novel was published, the narrative's too-easy collapse of racial differences highlights the complex nature of transnational Irishness as a global position at the turn of the twenty-first century. My reading of McCafferty's novel thus seeks to explain how her project speaks to global notions of ethnic identity and to situate it within the context of twenty-first-century transnational Irish writing.

BARBADOS AND BEYOND: THE LINKS BETWEEN RACE AND SLAVERY

To understand the cultural work that McCafferty takes up in her literary project, it is crucial to understand the history and the popular perceptions of the Irish as white slaves. McCafferty's stated purpose for the novel is to draw attention to this Irish experience of indentured servitude in the Caribbean, which she argues is 'most important, at the beginning of the twenty-first century, as part of a little-known history of affiliation, across race and ethnicity, between groups conventionally defined as incompatible' (p. ix). In terms of the scholarly world at least, however, her claim that it is 'little-known' is inaccurate. Hilary McD. Beckles, one of the foremost Caribbean historians (and one of McCafferty's main sources), frequently writes of the Irish presence in the Caribbean, most notably in *White Servitude and Black Slavery in Barbados, 1627–1715*. When the English faced two seemingly unrelated problems in the seventeenth century, the need to subdue the Irish people to shore up England's conquest of Ireland and a shortage of cheap labour to work in the Caribbean colonies, English administrators implemented a policy that promised to solve both problems: the trepanning of Irish children and young adults to the Caribbean colonies as labourers.[8] As Micheál Ó Siochrú records, beginning in 1649, when Cromwell sent the survivors of Drogheda to Barbados, thousands of Catholic women and children were shipped to the Caribbean; while the exact numbers are impossible to determine, 'estimates suggest that by the 1660s as many as 12,000 Irish resided in the Caribbean, compared with 50,000 African slaves'.[9] Historical counterparts of the fictional Cot were particularly vulnerable: Seán O'Callaghan reminds us that 'There was a special demand for young women, "marriageable and not past breeding", who were eagerly sought after by the sugar planters'.[10]

The attitudes that McCafferty's novel perpetuates and upon which it depends are well-ingrained, as Rodgers asserts; these attitudes are so integral to the novel that it is worth quoting Rodgers at length:

> The idea that people were sent to the West Indies, or more specifically to Barbados, as white slaves, is imprinted in the historical

> consciousness of both the Irish and the British. It features in popular history books, old and new, resurfaces again on television and radio. [...] Rooted in the political traumas of the seventeen century, it drew strength from knowledge of enforced and unremitting unremunerated fieldwork in tropical conditions which so often led to early death. For the bound servant dying while still under contract, the difference between indentured labour and slavery was not an obvious reality. But the notion of arbitrary removal from the homeland is an inextricable part of this sense of white enslavement in the West Indies. By the mid-1650s, the verb 'to be barbadoed' was being used to indicate such a fate.[11]

From the title onward, McCafferty unambiguously presents Cot's Caribbean experience as one of slavery, a move in line with both historical understanding and contemporary popular perception.[12] The Irish men, women, and children who arrived in the Caribbean as indentured servants quickly recognised the similarities between their position and the African slavery experience.[13] Life on Barbados was traumatic for the Irish: 'Almost from the earliest days of the settlement of Barbados, the indentured servants were treated as little more than slaves. For any sign of insubordination or malingering they were flogged with cowhide whips, leaving deep scars'.[14] Not surprisingly, such an awareness of shared oppression, as well as the possibility that it could lead to Irish participation in African slave revolts, worried English plantation owners.[15]

Beckles posits that seventeenth-century white indentured servitude in the Caribbean played a crucial role in the formation of the incipient slave economy, with Barbados establishing the pattern of agricultural developments that subsequent islands would follow.[16] As the plantation economy transitioned to slave labour in place of indentured service, servants found themselves 'forced to share their material deprivation, and its corresponding sociopolitical oppression, with slaves'.[17] In fact, he argues, white indentured servitude was the 'training ground' on which planters developed the necessary skills and attitudes for implementing large-scale black slavery.[18] The eminent politician and scholar Eric Williams concurs, noting, 'Barbados, a word of terror to the white servant, became to the Negro, as a slave trader wrote in 1693, "a more dreadful apprehension ... than we can have of hell"'.[19] Clearly, Williams links the experiences of bonded labour (as McCafferty wishes to do), while retaining important distinctions of degree. Beckles and Williams suggest that the ethnic distinctions that underpin the system of forced white labour that the British established in Barbados (with its reliance on the labour of Irish, Scots, and poor English workers) proved easy to intensify and transfer to the trade in Africans that the Caribbean plantocracy came to depend upon. While the progression from white to black slave labour was accomplished on the basis of ideologies of similarities between the groups, a reverse alliance was much more difficult to achieve.[20] Rodgers suggests that the descriptions of white servitude that positioned it in terms of slavery 'spring from an acceptance that slavery was for Negroes'.[21] In Ireland, this belief was manifested as a firmly-rooted 'horror of white people being on a level with blacks'.[22] At the same time, there is surviving evidence of Hiberno-African collaboration dating from 1655, and Rodgers documents the official belief in Irish willingness to participate in slave revolts.[23] Geographical location thus seems to be a crucial contributing factor in Irish attitudes toward racial alliances, with the Irish in the Caribbean much more sympathetic toward the enslaved Africans than the Irish at home in Ireland.[24]

In this context, McCafferty's attempts to stitch together this political alliance between the Irish and Africans in the Caribbean are particularly salient. In her testimony, Cot ruminates repeatedly upon the distinctions of race she has been taught to make and upon which her British overseers depend; these racial differences instigate the alienation she experiences. She tells Coote that she shuns any connection with her fellow Irish men and women because 'you do not trust even your own, once your own have sold and bought you' (p. 43). When Coote calls the differences between Cot and the Africans a 'natural difference, created by God himself', Cot contradicts him (p. 44). It is, rather, she argues 'not natural' and the result of being 'trained to see it' (p. 44). She ties her impulse to dismiss the Africans as 'unrefined' to the indoctrination that all groups impose on their young: 'all it meant was my fondness for the familiar, the fondness we are trained from our mother's apron to feel for a clan we learn to recognise as ours' (p. 45). Noting the similar reactions of the enslaved Africans to her difference, Cot avers, 'I believe that every tribe of people think themselves the yardstick of Creation, and feel fear and distaste and suspicion of outsiders. But still, I tell you this is learned' (p. 45). The alienation that she suffers is thus an exile from both those whose race she shares and those of the other race subjugated like her – but also, she suggests, potentially surmountable through proper maternal reactions to efforts to indoctrinate racism.

Neither Irish involvement with slavery nor their contact with Africans began in the Caribbean though, and historically the Irish have often been the beneficiaries of power imbalances between the two groups. The Irish have occupied shifting, complicated positions with respect to the institution of slavery. Rodgers outlines parallels between the Irish and African situations, noting that late twentieth-century medievalists have inconclusively debated whether external forces (the Vikings in Ireland, the trans-Saharan commerce of the Islamic trade between Africa, Egypt, Arabia, and Asia Minor) prompted increased slaving in either society in the fifth to twelfth centuries.[25] The Irish status as racialised colonial subject is well-established in scholarship; conversely, as Rolston and Shannon contend, 'the Irish have often met black people in situations where they, the Irish, have had relative social, economic or political advantage. The roots of Irish racism are in the history of those uneven power relations'.[26]

Within the historical context of Ireland, slavery was also practiced. Cot would have most likely had at least a sense of the important role as 'vital and venerable unit of currency' played by the *cumal* (the female slave) in early Ireland's economy, given its prominence in the *Táin Bó Cuailgne* and other early literary texts.[27] While the novel does not specifically reference the *cumal*, traces of this cultural heritage are found throughout. As Rodgers notes, '[i]n early Irish society the exceptional bondswoman could be influential, well dressed, managerial in position and boastful of her status'.[28] In *Testimony*, Cot finds herself oddly drawn to the captain of the slaver that brought her to Barbados through the bizarre comfort his attention offers her. On her first plantation, her looks draw the attention of the master as well, who sets her up in an empty barn stall where he visits her at night for emotional comfort. Cot aspires to the security of the high-placed *cumal*, calling her master 'the saviour on whom I had staked every desperate hope' (p. 76); this was a dream denied any of the African slaves who provided only sexual release and increased stock for their white masters. Although fulfilling a key economic role in Irish society, the *cumal* was still a slave, however, and we see traces of this marginalisation in Coote's treatment of Cot, whom he calls a 'common slut' (p. 32) in an echo of the perception of the *cumal* as purveyor of sexual favours that Rodgers notes.[29]

Initially, life in the Caribbean is bearable for Cot, who is 'relatively coddled' on her first plantation (p. 86). Cot's immature self-identification with those in power further insulates her, as well as prevents the formation of any solidarity between her and either the African slaves or other Irishwomen. Cot's experience of indentured servitude radically alters when she is joined on her second plantation by two Irishwomen. Cot first describes them as lively, telling 'silvery sly jokes' (p. 89). Her sense of loyalty has been corrupted, however, by her unconscious need to see herself as special; she confesses:

> I cannot say what changed in me so that one day I was planning how we three could build a little cottage altogether, but the next I drew away from where they stood. I averted my eyes as I passed by them. 'The dirty Irish mares,' Vaughton called them, and suddenly I felt them so. (p. 89)

When confronted with the dominant racialised view of her held by those in power over her, Cot can only cope by dissociating herself from her countrywomen. This distancing of herself from the other Irish indentured servants, then, is best read as indicative of the ways that Cot has been influenced by her masters' racial ideologies and has adopted them as protective measures. And this is the most tragic result of Cot's kidnapping: she is alienated from her heritage and rendered incapable of forming the kind of alliance that would affirm her identity. On the other hand, with her cultural alliances broken, Cot will ultimately be able to shift identification and form new alliances in future encounters with African slaves.

The American racial binary of black/white also strongly influences the text,[30] as we see when it positions Cot as black-like in direct opposition to her Irish and Scottish compatriots in Barbados; Cot describes her hair, for instance, as 'too snarled to pull smooth with my fingers: it had twined like African hair around itself into long plaits' (p. 143). This physical transformation marks a transitional moment for Cot: she makes this observation when she is preparing herself for her ordered breeding with Quashey. While Cot submits because she must, the experience is life-changing: Quashey does not just come to her hut and impregnate her. Rather, he sends his other wives to welcome Cot to their compound and to help her move into the new cabin he has constructed for her. As Cot shares this part of her history with Coote, she calls her co-wives '[t]hose two I came too late to call my sisters' (p. 144). The evolution of Cot's hair from the long-flowing locks she describes while she's on the slaver into dreadlocks thus presages her gradual recognition of her position within a racialised and racist system and her subsequent willingness to reimagine her clan and claim Quashey and his co-wives as members of it. Textually, McCafferty achieves this shift by drawing on both Caribbean history and Irish cultural notions of themselves as raced.

McCafferty alludes to this shared ground and race-based historical distrust between the Irish and Africans in Cot's experience of the uncanny in Barbados's similarity to and difference from Ireland. This little bit of home, the recovery of something that reminds one of home, proves more unsettling than a total lack of referents would have because it simultaneously induces the memory of home and the realisation that this is not home, thereby reproducing the separation from home. Arriving at her second plantation after her first master gambles her away, Cot re-experiences this uncanny homesickness: 'These were the first sheep I had heard of in Barbados. They made me sick with longing for Ireland, even after six years away, and seemed treacherous, like trusted beings from a peaceful realm who lead the dreamer, unsuspecting off of nightmare's cliffs' (p. 85). Additionally, though, Cot has a moment that night as she arrives at the Glebe in which she begins to develop empathetic understanding,[31] primed by this homesickness to reach out to another whom she categorises as like her according to gender and social status, not by race. A black 'woman look[s] at Cot in silence, lifting the infant from the water. "I half raised my arm in greeting, but saw myself through her eyes for a moment. So pale I seemed glowing in the dark, a huge glow-worm"' (p. 87); in this moment Cot sees through the other's eyes. The view of herself that she articulates simultaneously emphasises the privileges she enjoys as white through its reference to her paleness and its invocation of 'huge' stature and diminishes her by comparing her to a glow-worm. She thus captures the perspective of her that the African slaves were likely to have. This empathetic understanding is only possible when Cot ceases identifying with her captors, which in turn is only possible when a memory of home activates her critical assessment of her situation on the edge of 'nightmare's cliff'. Further, it is only possible with a woman whose actions identify her as a mother.

A MATERNAL ROMANCE

Operating under the critical premise that historical fiction is as concerned with the moment of its temporal composition as it is with the moment of its narrative setting (if not more so), my reading of *Testimony* reveals its deep concern with several dominant strands of Irish political discourse from the end of the twentieth century: reproductive issues, immigration, and religious pluralism. McCafferty uses Cot's initial wariness of Quashey, provoked by the racist attitudes socialised in her by the plantation system, and her subsequent understanding of him, birthed from extended exposure to his respect for her, to create a maternal romance that ostensibly forges a path through racism to solidarity. McCafferty only obliquely references racism in Ireland in her preface, but it throws a dark shadow over her project. As she explains in an interview included at the end of the novel, 'it was my intention to point to certain experiences and patterns of power that have gone on, and are still going on, and … are often smoke screened by issues like race'.[32] An attempt to decouple race and the exercise of power in a novel focused on Caribbean slavery is problematic, to say the least, given that race is an inextricable part of that experience of slavery. An important subtext is the coded discourse that Maureen Reddy articulates: 'anti-black racism in Ireland generally is both deeply disguised and firmly displaced onto the issue of immigration and asylum-seeking'.[33] Irish public discourse, she argues, manipulates racial codes to express deep-seated discomfort. In a culture as mono-racial and mono-cultural as Ireland, the visible presence of black people disrupts easy notions of Irishness and imbues immigration debates with deeper significance.

The novel thus participates in contemporary debates driven by anxiety over the ways that Irish women reproduce.[34] At the same time that 'Irish' women firmly bear the burden of 'reproducing the Irish national subject',[35] anxiety about immigrant women giving birth to babies who would be legal Irish citizens grows. And so in contemporary Ireland, the legitimacy and autonomy of specific bodies continues to be hotly contested. There are close ties between the concern evinced by women writers regarding reproductive issues and the social angst over race and immigration, and McCafferty cogently connects the two in her narrative. To borrow Luke Gibbons' phrase, the process of being bred together serves as a 'two-way mirror' for Quashey and Cot, allowing both cultures to 'see each other through the same darkened glass'.[36]

At the very moment when immigration into Ireland is rising and problematising Irish motherhood, *Testimony* imagines how multicultural integration might be achieved, narrativising it through maternity. Realities such as the fears over maternity tourism that led to the June 2004 Referendum or Savita Halappanavar's death from sepsis following a miscarriage when her requests for a termination were denied due to Ireland's constitutional ban on abortion,[37] however, suggests its improbability. We can thus read the reproductive politics explored in *Testimony* as reflective of the contested environment of Irish motherhood as they simultaneously engage with the complete lack of reproductive autonomy that characterised African slavery in the Caribbean. Thus, Afebwa practices birth control: 'Afebwa knew a weed whose cousin grows in Africa, and brewed it every month between her courses. Though Quashey wanted to have sons with her, she said that she would mother them only in freedom, after the Jihad' (p. 159).[38] While the novel is set during 'perhaps the most tumultuous [decade] of any in the long saga of Irish history',[39] McCafferty writes in another decade of great social turmoil, at the tail end of the Celtic Tiger, amidst great public, coded debate about racial understandings of authentic Irishness. It cannot be insignificant, then, that her heroine becomes mother to mixed-race children. Cot's reproductive powers are manipulated in service of the governing apparatus: 'Recently the first experiment of offspring bred between Irish and African had reached early maturity ... Vaughton bade her submit herself to Pawpaw Jack, the driver of her field crew' (pp. 126–7). Not only does Cot lack any agency in becoming a mother, since the fathers of her children are African slaves, her children are also 'chattel' for life (p. 195).[40]

Within the context of plantation slavery, we thus see McCafferty exploring concerns about parentage and citizenship, as well as echoing Irish rhetoric about the sanctity of motherhood. Cot becomes a mother in service of the plantation economy; there is nothing of the romanticised maternal instinct about the undertaking: 'Jack Vaughton ordered Cot Daley to prepare to breed' (p. 126). It is notable that the narrative records this momentous shift in the third-person voice that it occasionally employs to anchor Cot's testimonial remembrances to the present-day of the text; in this instance, however, it detaches her experience from her present. She submits to the breeding because she realises her only hope of ever becoming free lies in strict obedience to the managers of the plantation. When her first daughter is born, Cot sees potential redemption:

> But when I took her in my arms there in the shed, the sun rose here, inside my chest ... and I would not let her go. I knew then that to suffer breeding was not important if it gave me this. Holding my own perfect wee'n ... and to be a woman ... under all it was a wondrous, a mystic thing. (p. 131)

This experience fleetingly reconnects her with her heritage: although she is denied a priest and the opportunity to baptise her daughter, Cot names her Moya in honour of her mother (p. 132). Cot's postpartum reverie rhetorically mimics Irish ideologies of the Good Mother enshrined in the 1937 Constitution. However, only certain women can achieve this status, as mother of the nation, as late twentieth-century debates of citizenship reveal. Vaughton, the overseer, quickly corrects her delusion, reminding her that no freed white man will marry her after her servitude ends if she has 'half-Negra babies clinging to your skirts reminding him' of her sexual history (p. 132). Furthermore, because Pawpaw Jack is a driver, he is able to enforce his cultural tradition of having his kinswomen raise the child, and he takes Moya from Cot and renames her. Cot fights his attempts to take Moya away from her, but she has no concept of what motherhood in her condition would be like, friendless on the plantation and working in the fields. In her innocence, Cot believes that becoming a mother will prove her salvation, while the reality of her experience of motherhood is a total lack of control. Ultimately, Vaughton buys her cooperation with a length of cloth and two silver coins. Because life on the plantation has inculcated a Foucauldian discipline in Cot, she accedes to this lack of control. Now, Cot can only take comfort in the little she knows of Moya's life and end this portion of her testimony by fruitlessly asserting her claim on her daughter, calling her 'My firstborn child. My Moya' (p. 133).

Vaughton next pairs Cot with Quashey, a Muslim African, which affords McCafferty the opportunity to explore interreligious negotiations (a salient topic in Ireland since the partition and the Civil War) with a twist that contemporises Cot's meditations: motherhood is posited as the binding force between them, as Cot explains in the culmination of her testimony when she finally tells Coote about the conspiracy between the Africans and the Irish. Quashey feels that through ruining her health to bear his children, Cot has become 'flesh of his flesh, blood of his blood' (p. 179). Family formation is forced upon Cot, but familial bonds are carelessly rent, and she cannot yet distinguish between the overseers who disregard all family bonds and the members of Quashey's *umma* (brotherhood of fellow slaves) with whom she must share his loyalty. Cot is far from the perfect ally, as she herself admits; Quashey (through Mama Chiva, the only member of the family who can speak English) invites Cot to participate in the coming jihad, as sign of his total acceptance of her. Cot is neither ready to fully accept her position in this family nor to renounce it: '"I felt rancor, ill will, and contempt toward all of them who meant to steal my family"—here the prisoner begins to weep brief gritty tears—"the only family I would ever have, from me"' (p. 179). After witnessing a series of encounters between master and slave that should have prepared her to unreservedly participate, Cot still cannot. And it is her motherhood that simultaneously provides the impetus to join Quashey and the paralysis that precludes action. As he prepares for the jihad, Cot is terrified, thinking, 'Sold away, away, away! I looked at my one child and could not see how we could win this fight. Saw only many costs of losing it …' (p. 187). When the moment comes for Cot to act, the maternal sentiments that slavery has perverted overwhelm her:

> I sat upon a feed sack and picked up my child, but she was Ben, no she was Moya, no it was myself; it was 1651, it was 1681—the year I was to go free. But gaunt and starved and beaten, my term renewed, I would never now be free to go. I saw the Spirits of the Night batting me around like a wolf bats a rabbit; but no, that was my Betty they were batting, my Betty who I vaguely hoped to buy into freedom after myself. 'No,' I told my husband. 'Betty … Betty has a cold …' I undid my bodice and swirled her sweaty hair with my palm, pressing her to the safety of my pounding chest. (p. 188)

With Quashey and Mama Chiva standing in front of her, holding out the pen and paper upon which they need her to write travelling passes for the Africans leaving the plantation to purchase arms, Cot cannot make the necessary leap of faith to break with the indoctrination her overseers have inculcated in her. Although Quashey promises to take her to Montserrat, where they will be welcomed by 'the Maroons and a band of people like yourself, led by a man named Bat Fish' (p. 188), Cot cannot believe that such a fantastical end is possible. She screams in hysteria and Quashey capitulates, noting, 'Who knows if your fears are founded? For as the Prophet says, Heaven is found under a mother's feet' (p. 188). In their disparate reactions, we see an imperfectly achieved maternal romance: Quashey honours her inability to fully commit to the family he has welcomed her into, which she expresses as concern for her (not their) daughter. Without the protection Cot could have offered them with written passes, the uprising is brutally put down, and Quashey, Mama Chiva, Afebwa, and Cudjoe are arrested, tortured, and publicly executed.

Cot's eventual participation in the revolt is the product of her maternal identity, which enables her to overcome her antipathy towards her fellow Irishmen as well as her ability to embrace her place in 'Quashey's clan here in Barbados' (p. 197) and to believe that they await her in the afterlife to offer a 'welcome [that can be] taken for granted' (p. 196). Because Cot refuses to help Quashey and her co-wives, the revolt fails, but she is allowed to stay on the plantation until she finishes her indentureship. At its conclusion, Cot is cast off the plantation since the overseers do not trust her. She wanders the markets in a rum-induced haze until she hears that Betty has been sold off to be raised as an officer's concubine, a dehumanising treatment for her 'own Betty' that Cot cites as the impetus for finally joining the uprising. She weans herself from rum, gaining a new clarity that allows her to listen with 'younger ears, as if I had the ears of Moya and of Betty, my living daughters' (p. 199). When Paudi Isac, an Irishman whom she had toiled with at Arlington, contacts her (as Quashey's widow) to join the revolt, Cot agrees to carry maps and arms to bring about Quashey's jihad, the fruits of which will be freedom for people 'to discover their very destinies' (p. 202). Cot thus envisions an inversion of the racial project of the British Empire in which the Caribbean would become a 'garden-paradise' (p. 202). This is in many ways a hollow victory, as Cot is only finally convinced of its possibility by Afebwa's fortitude in the face of torture. Painfully, through this posthumous recognition of Afebwa's strength, Cot comes to understand that circumstances have woven unbreakable bonds between her and Afebwa, and it is ultimately out of solidarity that she participates, as she confesses in her last words of the novel:

> Yes, if you asked me why I carried pistols in with my papayas, 'tis because Afebwa is as much my ancestor as any Daley. And I have come to know that I too will become everyone's ancestor. So I must choose the right road for the progeny I've mothered: I have chosen

> where to set my mother's-feet. That this inverted paradise, sir, might become someday that garden-heaven, where people are at peace and plenty. Free to discover their very destinies. (pp. 201–2)

This new-found solidarity with Afebwa, this recognition of her as ancestor, cannot be read as acceptance of the polygamous nature of her family with Quashey, however. First, Cot can only see her with this sympathy once her physical presence—that which she finds threatening to her nuclear family—is permanently removed. Second, she calls Afebwa her 'ancestor' here, not sister, and then explicitly says she carried the weapons because of the one difference between herself and Afebwa that she does not erase: her maternal status. McCafferty thus links maternity with interracial solidarity, suggesting but only partially depicting a kind of transnational understanding that might lead to the end of war and oppression.

Afebwa's lack of voice in the novel also troubles any neat interpretation of racial solidarity, and Cot appropriates her actions into her own narrative of the uprising. While Cot claims Afebwa as her own sister, Afebwa is never given the option to reciprocate, and given the complicated fellow-oppressed/oppressor dynamic that defined historical relations between the Irish and the Africans in the Caribbean, this aspect of McCafferty's novel can potentially be read as undercutting her goal. Significantly, Cot does not claim to speak or act for Afebwa; rather her claim of solidarity is deployed as evidence that she has overcome the racial prejudices that shaped her interactions with Afebwa. Cot insists that her 'tale must be full told' because this is the only option remaining to assert the alliance she suggests can protect the 'progeny I've mothered' (p. 192, p. 201). Cot's growth is not unproblematic—it is predicated upon explicit expression of racist views of Muslims and Africans as well as misunderstanding (according to McCafferty) of the true goals of Jihad.[41] As Cot gives her testimony to Coote, she initially accedes to his view of the Africans as savages several times, and then contradicts him by drawing on rhetorics of the noble savage. What he wishes to dismiss as a failed uprising she insists was great and 'failed only at the moment' (p. 192); when he wants to cut off her testimony, she continues speaking in order to correct what she considers is Coote's failure to understand the truth of their respective positions in Caribbean society. She has, in important ways, appropriated the discourse of the slave experience in order to serve as an ally to those whose lives were radically reshaped by it. And she does this with an underlying purpose of illuminating an *Irish* experience. In his study of how Irish artists and intellectuals have 'used Afro-Caribbean culture as a way of fashioning Ireland as part of a cosmopolitan brotherhood', Michael Malouf dismisses *Testimony of an Irish Slave Girl* as a mere 'conventional morality play'.[42] The complexities woven into her novel, however, highlight the importance of *Testimony* in thinking about Irish literature and transnationalism.

SLAVE: MOTHER: ALLY?

Remembering Afebwa's fate, Cot laments 'the one I did not know was my own courageous sister until it was too late' (p. 189). In this claim of sisterhood is born a new understanding of racial differences: when Coote forces Cot to claim affiliation, asking her, 'By "your kind" do you mean those of the Irish nation?', Cot can now answer, 'Of the Irish nation: or the female nation: or of the nation of all chattel' (p. 76). Here, McCafferty's use of colons instead of commas or semi-colons enacts the very inclusiveness that Cot is theorising. Cot's narration troubles the hegemonic version of history that Coote is seeking to merely confirm. Cot tells Coote that 'there are two kinds of folk. People who look up, wanting to see themselves in their high-placed better; and people who find the best of themselves upon the midden of the humble poor' (p. 200), and she tries to present herself as the latter. And yet, the very vehicle through which Cot claims this breakthrough, motherhood, is also the reason she can only find posthumous solidarity with Afebwa. Cot is breathtakingly jealous of the bond Ben forms with his auntie, and when Afebwa dances to the tinkling sound of the spirits, Cot does not stop her even though she knows 'To dance to fey music is the beginning of the end' (p. 170). As Beckles observes, 'contemporary women activists recognise that future integrative, trans-feminist strategies for solidarity are likely to generate further fragmentations and contests'.[43] *Testimony* ostensibly presents exactly the opposite in its depiction of Cot and Coote's slave women, who offer her numerous kindnesses while in Coote's custody; but in Cot's primary relationships, she only ever produces fragmentations and contests.

In the end, McCafferty's utopian erasure of racial and ethnic differences impoverishes—though does not invalidate—her literary excavation. It's easy to dismiss *Testimony* as naively utopian in its blindness to the racial tensions that weave throughout it. The novel's oversimplification of race, however, is problematic precisely because it speaks to and signifies a moment of high interracial tension; as Evelyn O'Callaghan muses, 'it perhaps forces modern readers to confront slavery in a new way'.[44] A more nuanced discussion of race would, however, better serve such a confrontation and any related negotiations of race. While we might criticise McCafferty for appropriating the history of slavery to further her narrative ends, she is careful to not speak for the African slave women (and she does ground her novel in historical research). This narrative technique induces a frustration in the reader that surely mirrors the frustration Cot feels in being unable to communicate easily with Quashey and Afebwa. McCafferty thus depicts an imperfectly achieved solidarity in order to demonstrate the great difficulty inherent in achieving cross-racial understanding. Cot is only able to approach this solidarity with Afebwa through their relationship with Quashey—and we do not know how Afebwa experiences their encounters; it is possible that Afebwa sees no solidarity between them, especially after Cot refuses to provide the assistance that would have secured the success of their uprising. Overcoming the narcissism of differences evoked and stoked by the experience of colonialism is, McCafferty suggests, a life-long project with rare success. Coote, for example, is never able to admit the similarities between himself and Cot, so consumed is he by chasing colonial fortune—even when he fathers a child with his slave Lucy. Even when formulating the thesis he draws from her testimony leaves him 'tangled, melancholy, frustrated', he cannot admit the possibility that her understanding is the true one: 'He will never consider changing the hypothesis' (p. 202). Ultimately, then, *Testimony of an Irish Slave Girl* exposes fault lines in Irish racial discourse through its own attempts to bridge them.

Transnationalism, sexuality, and Irish gay poetry: Frank McGuinness, Cathal Ó Searcaigh, Padraig Rooney

ED MADDEN

Because Irish poetry is so often assumed to be grounded in the local and the national, Jahan Ramazani argues in *A Transnational Poetics* that Irish poetry 'deserves special attention in an exploration of what a transnational disciplinary paradigm can reveal and a national paradigm can make harder to see'.[1] A narrow, national framework, he explains, fails to adequately address the 'powerfully intercultural dynamics' of Irish poetry, such as the imaginative topographies and 'multilingual dislocations' in the poetry of Seamus Heaney. Ramazani further points to the influence of Anglo-American feminist verse on Eavan Boland, suggesting that she adopted their poetic strategies in order to 'break the grip' of Ireland's patriarchal poetic ideologies.[2] Despite that recognition of gender as interpretative category and feminist poetics as an emancipatory project, Ramazani is markedly silent throughout his book on the subject of sexuality. If Irish poetry 'deserves special attention' in a discussion of transnational poetics, queer sexuality doesn't seem to merit even a mention.

Indeed although Gertrude Stein, Elizabeth Bishop, Amy Lowell, June Jordan, and Jackie Kay all appear in the book, lesbian sexuality is unmentioned or, at best, elided in the rich and otherwise nuanced analysis of a single poem, Elizabeth Bishop's 'In the Waiting Room'.[3] Moreover, although gay and bisexual poets John Ashberry, Hart Crane, Robert Duncan, Allen Ginsberg, Langston Hughes, Claude McKay, James Merrill, Frank O'Hara, Wilfred Owen, and Walt Whitman also appear in the book, male homoeroticism is invisible. Yet the question of same-sex desire is inevitably provoked by Bishop's deconstructions of gender identity, and homoeroticism could be said to animate if not compel the deeply humanising, affiliative, and boundary-crossing empathies Ramazani locates in Owen's elegiac war poetry.[4] In the analyses of Bishop and Owen, sexual identity seems to have been effaced precisely where it could offer a complicating and enriching lens of identity and difference, and precisely where erotic desire might, in fact, underlie the affiliating or disaffiliating transcultural impulses of the poetry.

In this essay, I hope to demonstrate the importance of sexuality to transnational literary analysis through an examination of gay Irish poetry.[5] Because gender and sexuality inevitably inflect and inform national and transnational forms of belonging and identification, sexuality is a critical lens for understanding national identification or disaffiliation, thickening our sense of the cultural specificities, social materialities, and legal exigencies of national and sexual identification. Moreover, sexuality—manifest in queer forms of belonging and identification, queer desires, lesbian and gay relationships and cultures—may also animate and compel the intercultural dynamics and interstitial identities that Ramazani locates in transnational poetry. I hope to demonstrate further that Irish gay poetry—like much of Irish lesbian and gay literature, especially before decriminalisation—is almost inevitably transcultural in reference and transnational in scope. Identification as *gay* seems to depend, in Irish poetry, on cross-cultural influences, and (homo)sexual identity formation may trouble, even dislocate, identification with(in) the nation.

As I will illustrate through readings of poems by Frank McGuinness, Cathal Ó Searcaigh, and Padraig Rooney, queer forms of identity and belonging intensify what Ramazani calls the affiliative and disaffiliative energies of transnational poetry. Though readers of Irish literature are familiar with Frank McGuinness (his plays if not his poetry) and Cathal Ó Searcaigh, Padraig Rooney has largely escaped critical attention. As I have argued elsewhere, Rooney's work emphatically dislocates the ethnically (dis)identified Irish queer into transnational networks of queer and consumer cultures.[6] In the following I will focus my analysis on three emblematic figures: the resident alien, the migrant *flâneur*, and the escape artist, three figures that suggest complex transnational forms of identity and belonging and key themes of alienation, mobility, and escape.

TRANSCULTURAL CONTEXTS AND GAY IRISH IDENTITIES

Irish lesbian and gay culture—at least before the decriminalisation of male homosexuality in 1993[7]—often seemed driven by a double-bind of identitarian politics, at once indigenous and foreign, resident and alien. On the one hand, there is an insistent emphasis on *indigenous* queerness, on *Irish* lesbian and gay practices, cultures, and peoples, even if coded and covert, unrecognised or unrealised. When the first book on Irish lesbian and gay culture, *Out for Ourselves*, appeared in 1986, its editors insisted on the first page, 'Let us make one thing quite clear, we are everywhere in the thirty-two counties. We are Irish born and bred, not an imported vice or the product of foreign influence'.[8] On the other hand, while Irish people may be lesbian and gay, the ability to name oneself and imagine a different culture is more often than not located outside of Ireland. There was an insistent turn to international contexts for gay identity formation and gay liberationist politics, recourses both legal and cultural, and a simultaneous displacement of representations of homosexuality elsewhere in order to imagine its possibility.[9] As Eoin Collins admits in his personal introduction to *Lesbian and Gay Visions of Ireland* (1995), his 'reference points for "gayness" were to be British and American: Bloomsbury, Berlin decadence, and, eventually, Stonewall and Gay Liberation', a transcultural bricolage of identify formation.[10]

In 1978, Jeff Dudgeon, who successfully challenged the criminalisation of homosexuality in Northern Ireland, stated emphatically in *Gay Left* magazine: 'The dominant influences on the lives of emancipated gays cannot be their native communities, which do not recognise or consider their position. Rather, they are influenced by ... Anglo-American cultural factors', among which he cites both the gay disco of Sylvester and the punk rock culture of Belfast.[11] The sources of gay emancipation, Dudgeon suggests, lie outside the nation. At that moment, his own legal complaint was at the European Commission on Human Rights. Within the year it would be ruled admissable to the European Court of Human Rights, which would ultimately decide in his favour in 1981; as a result, male homosexual sex was decriminalised in Northern Ireland in 1982. In the South, David Norris followed Dudgeon in appealing to the European Court of Human Rights, which ruled in his favour in 1988; homosexuality was eventually decriminalised in Ireland in 1993. Decriminalisation resulted from legal appeals beyond the nation, but Norris and fellow activist, Kieran Rose, consistently relied on a nationally-inflected rhetoric—insisting on a social tolerance that was intrinsically Irish and homophobia as the cultural import. If Dudgeon's case argued that Northern Ireland should have the same laws as England, Norris argued that English laws were the problem.[12]

Despite these seemingly contradictory political positions in relation to nation—the disaffiliative politics of Dudgeon and the affiliative politics of Norris—both appeal beyond the borders of the nation to international courts, and on both sides of the border, the gay rights movement was driven by transnational networks of information and community. Tellingly, the names of the first gay community centres in Ireland invoke their respective influences—the (Edward) Carpenter Centre in Belfast and the (Magnus) Hirschfeld Centre in Dublin, outposts of transnational gay culture invoking British and European ancestries and acknowledging the transnational grounding of an Irish gay movement.

FRANK McGUINNESS AT HANOVER PLACE

'Wrap my nearness round you like our flag.'[13]

Frank McGuinness's poem 'Hanover Place, July Eleventh', which concludes his first collection of poetry, *Booterstown* (1994), portrays a gay couple in Northern Ireland as 'aliens at home', suggesting the double-bind and displacement of gay identity in Ireland or Northern Ireland before decriminalisation—'at home' but alienated. In the poem, two men, one Irish and one English, prepare for bed in a nation that does not accept them: 'Aliens at home, this is where we live', McGuinness writes, 'Ireland and England with no right to love' (p. 85). National borders inflect the relationship—to the extent that each man seems synecdoche of his nation—and both men are marginalised by and within the nation. The figure of homosexuality in the poem is the resident alien, and the slant rhyme of live/love foregrounds the incompatibility of nation ('where we live') and sexuality ('no right to love').

The poem first appeared in the literary magazine *Cyphers*—a journal Anne Mulhall describes as 'outward-looking'[14]—in 1980, the year before the Dudgeon decision in the North. Readers would have been aware of the Dudgeon case at the European court, but they might also have recalled the Provisional IRA bombings in Coleraine, the poem's setting, only a few years before, in 1973 and 1975. When the poem was republished in *Booterstown* in 1994, the year of the IRA ceasefire, it came with the imprimatur of Gallery Press, a press devoted to Irish literature and thus more inward or nationally focused. It also appeared in the midst of a burst of lesbian and gay cultural production in the Republic following the 1993 decriminalisation.[15] In its publication history, the poem thus straddles the years of legal reform and European court challenges, as well as marking the transformed literary scene for queer Irish writers.

If the poem thus seems to move from the margins to the centre—in politics, publication venues, and timing—it is still emphatically about marginality, specifically the marginal status of gay men in Ireland and Northern Ireland. This marginal status is enhanced by the poem's historical setting, its representation of temporal and geographical liminality, and the transnational romance it portrays. 'Hanover Place, July Eleventh' is a liminal place at a liminal moment, the poem's title and setting emphasising boundaries. Hanover Place is a major street in Coleraine's city centre, next to the River Bann that divides the city, as McGuinness writes, 'from the working-class estate'. That is, the river divides the predominantly Protestant city from the Catholic estates, just as it is also imagined to divide the urban Protestant and Belfast-centric regions of Northern Ireland from the more rural and Catholic regions to the west. July 11, Eleventh Night, is a night of celebratory bonfires before the Protestant Unionist Orange marches on July 12. 'Come midnight the eleventh of July, / A powerful water music pounds our ears'—the poem thus moves from quiet ('the quiet Bann') to noise, the temporal pivot of midnight further emphasising the poem's liminal status. The Bann surely also suggests the traditional *banns* or public announcements of marriage, the geographical infused by pun with the heteronormative—as if to emphasise that this particular union is 'quiet', unproclaimed.

If the poem's setting is marked by boundaries, its movement is predominantly one of contraction and retreat. Space constricts from the town and river of the first stanza to the Georgian house (a 'refuge of books and papers') of the second stanza to the lovers' bed of the conclusion. The house is not only a refuge but also a 'haunt', as if the two men are spectral, dislocated or translocated here, not of this time and space.[16] The use of the term haunt here, along with the social isolation marked in the steady reduction of social and geographic scale, registers the dislocation the speaker and his lover experience, their sense of alienation from the national *and* sexual politics of the North. Drawing on Jacques Derrida's concept of 'hauntology' as a logic of alternative temporalities and narratives of political being, Eugene O'Brien reads spectral figures in Irish literature as attempts to 'define Irishness otherwise', to resist fixed versions of Irish identity.[17] McGuinness's use of 'haunt' surely registers the men's status outside (hetero)normative versions of Irish identity, as well as perhaps the forms of social (if not literal) violence that render them other, alien, spectral.

Because of the poem's constrictive spatial movement from border town to bed, one might read this poem in the tradition of 'romance-across-the-divide' narratives Joe Cleary describes in Northern Irish literature, in which the love of the two symbolic figures can only be realised 'in a private sphere where sexuality and politics are completely disassociated'.[18] Of course, sodomy laws inevitably make the personal and the sexual *political* for gay men; there may be a social retreat into privacy in the poem, but that is as much an effect of social stigma and legal interdiction of homosexuality as it is the exigencies of border romance.

Because of the alien and spectral status of the men, the constriction of the poem seems more about refiguring the status and nature of home and citizenship than, *pace* Cleary, an abdication of national politics: 'Aliens at *home, this is where we live*' (my emphasis). They are at home, but not really 'at home' here because of their sexuality. Ramazani suggests that 'what is meant by home' is a question that much contemporary Irish poetry 'more often raises than answers',[19] but *home* is a particular concern in lesbian and gay literature. Anne-Marie Fortier argues that queer diasporic narratives foreground a 'desire to *feel at home*' in a reconstituted physical or symbolic space;[20] queer migrant narratives must 'reprocess' figures of home, she says, in order to question the forms of sexual and social belonging it represents.[21] For the queer Irish migrant, *home* must be negotiated as a site of estrangement and nostalgia, especially as 'home' (domestic space or place of origin) is linked to heterosexuality.[22]

'Hanover Place, July Eleventh' is not a migrant poem, but its placement in the book almost allows it to function as such. *Booterstown* is a book of travel, with poems wandering from Carraroe to Venice, Japan to Maynooth. As the poems traverse geographic and temporal locations, the book includes transcultural queer references as well—a poem about artist David Hockney, a prayer to filmmaker Derek Jarman. A modern Achilles cruises Ireland in 'Patroclus', lusting for boys in Dublin, Blackrock, Galway, and seeing a 'blond Brit' in Derry, about whom he wishes 'love were a language they could speak'.[23] By the time the reader arrives at Hanover Place at the end of the book, where the lovers are 'aliens at home', the meaning of *home* is clearly at stake.

The poem concludes: 'Colonise this bed, stop time in its tracks. / Wrap my nearness round you like our flag'. The verb 'colonise' echoes and queers Seamus Heaney's 'Act of Union', which appeared only five years before in *North*.[24] Indeed, the poem seems to reverse Heaney's use of vehicle and tenor; rather than sexualising the historical as Heaney does, McGuinness politicises the sexual. Indeed, the poem enacts in miniature a repeated strategy Elizabeth Cullingford locates in McGuinness's plays, in which sexual and political border crossings are deployed as 'reciprocal metaphors', one amplifying the other.[25] The sexual becomes the means by which to claim social space, no matter how limited. Moreover, private spaces remain marked by public conflicts. To stop time might be read as an attempt to block out the politics of time and place, but to stop time would also prevent the Orange marches (and perhaps the related violence), allowing the substitution of one form of belonging (sexual) for another (national).

The poem's final image—'wrap my nearness round you like our flag'—metonymically suggests political pacification (white sheets), but the flag is actually the 'nearness' or the body of the lover. As a banner of identity (wrapping oneself in a flag), the line suggests a queer nation that resists the existing norms of the national or the sexual, the Bann or the banns. As if to make clear that the allegiances of gay identity *must* lie beyond or outside of national identity, the speaker of 'Hanover Place', on a night associated with Unionist politics, insists that their *union* is 'like our flag', the simile's 'like' suggesting its approximation of belonging, but the image of the flag itself declaring the sexual relationship's primacy over national or ethnic affiliation as the grounds of identity, citizenship, or belonging.

CATHAL Ó SEARCAIGH AS *FLÂNEUR*

> I hardly ever went to any of the pubs or the dance halls where the Irish socialised in London . . . I found their localist outlook stifling and didn't engage with it at all. I went elsewhere. The West End was a thrilling stomping ground for an eager youth. I spent most of my free time there: a West End *flâneur*, if that word can be appropriated for strolling in any city other than Paris.[26]

Though usually associated with rural Ireland, gay Irish-language poet Cathal Ó Searcaigh is a transnational poet. In fact, Ó Searcaigh's work illustrates Ramazani's suggestion that 'poetries that seem native or provincial or local often turn out to be vitally exogamous', because of their linguistic and cultural hybridity and their transnational geographies.[27] This is especially true of a series of poems Ó Searcaigh wrote about the experiences of gay Irish migrant men in 1970s' London. In these poems—in particular 'Cainteoir Dúchais'/'Native Speaker', 'Cor Na Sióg'/'The Fairy Reel', and 'Déagóir Ag Driftáil'/'Drifting'—

transcultural poetics and transnational sexual relationships are so inextricable that the poems also illustrate the very point Ramazani ignores: that a transcultural poetics may be inflected by, if not driven by, the poet's sexuality. In these poems, as Lillis Ó Laoire and Frank Sewell argue, Ó Searcaigh incorporates Beat poetics and Anglo-European influences into his work in order to find a language for homosexuality.[28] Indicative of the sexual autonomy he found abroad, these poems also represent what Kieran Kennedy calls 'the predicament of the rural gay man, drawn towards the sexual opportunities of metropolitan life, yet attached also to his place of origin'.[29]

The Irish migrant in the London poems must negotiate between ethnic allegiance and sexual autonomy—a sexual autonomy he finds both outside of Ireland *and* outside of the London migrant community. In these poems, Ó Searcaigh portrays the queer Irish migrant as *flâneur*, emblematic figure of urban wandering, but he transforms him specifically into a sexual cruiser, wandering the urban scene in search of sexual partners—a figure in search of visual, aural, and other pleasures, and one that seems often unmoored from ethnic or local ties. When Ó Searcaigh calls himself a 'West End *flâneur*' in his memoir, he defines it in opposition to the ethnic migrant community, which he disavows as 'localist' and 'stifling'. 'I went elsewhere', he insists.[30]

Ó Searcaigh's identity formation as a gay man was made possible through non-Irish sources—the *elsewhere* and other, both non-Irish literatures and migrant sexual experiences. Although he describes adolescent sexual desires for (and encounters with) other young men growing up in rural Ireland in his memoir, *Light on Distant Hills*, he clearly ties sexual self-awareness to non-Irish literature. 'I came to accept that I was gay', he writes, though 'a chance encounter with a book', a copy of Gore Vidal's *The City and the Pillar*, which his father picked up in Scotland. 'It was the first time I had read about a romance between two men in a book', he says,

> and, although their relationship was a tortured one, frightened and doomed to failure, it was an acknowledgement of the public reality of homosexuality. For me, a young adolescent in the wilds of Donegal, coming to terms with my sexual difference, it was an assurance, a guarantee even, that I wasn't on my own. Out there, somewhere, were others of a similar bent.[31]

It is not just that the book enables self-awareness, but that it ties that identity to a community and a discourse that is 'out there, somewhere' beyond the nation. What is transnational in Ó Searcaigh's work is connected to the homoerotic, and what is homoerotic is made possible by the transnational.[32] Specifically, as Kieran Kennedy notes, 'A new language of lived gay experience and a subculture of gay identities became available to Ó Searcaigh in English' and abroad in London, though he notes further that 'the process of [sexual] self-recognition' in Ó Searcaigh's work quickly shifts into an 'interrogation' of ethnic origins and allegiances.[33]

The poem 'Cainteoir Dúchais'/'Native Speaker', which both Kennedy and Brian Ó Conchubhair emphasise for its linguistic hybridity and representation of migrant sexuality, perhaps best represents the difficult (dis)affiliations of the gay Irish migrant.[34] In this poem, Ó Searcaigh's *flâneur*/cruiser searches for erotic connection, but he is open to the possibility of both erotic and ethnic connections, as if the embrace of one is not, always, the rejection of the other. In the poem, an Irish migrant has cleaned his apartment in preparation for going out cruising. The poem ends:

Bhí sé *shag*áilte, a dúirt sé
ach ina dhiaidh sin agus uile
rachadh sé amach a *chruise*áil;
b'fhéidir, a dúirt sé, go mbuailfeadh sé
le boc inteacht
a mbeadh Gaeilge aige.

He was shagged-out, he said,
but even so, he was all set
to go out cruising;
you never know, he said,
he might run into someone
with a *cúpla focal*.[35]

In London in the 1970s, a gay man might find sexual freedom, but he might also find anti-Irish racism. The complexities of cruising here are rendered in his desire for a sexual other who might, in fact, be ethnically similar—as registered in language. If the *flâneur* is generally a visual figure, Ó Searcaigh's is also aural, his sexual cruising threaded with linguistic affinities, the possibility of hearing ethnic difference (a *cúpla focal*) and thus a different kind of sexual desirability within a domain of visual tourism and sexual cruising.

Ó Conchubhair says the poem would appal 'any old style Nationalist *Gaeilgeoir* on two counts', the use of English words and syntax 'a total corruption for a traditionalist' and the very idea of a gay 'native speaker' of Irish. Linguistically hybrid, the poem imports English brand names into Irish as verbs ('Rinne sé an t-árasán a *hoover*eáil' and 'an *bath* a *vim*eáil', or 'He had the place all hoovered' and 'the bath vimmed'). Ó Conchubhair says the poem also subverts stereotype by substituting an urban gay man (who subverts gender as well as ethnic ideology by doing domestic work) for the traditional figures from the West.[36] Kennedy further notes that the phrase 'a *cúpla focal*' is the translator's attempt to replicate in English the complex borrowing of idiom and vocabulary in Irish.[37] The translator, Frank Sewell, says the ideal reader would be bilingual, and he says of his own practice that 'to be true to the sense and sensibility of a whole poem, one must be prepared to play around with the individual word or phrase'.[38] If these poems are, as Sewell insists, sexy, then this particular phrase calls for a particular reader, like the cruiser's preferred lover, bi(lingual) enough to hear that sexualised ethnic difference.

While McGuinness describes the gay Irish as 'aliens at home', Ó Searcaigh at times finds himself more 'at home abroad', as in 'Is Glas Na Cnoic'/'The Grass Is Always Greener' (pp. 174–5). In part, this sense of being at *home* is an act of poetic transfiguration: he reimagines the urban as rural landscape, figuring traffic as sheep, office-blocks as mountains. Ó Searcaigh enacts what Ramazani calls 'geopoetic oscillation', an 'imaginative movement back and forth between discrepant topographies';[39] he juxtaposes Irish and English landscapes, or he maps American, Irish, and English cultures onto the urban landscape as a contact zone. In 'Déagóir Ag Driftáil'/ 'Drifting', for example, a probably-English woman flirts with the young Irish poet in an American café in Covent Garden among the tourists—just after he encounters his Irish 'brothers' in the Bell and the Crown and buys American Beat poetry in Charing Cross Road (pp. 158, 159). London is a cultural contact zone, a geography crisscrossed with the influences and affiliations that drive the poet.

Similarly, in 'Cor Na Sióg'/ 'The Fairy Reel', Ó Searcaigh connects Soho to Prochlais Wood, using the pun of 'fairy' (slang for gay man) to imbricate the two geographies: 'Anseo tá na síoga ag *cruise*áil sa chlapsholas / Tá siad tagtha amach as liosanna na heagla, as rathanna an uaignis', or 'Here the fairies come out from fear's ring-forts / and the raths of loneliness to cruise the waves of twilight' (pp. 162, 163). Tellingly, Ó Searcaigh's fairies are *cruising*, the importation of the English verb into the Irish poem modernising and sexualising the folkloric.[40] Sexual desire threads the *flâneur*'s London wanderings, and the poet repeatedly displaces ethnic identification for sexual or poetic forms of belonging.

Even more than 'Cor Na Sióg'/'The Fairy Reel', which Ó Conchubhair convincingly reads as a psychological journey that enacts the poet's 'rejection of heterosexual love',[41] 'Déagóir Ag Driftáil'/ 'Drifting' repeatedly stages the rejection of heterosexuality, and it does so in transcultural terms. The poem opens on a tableau of desire and choice, the poet in a public park looking at a young woman with a child and at a soldier who is 'more to my liking' (p. 153). This opening scene is cross-cultural and queer in reference, a poetic echo of Lord Alfred Douglas's 'Two Loves', the poem that famously concluded, 'I am the love that dare not speak its name'. Not only does Ó Searcaigh locate two versions of love in a staged garden scene—one version clearly reproductive, the other a male object of the speaker's desire—but he also fills the scene with symbolically suggestive flowers (love-lies-bleeding, pansies) and as in a *fin-de-siècle* poem, the male object of desire is explicitly tied to poppies. After this tableau of rejection, the speaker encounters Irish 'brothers' but distances himself from this fraternally figured ethnic connection and their (heterosexual) loneliness, and he turns from them to the Charing Cross bookshops and the language of the Beat poets. Tellingly, the poet again hybridises his own language: as he browses the Beat writers, he imports the words 'Beats', 'voodoo', and 'vibe' into his Irish language poem (pp. 156–157).[42]

After a flirtation then with the waitress in the American café, he has a sexual encounter with a young man in a Piccadilly toilet, moving from heterosexual possibility to homosexual pleasure (pp. 158–159). This encounter is a 'cottaging episode', as Ó Conchubhair notes, 'an ephemeral encounter' in a public washroom.[43] That said, *cottaging* (and surely the term itself ironically refigures the idea of home), the practice of finding sexual partners in public restrooms, has an important subcultural history, in Ireland and elsewhere.[44] As if to emphasise his transvaluation of this moment, Ó Searcaigh casts this urban scene in pastoral terms: the young man a dove, the toilet a 'mystery-branching wood that binds our senses', again mapping the rural onto the urban through poetic figure, but thus reclaiming the importance of a counter-public queer space of identification and belonging that the dominant culture would dismiss.

It is clear that when the speaker finds himself 'at home abroad' in 'Is Glas Na Cnoic'/'The Grass Is Always Greener', that sense of being at home is grounded in the fact that he is 'more sure of myself / than I've ever felt before', a poetic and invariably sexual self-awareness at the heart of his new sensibility (p. 175). Tellingly, Ó Laoire says of this poem that Ó Searcaigh is 'now at home *within himself*, regardless of his physical location' (emphasis mine).[45] His experiences abroad enable both sexual and poetic awakening, an epiphany so profound that when he has sex with 'a handsome boy of the fairy family' in 'Cor Na Sióg'/'The Fairy Reel', he says he feels like Moses before the Burning Bush (pp. 164–65)—a possibly bawdy pun that locates spiritual and sexual awakening in or on a young man's naked body, and an image that evokes not only a sense of revelation but also an emblematic narrative of a disaporic people seeking freedom.

To conclude with the image of Moses would suggest a reading of Ó Searcaigh within what Eithne Luibhéid calls the 'liberationist narrative' of queer migration, a movement from repression to freedom. As she warns, however, the liberationist paradigm can easily become a reductive myth that obviates the complexities of migrant experience.[46] Ó Searcaigh's poems resist that narrative, suggesting complex networks of identity and belonging, not easy liberationist tropes. Further, a constant and perhaps worrying sense of consumer culture underlies his representations of gay sexuality in these London poems, denoting consumption more than liberation. Kennedy argues, for example, that the insistent use of brand names in the London poems marks 'a parallel between the market in products and the market in bodies', the poem thus connecting modern gay male identity to global consumer capitalism.[47]

When gay sexuality appears in discussions of globalisation, nationalism, and sexuality, as Jon Binnie remarks in *The Globalization of Sexuality*, 'it often does so in a homophobic sense'—specifically he notes the 'discourses of sex tourism', that portray Western gay men as predatory, even paedophilic.[48] Ó Searcaigh has recently been vilified in precisely these terms after the 2007 documentary film, *Fairytale of Kathmandu*, suggested that his (sometimes sexual) relationships with Nepalese young men were marked by imbalances of power if not actual exploitation.[49] Setting aside the difficult and unresolved arguments about Ó Searcaigh's sexual and economic relations with young men in Nepal, we must still acknowledge that the London poems may invoke discourses of consumption as easily as confirmation and liberation. 'Déagóir Ag Driftáil'/ 'Drifting' depicts the city of the Irish migrant-*flâneur*-cruiser as a geography of consumer culture and sexual tourism, but as it turns from heterosexual invitation at the tourist cafe to the encounter in the washroom, it gestures toward the *elsewhere* and other ('I went elsewhere'), toward queer networks of connection beyond or beneath or screened by (even enabled by) the visible and visibly heteronormative cultures of global capitalism. Pastoral or perhaps Dantean, these 'mystery-branching woods that bind our senses' and these subterranean tunnels indicate networks of connection, affect, and pleasure that subtend and resist the normative geographies of citizenship.

PADRAIG ROONEY'S ESCAPE ARTISTS

'nomadic heart by nomadic heart'[50]

Padraig Rooney's poem 'Ash', which was first published in *The Irish Times* 26 Feb 1994, exemplifies what Ramazani calls the 'travelling poem': it is a poem that offers imaginative enactments of geographic displacement and also literally represents how poetry as a text may travel.[51] In this case it is an Armed Services edition of Ted Hughes's *Crow*, which ends up in the hands of a poolside reader in Bangkok. First imagining the book in the hands of an American soldier, and then identifying with him ('like him') as 'flaked out' reader, Rooney quotes a line from the poem 'Crow's Account of the Battle': 'what was left look[ed] round at what was left'.[52] His transformation of the past tense 'looked' into the present 'look' collapses time and space, as well as collating the three figures of the mythic Crow, the American soldier, and the poolside slacker, all among those left.[53] Thus the remnant 'left'—the book left behind or the survivors—can be transformed into a political 'left'. In the hands of a dope-smoking Irishman in exile, an Armed Services edition becomes an anti-war poem. Rooney's poems repeatedly enact these kinds of trans-cultural juxtapositions as goods and peoples circulate in transnational contexts, and they may also collapse time and space, one topography or history inflecting or enacting another. However, acts of identification, like this with an American soldier of that 'long ago' war, are more often impelled in Rooney's work by erotic desire than by political sympathies.

Elsewhere I have traced some of the complex representations of identity and desire in Rooney's poetry, particularly in his second book, *The Escape Artist* (2006). Central to several of the book's poems and the title figure, the escape artist is Harry Houdini, Rooney's version of Stephen Daedalus. Born Eric Weisz to Jewish parents in Hungary, Houdini changed his name and later claimed Appleton, Wisconsin, as his birthplace, escaping thus national identity as well as the locks and chains of his stage act. Currently living in Switzerland, Rooney is himself a migrant, and his poems are filled with images of travel and transcultural encounter. Houdini reappears in Rooney's most recent book, *The Fever Wards* (2010), in the poem 'Wire', in which he attempts to escape both death and 'the world he spurned', but he does so while imagining a wire across 'the childhood ghetto in his mind', the air awash with the sounds and scents of the culture he disavowed—klezmer music and 'canted prayer', almond milk, 'sweet liqueurs and fusty gabardine' (p. 8). It is a return to the geography of the past, not simply via imagination but by means of the affective appeals of the sensory. As I argue elsewhere, if *escape* suggests an emancipatory impulse (or the liberationist narrative), the figure of the escape *artist* registers a self-consciousness about that impulse, about the parameters and possibilities of escape, about the self-fashioning of identity. It also registers the centrality of aesthetic experience to Rooney's work; indeed, often the sexual is imbricated in some form of aesthetic experience or object, erotic encounters involving not only sexual and national others but also representations thereof.[54]

As in Ó Searcaigh's work, Rooney's poems suggest that sexual experiences elsewhere allow the Irish migrant to reimagine the possibilities of queer identities and experiences *within* Irish cultures. In 'The Carpet', a man sends home to Monaghan a carpet he has bought in a North African market—the rug both aesthetic object and synecdoche for experience in a foreign culture (p. 28). It is inscribed with 'a tale of flight' written in Tifnagh, the Berber script of the nomadic Tuareg tribes—the tale suggesting Rooney's theme of escape and the alphabet his emphasis on exile. Purchased 'for a song' in Africa and then sent back to Ireland as a gift, the commercially purchased rug is resituated in networks of aesthetic and affectional exchange—and the tale of flight becomes a tale of return, but not without the experience abroad inscribed in the rug as well. The speaker says of the rug, 'I smelled the goatherds / who lay on it'. As in Houdini's fantasy of the ghetto, sensory appeals connect the present to the past, but scent here is not only affective but also erotic, and the sensory reinscribes the present with the sexual experiences of the past, transforms the local with the elsewhere. Rooney continues, 'And love was woven into goatishness / that year beneath us on the sandy floor, / nomadic heart beside nomadic heart'. This network of belonging is small, nomadic, and randy. A strictly delineated location of sexual relationship like McGuinness's Hanover Place bed, the rug allows for a form of imaginative resistance to the isolations of geography; rather than retreat, it is a figure of imaginative escape, a kind of Arabian magic carpet that can take them across 'half the towns of northern Africa' even as it remains on the floor of a home in Monaghan.

An earlier poem in the book, 'His Dark Companions', also brings the sexual experiences of the gay migrant back to Ireland, but it does so within the context of nascent community formation. That is, sexual experiences abroad not only transform the literal home (in Monaghan), they also transform the cultural home. In the poem, an Irishman whose homosexuality finds expression abroad comes back not with a carpet but his memories of the 'dark companions' he met in New York, 'black and Puerto Rican boys who died / a decade later in Korea' (the reference echoing the anti-war sentiments of 'Ash') (p. 12). But, as Rooney writes, 'So much was left unsaid / when he came back to Ireland, married, / and fathered children of his own'.[55] The man spends his winters in South Africa and returns to Monaghan where his wife has died and his children grown. The poem thus twice marks Ireland as heterosexual and reproductive space, homosexual desires displaced abroad. The poem ends:

> I saw him once in Bartley Dunne's
> and later at the disco in the Hirschfeld
> in toupee and designer jeans.
>
> He stood half in and out of shadow—
> the shade who stood for me when I was born. (p. 12)

The poem gestures toward early gay community formation in Dublin: Bartley Dunne's was one of the first gay bars, and as noted above, the

Hirschfeld was the first gay community centre in Ireland, its name affirming European affiliations. In marking the early sexual geographies of Dublin's gay community, the poem suggests that experience abroad impels and enables a new cultural and sexual geography at home.

Tellingly, the last couplet describes an interstitial identity, 'half in and half out of shadow', as if half in and half out of the closet, half in an identity formed abroad and half in an identity based in Ireland. He is a 'shade'—a spectral figure, like those spectral men haunting McGuinness's Hanover Place—who 'stood for me', an ambiguous phrase that echoes church phrasing, the godparent who stands in for the baptised infant, who offers a profession of faith and promises as proxy to provide religious training should the parents be unable to do so. This closeted man is like a godparent, standing in for a different profession of faith. Or, read differently, he 'stood for me' because he represented what the speaker might have been, given a different place and time.

In the work of all three of these poets, Frank McGuinness, Cathal Ó Searcaigh, and Padraig Rooney—especially as represented in the emblematic figures of the resident alien, the migrant *flâneur*, and the escape artist—queer forms of identity and belonging intensify what Ramazani calls the affiliative and disaffiliative energies of transnational poetry. All three illustrate the fundamental arguments of this essay: that (queer) sexuality must be a critical interpretive element of transnational literary analysis since sexuality critically inflects forms of national identity and belonging; that sexuality can animate and compel the intercultural dynamics of transnational poetries; and that Irish gay poetry is inevitably transcultural in reference and transnational in scope. Further, if these three emblematic figures suggest the fundamental themes of alienation, mobility, and escape, Rooney's poems also suggest the possibility of transformation; that is, the transcultural and transnational inevitably refigure the local.

A longer version of this study would take into account the insistent cross-cultural references and geopoetic oscillations in the work of James Liddy—'Innisfree was still and churned, / as much as Thoreau's pond'[56]—as well as the peripatetic poetries, varied geographies, and translations of Pearse Hutchinson, and Padraic Fiacc's homoerotic empathies with both perpetrators and victims of violence in Northern Ireland. It could also consider the sexual geographies of Greece and Dublin in the work of Richard Riordan, the evasively local poetics of Aodhan Madden, the sexual polemics (and anti-identity politics) of John Grundy, and the

European frames of reference and Irish locales of John Jordan.

National boundaries remain critical, because of the cultural specificities of lesbian and gay lives and communities and the exigencies of legal reform, but a focus on those boundaries is inadequate and inaccurate, given the translocational (or dislocational) influences and impulses of Irish queer culture. Irish gay identity and culture has been grounded in transnational exchanges; Irish gay poetry, consequently, is almost inevitably transnational in both cultural reference and poetic practice, negotiating local and global cultures, representing the cultural and material experiences of gay men who located their sexual identities outside the nation when the nation did not welcome them.

'Home with a Queasy Nudge': Transnationalism and the persistence of Irish identity in Julia O'Faolain's *Three Lovers*

KELLI MALOY

Born in England to Irish parents—the writers Eileen Gould and Seán O'Faoláin—and having lived, as her characters have, in England, France, Ireland, Italy, and the United States, Julia O'Faolain and her work can easily be characterised as transnational. This essay focuses on the transnational dimensions of her novel *Three Lovers* (1971), which examines the complexities of escaping and reinventing Irish identities inscribed by history, mythology, and nationalism.[1] The novel's treatment of these issues is distilled by genre: *Three Lovers* is an Irish *bildungsroman*, a form with unique complexities concerning subjects' maturation and independence. With Joyce's *A Portrait of the Artist as a Young Man* as a familiar referent, the genre of the Irish *bildungsroman* has been widely studied as a representation of Ireland's colonial and postcolonial history. One notable study is Jed Esty's reading of Elizabeth Bowen's *The Last September*, in which he characterises female protagonist Lois Farquar as a 'frozen-adolescent figure', a product of the 'temporal oddities of the surrounding colonial history'.[2] More currently, Irish literature has been considered within the context of Ireland's economic coming of age.[3] As it has taken its place in the global economy, through the Celtic Tiger and its aftermath, the Irish *bildungsroman* subject has become less bound by geographical borders and political constraints. As postcolonial subjects with greater mobility, Irish literary characters as travellers, émigrés, and exiles—particularly female characters—have become increasingly likely to engage in international experiences and to emerge as subjects with transnational or cosmopolitan capital. As recent scholarship shows, however, the complexities of the modern Irish subject defy easy correlation of mobility and liberation. Although it is lesser known than O'Faolain's novel *No Country for Young Men*, *Three Lovers* is a predecessor of the Celtic Tiger-era *bildungsroman*, foreshadowing the limitations of the genre and the ways in which readerly expectations are shaped by the cultural moment.

The terms transnationalism and cosmopolitanism—and related terms such as localism and 'glocalism'—imply complexities that have been considered and problematised widely. Stephen Clingman posits that the term 'transnational fiction' fundamentally connotes and presumes the underlying existence of a 'national fiction',[4] a notion with great theoretical freight in any context but with particular valence in the context of (post)colonial Ireland. The nascence of Irish independence undergirds the narrative of *Three Lovers*, which takes place somewhere between 1954 and 1962. Juxtaposed with a war-torn Algeria, the Irish republic serves as a narrative construct that lends possibility and optimism: the Irish characters are not only citizens of a free Ireland but also citizens of the world in a way that they had never been before. However, O'Faolain's interest in nationalist rhetoric—especially the ways in which mythology and the language of the 1937 Constitution render the role of women in the new Irish republic—undercuts this optimism and should heavily influence a transnationalist reading of the novel.

Ulrich Beck's notion of 'transnational social spaces',[5] with its emphasis on loci rather than transformative experience, offers an alternative to the expectations conferred upon transnational narrativity in literary forms, especially the *bildungsroman*. Ascribing transnationality to the spaces rather than to those who occupy them resists the easy tendency to correlate travel and transnationality, transnationalism and cosmopolitanism. Paris as a locus in *Three Lovers* is a space conducive to transnational experience but one that is value-neutral, as are those who inhabit it. For O'Faolain's Irish characters, transnationalism as a means of crossing borders and existing outside the purview of the national narrative is employed to enhance and, more directly, correct some aspect of Irishness.

Three Lovers is the story of Sally Tyndal, a graduate student at the Sorbonne, and the three men with whom she interacts romantically. The first is Mesli, an Algerian revolutionary and medical student. The second is Fintan McCann, an Irish artist with whom Sally has a platonic relationship. The third is Raimondo, an unappealing older Italian man who offers financial security. In Paris, Sally encounters a range of Irish characters, and as students, artists, and socialites in a transnational social space, they are to some extent successful in displacing or correcting their Irish identities. Sally in particular quickly creates the life she could not have in Ireland, a bohemian existence built around a passionate, satisfying sexual relationship. This life is fleeting, however, and serves only as temporary displacement of her Irish identity. Furthermore, the extent to which the novel's Irish characters attain a cosmopolitan outlook is a murky and ultimately unresolved issue. This ambiguity is particularly evident in Sally's transnational experiences.

As a citizen of independent Ireland, Sally is theoretically poised to offset a colonial past that she cites as the source of her guilt and inadequacy. She immerses herself in French culture and initiates a sexual relationship with Mesli in order to displace her provincialism. Her privileged position in Paris does to an extent offer the cultural capital with which to resist the stunting forces of her life in Ireland. In order to be 'finished'—both in terms of her education and as a developing self in the context of the *bildungsroman*—in theory Sally must be not merely transnational but also cosmopolitan. Ulf Hannerz defines cosmopolitanism as 'a willingness to engage with the Other' characterised by a narcissism that promotes the discovery of the self 'in the space where cultures mirror one another'.[6] This definition is helpful in two ways. First, it suggests a dialogic exchange not necessarily present in a transnational subject's grappling with his or her own national identity. Second, it argues that cosmopolitanism is often a solipsistic endeavour, one in which openness to Otherness masks the desire to locate a familiar self in unfamiliar surroundings. This framework resists the tendency to essentialise cosmopolitanism as fundamentally benign. Sally's 'willingness to engage' with Mesli, who becomes her lover immediately following her arrival in Paris, is not merely a sign of her progressiveness, or of rejection of her Irish identity. Rather, she attempts to create a cultural narrative for herself by co-opting Mesli's, and to re-create her image through a lens more flattering than the Irish one. Although her experience suggests the potential for transnationalism and the concomitant liberation of transnationality, its reliance on consumerism and exoticism results in a state of subjectivity that is highly prescriptive and performative. O'Faolain's satire of the romantic novel and the transnational narrative demands examination of the expectations projected onto these forms, and onto the Irish *bildungsroman*.

ALL ROADS LEAD OUT OF IRELAND

Transnational narratives are often assumed to be emancipatory. While it is widely accepted that socioeconomic factors dictate the level of cosmopolitanism that can reasonably be correlated with transnationalism —for example, we do not ascribe the same outcomes to the life experience of a migrant worker as we do to an expatriate who has chosen to relocate to a less politically turbulent environment—literary narrativity confers unique expectations. A *bildungsroman* set in an international location implies a transformation of the self attained through engagement with Otherness. The storyline of *Three Lovers* initially suggests that Sally will circumvent the constraints of Catholicism and de Valera's nation-state, as she is transported to a centre of intellectual and cultural freedom. However, the novel's conclusion implies that, although she may find a way to stay in Paris, this will be possible only if she takes up with Raimondo, a stand-in for Sally's controlling father. Moreover, it seems just as likely that her father will return her to Dublin and arrange a loveless marriage. The novel's conclusion not only confounds genre expectations; it also prompts questions about the outcomes of transnationality. For O'Faolain's characters, transnational experiences reinforce their national affiliations, and their Irish identities are simply re-enacted in new contexts. Sally's uncertain future also parallels her abortive attempts to develop a cosmopolitan perspective: her willingness to engage with the Other and her ability to recognise herself in transnational social space, narrativised in her adolescent journal entries and performed in public spaces such as the bathhouse, never take root or thrive.

Sally finds herself part of a group of Irish expatriates who are linked to her parents and the safety of home, and whose model of Irishness offers a specific manifestation of transnational identity. Family friend Letty, characterised by her 'loud, Anglo-Irish hunting-voice', left Ireland after it attained independence.[7] Though she refers to herself as a professional in 'the rag trade', Letty does little but throw parties and seduce men. Her friends are English and, according to Sally, 'disembodied . . . [l]ike heads, in history-book pictures, stuck on lances' (p. 69). They regard Paris as an outpost of British colonialism and are vocally pro-French, aligned with locals who characterise Algerians as 'Wogs' incapable of 'running anything bigger than a Turkish bath' (p. 77). Although technically 'Irish abroad', this group of expatriates cannot be evaluated in the same way, as in Ireland they were already transnational in Victor Roudometof's sense of being people 'out of place'.[8] This group replicates its out-of-placeness in Paris, relatively unaffected by its surroundings.

Fintan, Sally's second 'lover', offers perhaps the most familiar signifier of Irish transnationalism—that of the Irish artist-in-exile. A Stephen Dedalus stand-in affiliated with an American bookshop owner who 'fancie[s] himself as heir to Sylvia Beach' (p. 25), Fintan fails as both a businessman (he considers commercial art to be 'prostitution') and an artist (his days are spent recovering from bouts of heavy drinking), and, while transnational in the most literal sense, he is more an exile, fleeing, among other undesirable aspects of Irish culture, a possible pregnancy. Moreover, he learns no French, being 'suspicious' of new languages, and has no need for them, having relocated to Paris 'to be alone' (p. 17). His limited livelihood consists of public performances staged for the amusement of the French literati through exaggerated vernacular and the grotesquerie of stage Irishness.

In sharp contrast to Fintan, Sorbonne student Shevawn Donnelly is portrayed as a token of Irish nationalism, with her own highly performative version of Irishness. Introduced as 'home intruding with queasy nudge', she has a 'seesaw Southern-Irish accent . . . considerably more pronounced now than when she'd lived at home', and is marked by her 'folksy' language and rosary beads. Shevawn regards Irish culture as a pure form poorly replicated elsewhere, describing the French as 'desperate robbers' and French clothing as inferior imitation of Irish tweed, lacking the smell of turf smoke (pp. 5–6). The previous year's Irish scholarship student and in theory Sally's mentor, she is the voice of the colonially oppressed. At a cocktail party, she responds to a British national's racist remark about the English having saved Africans from 'sitting in the dust' by asking, 'Do you not think . . . that would be the *safest* place for their bums? Considering the British buggers who went out to occupy them?' (p. 79). Sally is repulsed by the thought of modelling herself after Shevawn, whose identity is overtly bound to an outmoded Irish identity, one that Sally finds anachronistic, superstitious, and fusty. As a mobile representation of Ireland, Shevawn is transnational, though her fierce representation of Irish 'authenticity' with disregard for other cultural influences prevents her from attaining any degree of cosmopolitanism. Moreover, she gauges Irishness superficially, through commodities and signifiers. Exported for continental consumption, she is a virtual map of Ireland, with Connemara marble and turf-infused Donegal tweed as essential elements of her identity. Her anti-colonialist stance is made ironic, though, as the Irish authenticity she defends so insistently is parodied in her name's Anglicised spelling.

Amidst these stock representations, Sally is a more complex character. In Dublin, her identity was prescribed by her geographical location and by the landscape itself. Her diffidence about her abilities as a student can be traced to the comment of a visiting French instructor who told his Irish students that their minds are like bogs, a remark that prompted her to take a logic course in an effort to impose order on an ostensibly murky, unmanageable, essentially Irish part of her being (pp. 14–15). Having been awarded a prestigious scholarship by the Sorbonne indicates some success in these efforts, and her professional and social options are thus expanded. Sally may be groomed for a lectureship in France or could return to Ireland with greater social mobility conferred by continental 'finishing'. Confined by the 1937 Constitution not only to the space within national borders but more specifically to domestic space, women as agents of the nationalist enterprise were charged with producing and rearing sons to be productive and devoted members of the state; therefore, leaving is a performative act of independence with political repercussions. However, Sally does more than remove herself physically from Ireland, and her resistance takes the form of a manifesto:

> *I* did the right things all that time: wore the Loretto, Foxrock, uniform in the bus (cinnamon and green-for-Old-Ireland, it clashed with my hair), came home at five, did my homework, learnt Christian Doctrine and Gaelic, went to mass, won prizes, went to college, provoked no scandals. [My father] thinks I'll marry the solid son of one of his friends and start the cycle again for the honour and glory of the RC republic. The contract's up! Finished! (p. 181)

Her efforts to assimilate in Paris are an attempt to reject a variety of elements of Ireland's nationalist narrative, particularly what James M. Smith refers to as the 'culture of containment'. While she can be exported temporarily as a student groomed to return home and contribute to Irish society, the constraints of containment attempt to prevent her from being exported as a sexualised Irish body. In the novel's opening scene, as they arrive in Paris, Sally's fellow Aer Lingus passengers warn, 'Don't do anything we wouldn't', which O'Faolain follows with the line 'She would if it killed her' (p. 5).

Smith's study of the 1931 Carrigan Report examines ways in which church and state colluded to discourage public discourse on sexual issues and to 'export sociosexual problems through emigration'[9] in an effort to develop a containment culture that 'constitute[d] and perpetuated the fiction of Irish purity'.[10] Efforts made within the state to contain sexually aberrant citizens in reform schools, homes, and asylums were paired with attempts to expel women who challenged fictive Irish purity in spite of perceived 'proselytism and moral decay in Britain' and elsewhere.[11] Such efforts were indirect, and emigration (along with prostitution and infanticide) was a result of the 'inhospitable environment stigmatising illegitimacy'.[12] Exile as a punitive response to unruly elements of the body politic became an agent of state regulation of sexuality; however, those with the means and the inclination to pre-emptively choose emigration as a way of circumventing church and state control could pose a serious threat to the containment of sexual immorality. Unlike her family's maid, who 'had to be sent to the Magdalene Homes', Sally can cross borders freely and return permanently if she so chooses (p. 48).

The degree of freedom conferred upon Sally by her socioeconomic status, combined with her eye for high fashion and her public relationship with an Algerian man, allows her to temporarily escape her Irish affiliations and redefine her cultural ties, interpreting signifiers and 'passing' as continental. She can communicate with the locals in French and uses the public baths with Mesli, adopting a seemingly liberated lifestyle in an effort to offset her self-perception as a 'mud creature . . . whose native habitat is a swamp of undefined guilt' (p. 34). She also attempts to correct her lack of sexual experience—previously limited to an encounter with an Irish man that left her unsure of whether she was still a virgin—through a sexual relationship with a man she perceives as innately sexualised. This Orientalist perspective recalls Edward Said's notion of 'flexible *positional* superiority', through which a Westerner can attain 'a whole series of possible relationships with the Orient without ever losing . . . the relative upper hand'.[13] During her first sexual encounter with Mesli, the authority that Sally both resists and assumes is literally positional as well as sexual: 'Arabs were from the dark underside, south of the Mediterranean, below the European belt, mildly pubic, male, suspect and unknown. She was getting truly away from Ireland, she thought with satisfaction and terror' (p. 57). He similarly projects sexual experience and freedom onto her, distinguishing European women from 'our women'. Although she uses her European identity to pass in Paris, she attempts to define Irishness to Mesli, explaining, 'Celts aren't quite Europeans. We're from the fringe. Almost Eskimos' (p. 62). In doing so, she posits Irishness as polar, the product of a cold climate inhospitable to sexuality. On the fringe of European culture, Irishness lacks and lags in terms of modernity, but within the Orientalist framework of positional superiority, European culture is more cosmopolitan and liberated than non-European cultures. Mesli's Otherness can potentially offset Sally's 'Eskimo' asexuality, and for Sally, Paris is recalled as a sensory experience of 'animality and dark tobacco' (p. 5).

Ultimately, Sally's relationship with Mesli is less cosmopolitan than colonial. A modern Othello, Mesli is referred to throughout the novel as 'the Arab', 'the Moor', or 'the Blackamoor', including by Sally's father, and his Otherness is, within Sally's Orientalist perception, conflated with sexual desire. In her diary, she recounts their first date, writing, 'His nostrils began to pump and splay splendidly and I almost felt I was in love with him though I was terrified of him, too. He had black eyes and brows and black crevices full of the deep shadows you get in sunny countries and I imagined him camouflaged in shadow like a lizard in the crack of a stone' (p. 32). She is also ambiguous about her relationship with Mesli and considers that his being Algerian makes him 'romantic' but 'unreliable' (p. 31). Unwilling to recognise him as a subject colonised and potentially emasculated by the French, Sally assumes the role of coloniser herself, dehumanising him and reducing him to property: 'You're like a bit of Mediterranean land . . . [a]ll folded up with fuzzy shadows between the folds'. When he replies, 'They're fighting over my Mediterranean land', she asks, 'Who can I fight for my bit of it?' (p. 125). In this imperial role, she also attempts to erase her primeval and boglike existence by positioning herself beyond Mesli's own cultural development. When Mesli questions her simultaneously dating Raimondo, she replies, '[D]on't be so damn sure you've got it all sized up. Remember the cultural lag', which prompts him to strike her (p. 126).[14] Though it is not conspicuous in the cosmopolitan context of Paris, Sally becomes more aware of her Irishness in contrast to Mesli's Otherness, and of her Irishness being out of place in its new setting.

Her existence outside of Ireland is dedicated almost entirely to correcting her Irish identity, one that is clearly inescapable. In his reading of *Othello*, Daniel Roux argues that the modernist subject is characterised by its self-estrangement and that 'it is only from within the symbolic order itself that the subject acquires its sublimated traumatic existence and thereby retroactively locates itself'.[15] Estranged from her national narrative and her role within it, Sally attempts to locate herself in transnational social spaces; in order to do so, she must maintain what she perceives as social order. In replicating the colonialist model, she not only finds herself 'out of place' but also fails to attain any degree of cosmopolitan consciousness, lacking the ability to recognise or empathise with the Other. Her development seems to be stunted by the realisation described thusly by Carmen Kuhling and Kieran Keohane: the 'strangeness of the Other's way of life, its difference, raises the possibility that our own way of life, our own identity may be strange, uncertain and insecure too'.[16]

Yet her focus on colonialism also allows Sally to make connections between Irish and Algerian history and identity. Ireland's colonial past is alluded to fleetingly, and Sally's links to this history are tenuous, formed by her grandmother's 'chilling tales about the Famine, the pitch-cap and the Penal Days' and her mother's love affair with an ill-fated gunman (p. 97). To Sally, the Irish revolutionaries are vague and romantic: she and her friends 'had heard too much about them to think of them as people. A crust of reverence covered their memory like the glass bells placed over grave flowers' (p. 48). Now close to the age her mother was when the gunman was killed, Sally craves a romantic narrative of her own but, failing to find it in Ireland, attempts to create one through her relationship with Mesli. Her romantic view of the soldiers of her mother's generation is the foundation for her highly sexualised narrative of the Algerian revolution. Having missed a defining cultural moment, Sally attempts to create a 'national fiction'. Without this foundation, she is ill-equipped for both transnationality and cosmopolitanism. While she adopts the Algerian revolution as her own, in part because of its parallels to Ireland's, she also refuses to recognise Mesli as a colonised subject. To do so would be to align him with the emasculated Irish men whose pale skin and lack of sexual prowess drove her to France. The presence of Algerian nationalists in France at this time provides Sally with a narrative to fill the void, though she is able to engage with it only from a consumerist perspective. She learns nationalist songs and eats in Algerian restaurants but is prone to naiveté and political missteps, failing to recognise France as a colonial oppressor. She refuses to believe, for example, that the French are using torture: 'The British were known to be capable of this—Sally had been reared on stories about *them*—the Germans, the Portuguese, the Spaniards, yes, but surely not the French?' (p. 66). This romanticisation of France indicates how Sally's flexible positionality extends beyond herself to include Ireland, which she sees as having parallels to both France and Algeria—countries on the opposite sides of a war. Her romanticised yet colonial perspective is similarly contradictory, being both progressive and conservative, cosmopolitan and parochial. This paradox not only reflects the xenophobic paranoia of post-World War II Ireland, where emigration rates soared in response to widespread unemployment brought on by Eamon de Valera's isolationist policies, but also foreshadows contemporary responses to immigration in Ireland, which I will discuss later.

Sally's co-opting the Algerian nationalist movement suggests both the narcissism Hannerz describes and a naïve appropriation of a revolution that she associates with the sexual pleasure and masculinity she has found to be lacking among Irish men. Her romanticisation and sexualisation of the Algerian struggle conveniently reduces it to one devoted to her independence, one available to rescue her from her father and from Ireland. Sally's love affair with the Other posits her as an authentic cosmopolitan by Hannerz's definition but also as a transgressive cosmopolitan, one who resists containment. For Sally exports herself as a sexual subject, disrupting both the Catholic model of Mariolatry and the Kathleen ni Houlihan narrative when she becomes pregnant with Mesli's child.[17] Her conflation of sexuality and her adopted nationalist movement is most stark in a scene in which, shortly after realising that she is pregnant, Sally dances naked in front of a mirror: '"Bang! Bang!" Tilting her (swollen) nipples as if they were gun-barrels. "*Vive la Carmagnole!*" Like the African nations, I demand the right to govern myself badly' (p. 181). Her transnationality allows Sally to achieve a pleasurable sexual experience, one that provides relief from the threat of sexual combustion implied in her being a 'leaky gas jet', and to temporarily reject the Irish nationalist narrative. In aligning herself with the revolutionaries, however, she simultaneously characterises them as incapable of successful self-governance, unwittingly adopting both the British and French colonial positions. In paradoxically playing the roles of both coloniser and colonised, she finds that no form of resistance will successfully displace the persistence of Irish identity.

Moreover, though she ostensibly recognises her own Otherness in Mesli's, her mimicry of the colonial process suggests a fundamental lack of genuine understanding of Otherness. Pico Iyer defines a true cosmopolitan as 'not someone who's traveled a lot so much as someone who can appreciate what it feels like to be Other'.[18] Both a helpful way of distinguishing transnationalism and cosmopolitanism and a less cynical alternative to Hannerz's definition, Iyer's model of cosmopolitanism implies an ability to detach from one's national identity and subjectivity in a new space. As an Irish national desperate to detach from her Irishness, Sally would seem to be the type of transnational subject with the empathy required for her to fit this model of cosmopolitanism. The persistence of her Irishness, however, and the superficial way in which she engages with French culture and with Otherness prevent her from truly appreciating what it feels like to be Other. Whether this is an artifact of immaturity, of cruelty, or of the insidious ability of oppression to promote a cycle of repetition is unclear. Sally is written more as a naïf than as a character driven by cruel intentions, but her opportunism, both latent and active, may be a response to her own colonial legacy. Edward Said characterises the exile as one whose life is 'taken up with compensating for disorienting loss by creating a new world to rule'.[19] Given all its complexities, the term 'exile' cannot easily be applied to all of the Irish characters in *Three Lovers*, though Sally is in many ways more an exile than is Fintan. She is more likely than he to return to Ireland but more vulnerable to the deprivation of exile, to what Said calls a 'discontinuous state of being'.[20]

That O'Faolain, given her own strongly international background, devises characters so directly bound by concealment and performance of Irishness abroad suggests that transnational mobility is more elusive and that the reach of nationalism is more extensive than readers might suppose. If the re-enactment of Irish identity is viewed as a process by which subjects seek, narcissistically, to engage with cultural influences beyond their own in order to see their own national identity reflected in a more pleasing way, then the value of cosmopolitanism becomes highly questionable. The Irish *bildungsroman*—again, Joyce's *Portrait* stands as an obvious example—is built on the premise that cosmopolitanism will save the provincial subject from his own Irishness. Though readers can look to Joyce's biography for a conclusion to Stephen's maturation, his narrative is unfinished. The same is true of O'Faolain's novel. While the subject of such a narrative might easily be regarded as a failure in the context of an incomplete transformation, the more problematic aspect of such a narrative is the emancipatory essence ascribed to cosmopolitanism. Even if it cannot be reduced to an internationally staged exercise in narcissism, cosmopolitanism in its many forms surely cannot be expected to confer subjecthood on all those who seek it, particularly those emerging from a colonial past.

THE ILLUSION OF CULTURAL HYBRIDITY

Despite the presence of a familiar island/continent, tradition/modernity dichotomy, relocation to a transnational social space does not automate a sort of cosmopolitan consciousness in O'Faolain's Irish characters, particularly Sally and Fintan. Although both view Paris as a mecca for sexual and intellectual liberation, its ability to offer Irish transplants a transcendent cultural experience is limited and often superficial, and artistic or intellectual expression is unsuccessful. Sally, though in France to represent Ireland as an accomplished scholar, cannot think of a thesis topic, does not attend classes, and never completes a single written assignment. Instead, she writes only in her diary, an adolescent cataloguing of her academic failures and her desire to meet men. Similarly, despite his engagement with Paris's literati, Fintan, who describes himself as a '[v]erbal onanist', is unable to produce effective communication of any kind: he telephones women and hangs up, cannot speak at his own lecture, and copies documents illicitly in the library lavatory for illegal publication (p. 85).

In addition to being incapable of communication or creation, both Sally and Fintan are unable to dissociate from Ireland. For Sally, Paris is an almost panoptical construct: she must use public baths and pass through a common area as she enters and leaves her flat, and is permitted to enter Mesli's building only with the approval of his cousin, who assumes the authority to override building policy and to determine if Mesli is spending too much time with a woman and not enough time with his revolutionary 'brothers'. Most pervasively, her parents have friends throughout the city who monitor Sally's behaviour and report back to Dublin. Consequently, Sally receives probing letters and telegrams from her parents warning against romantic involvement. Fintan, too, is followed by the mail, which in his case bears news of an unplanned pregnancy. The news and its vehicle, 'the genteel, linen-weave envelope . . . that squat little map on its stamp: foetally folded Ireland, stretching out embryo arms' (pp. 17–18), become a grotesque, suffocating embodiment of Ireland—and, as Antoinette Mastin has suggested, a variation on Stephen Dedalus's characterisation of Ireland as the sow that eats her farrow.[21] The written products of Ireland, intended primarily to warn the expatriate of the consequences of sexual activity, prevent both Sally and Fintan from contributing to or benefiting from Parisian culture in any significant way. Paris, then, acts as a transnational space in permitting communication but becomes an outpost of Ireland, explicitly proscribing interaction with Otherness and, by extension, cosmopolitanism.

Furthermore, cultural hybridity, typically viewed as a signifier of cosmopolitanism, is characterised by O'Faolain as having a range of reinscriptive consequences, among them literal and figurative incestuousness and impotence. When she returns home for Christmas, pregnant, Sally is sent to Mass with an older family friend thought to be an appropriate suitor. The scene depicting his advances, juxtaposed with the 'backsliders' Mass (the late service attended by the less devout) suggests both the endogamous nature of the Irish nationalist narrative and the role of the church in reinforcing it through the family model, and posits Sally as a Madonna/whore figure. This tendency toward endogamy is also felt by Sally and Fintan when they are outside Ireland. Though she gravitates toward Mesli and his Algerian circle of friends, Sally is compelled to interact socially with the Irish expatriate group—first at her parents' urging and then, more significantly, as a return to the familiar. When she leaves Mesli to attend a party with her Irish acquaintances, she has 'a moment of delight feeling like a newly detached Siamese twin, a pupa getting its wings, an animal released from hibernation' (p. 69).

Fintan resists engagement with the Other and keeps company almost exclusively with fellow Irish expatriates; in contrast to Sally, he does not need or attempt to pass as vaguely European, nor is his sexuality subjected to the process of containment. However, in France he is both sexually and socially impotent, less virile than Mesli and attracted only to Irish women, particularly Sally, to whom his advances seem 'brother-and-sisterly' (p. 114). He does, however, signify comfort and familiarity. Sally sees him as an emasculated exemption among men, whom she describes as 'the enemy', yet she also endows him with the romanticism of pre-colonial Irish mythology, proposing, 'Let's be brother and sister like the pair in the old fairy story who lay in the wood comforting each other and for whom the birds made a coverlet of leaves' (pp. 114–115). Sally's unwillingness to engage with him sexually, as a rejection of either tribal or filial endogamy, is for Fintan emotionally devastating, psychically fatal. After she rejects him, he thinks, 'Here lies one who little layed. RIP. They say there's no word in Gaelic for fuck' (p. 116), suggesting that Irish culture has no language or capacity for sexuality. However, both Sally and Fintan were sexually active in Ireland, albeit with less than ideal outcomes. Irish containment is the cause of Fintan's metaphorical death, its reach extending to his attempts to develop a sexual self beyond Irish borders.

With its 'almost Eskimo' frigidity, Irishness keeps Sally and Fintan on the fringes of transnational social space. In her reading of the novel's

Joycean elements, Mastin posits that Fintan, '[s]teeped in neo-colonialism . . . is determined to escape colonial domination, to throw off the mores of a post-colonial society'. The result, she argues, is his inability to assume 'the dominant Irish male role of colonial hegemony [which] leaves him in an ambivalent position with Irish women'.[22] Women see him as asexual or sexually unattractive, as a brother, or as a submissive partner to be dominated sexually, illustrated most starkly in the scene in which Letty performs fellatio on him against his will. Sally's efforts to replace Irish men with Mesli fail when he leaves her for the revolution—an echo of her mother's doomed romance—and it seems plausible that she would have resigned herself to a life of celibacy with Fintan had he remained in Paris rather than leaving abruptly for Barcelona at the novel's end. This would recast her as a perpetual exile and doomed lover, a role consistent with the reinscriptive consequences of her transgressions and her desire to escape.

Yet the novel's most overt rejection of potential cultural hybridity is symbolised by Sally's abortion. As a woman who challenges Catholic codes of purity and morality, the perpetuation of Irish bloodlines, and the law, Sally becomes an unruly body. Her public haemorrhage is an example of Julia Kristeva's 'signs of horror', which Lorna Rooks-Hughes has cited as a trope used by both O'Faolain and Edna O'Brien to illustrate threats to Irish identity presented by transgression of borders.[23] As an unruly body that temporarily eludes containment, she must be regulated. Conceived as the product of the Irish and Algerian nationalist narratives, the unborn child represents the sacrificial son of Kathleen Ní Houlihan given over to the Algerian nationalist movement. As Sally reflects on the pregnancy, she thinks, 'Poor brownish, pinkish Irish-Algerian never-to-be! I'm sorry, my fine *fellagha*, with your gun in one hand and prick in the other!' (p. 182). The abortion is not accomplished easily, however, and Sally enlists the help of both Fintan and a bumpy bus ride to expel 'the tough little Arab . . . holding on to his terrain' (p. 214). The tensions implied in this act of expulsion are embodied by Fintan, who assists despite his moral opposition, symbolically interceding on behalf of the nation that Sally's child theoretically threatens. Ultimately, his acting as an agent of expulsion serves as an unlikely and inverted form of containment that perpetuates the myth of Irish national and sexual purity.

The novel's conclusion is ambiguous, making *Three Lovers* another unfinished *bildungsroman*. Raimondo, the 'fossil-faced' antiques dealer, is a self-described 'Marauding Male' whose objective is to permeate the layers of 'ideal femininity' in order to discover in the Irish women he dates their 'secret simian and hidden hairinesses' (p. 70). Originally from Florence, an 'outpost of England' (p. 46), he spanks Sally in a public place and fondles her painfully under the table while on a date with another woman. Paternalistic and sexually oppressive, Raimondo is also impotent, taking tonics for his 'failures'. Sally is drawn to Raimondo because he can support her, allowing her to stay in France. However, he also represents a hybrid of her other two lovers, one who simulates the sexual aggressiveness she sees as lacking among Irish men but who will not impregnate her or abandon her for politics. He is safer than the gunman of her mother's youth and than Mesli, and her role in this narrative will be to remain young, beautiful, and Irish. After Sally lures him with her youth and vulnerability, describing her own mirror reflection as 'frail and innocent and victimised', Raimondo breaks off his relationship with Letty, 'wish[ing] women stayed young and attractive' (pp. 249–250, 254). As she continues to imagine herself as romantic French cinema heroine Dany Robin, Sally's fictive transnational identity is only superficially different from the one prescribed by Irish mythology. Her youth and beauty, which posit her as a Kathleen Ní Houlihan figure, act as international currency in all three of her relationships, whether as European adventurousness, Irish familiarity, or archetypal youth, and her beauty is ostensibly her only practical asset.

Ultimately, Sally's efforts to resist her prescribed Irish identity are futile. She can interpret the signs of the Algerian movement only as they resemble European history, and her presence in France is inextricably connected to her Irish identity. Although transnational mobility can temporarily dilute Irishness and the perceived constraints that accompany it, Sally is finally resigned to the legacy of de Valera's idealised Irish mother. The cultural role she attempts to escape by leaving Ireland is replicated in her relationship with Mesli, who finally abandons her for the revolution, one he may not survive, and in her sacrificing their unborn son. While she rejects motherhood and marriage, she is reinscribed at the novel's end through traditional iconography, specifically that of Kathleen ni Houlihan. A blood sacrifice made in the name of Irish and Algerian nationalism leaves Sally to wander at the novel's end without a home. This ending typifies a phenomenon described by James Goodman, one in which transnationalism serves to resurrect the nationalistic forces it is perceived to threaten: '[A]s transnational forces side-step state structures, national states strengthen their authority; as transnational identities become more important, nationalisms are re-geared to meet new, more "externally"-driven aspirations. Paradoxically, then, transnational pressures may broaden the options for official Irish nationalism, not close them off'.[24] Both paradoxical and predictable, this action/reaction dichotomy is evidenced in many ways in the novel. It is also clearly evident in more recent Irish history, specifically in the Irish response to immigration.

HOMELAND (IN)SECURITY

A contemporary reading of *Three Lovers* prompts the question of how today's more multicultural Ireland utilises containment culture, exile, and expulsion to safeguard against immigration's perceived threat to its nationalist narrative. Resistance to immigration has perhaps been most overt in the language and enforcement of citizenship laws: by using nationalist rhetoric to develop exclusionary policies, the framers and supporters of the twenty-seventh amendment have embraced bio-political containment as an answer to multiculturalism. Gerardine Meaney argues that throughout the twentieth century 'Irish nationalism may have had within it the potential for all kinds of hybrid, liberationist, adulterated and inclusive versions of Irish identity', potential that was squandered by 'extraordinarily narrow and exclusive' state policies.[25] As this has become truer in the twenty-first century, containment culture has taken the form of border control and denial of legal and civil rights designed to maintain the myth of racial purity. With a centuries-long history of colonialism instilling apprehension about porous borders and a sense of self-strangeness, Irish resistance to immigration is on one hand predictable. On the other hand, a lack of empathy for those fleeing substandard conditions at home seems paradoxical, the difficulties the Irish have faced abroad notwithstanding.

Yet one critical difference between the Irish abroad and many of the most violently rejected immigrants in Ireland today is the former's access to whiteness and the privileges of this racial affiliation. Sally's ability to pass in Paris, in contrast to Mesli's persistent Otherness, is a dubious privilege implied in the Irish right to emigrate and to police those who penetrate Irish borders. Irish resistance to immigration is not paradoxical when we note, as Meaney does, that calls for sympathy based on common experience 'ignore the extent to which the Irish cultivated, traded in and still exploit the valuable commodity of their white identity both abroad and at home'.[26] Although white identity has not always been advantageous to transnational Irish, it has at times served an insidious mimicry of colonialist practices, echoed in the eugenically driven nationalist fears so clearly outlined in the constitution.

O'Faolain's treatment of these themes in *Three Lovers* both reflects and anticipates Ireland's racial ideologies. Timothy Brennan suggests that cosmopolitan characters in literature 'are not the agents of historical change but the comic register of our common inadequacies, gullibilities, creativities, and desires'.[27] O'Faolain's comic novel does offer a sensitive and sympathetic critique of the Irish naïf. Simultaneously, from the spaces between contemporary feminist movements and periods of sectarian violence, Sally embodies what Raymond Williams refers to as '*pre-emergence*, active and pressing but not yet fully articulated'.[28] As the subject of a *bildungsroman*, Sally can be compared to the protagonists of writers such as Clare Boylan and Edna O'Brien, who typically asserted their independence by detaching from their families and from the church. However, the ability of these subjects to transcend the confines of female identity as constructed by nationalist iconography and mariolatry has traditionally been limited and, more often than not, illusory. Though maturation in these works often takes the form of sexual liberation or emigration, freedom is interrupted by persistent Irish influences.

One possible explanation for the failure of the Irish *bildungsroman* is its attempt to chronicle development prevented and cut short by colonialism. Sarah Townsend posits that the genre has failed in Ireland for a number of reasons, namely that a state of belated development, born partly of 'racial and/or cultural primitiveness', has resulted in narratives in which the subject's development is aborted. The promise of modernisation, she contends, is a 'developmental mirage' resulting in 'zones of hypermodernity' interspersed among areas left 'virtually untouched'.[29] One response to belatedness, Townsend contends, is an effort to accelerate the process of maturation, whether social, economic, or sexual, one that tends to miss a critical phase, and to fail. Townsend's claim is useful in reading *Three Lovers*, in which Fintan is a Dedalusian parody, a character whose physical journey surpasses that of Stephen's but whose capacity for existential analysis is nonexistent. Stephen's objective to 'fly by those nets' proves in Fintan's case to be a mirage, one promising release that Irishness will forever confound. Shevawn embodies a fiercely anti-colonialist mode perpetually hinged to colonial identity and therefore incapable of transcending it, despite the narrative promise of transnationality. Sally is defined by her belated development and marked and haunted by her 'primitiveness' as a 'specimen of the traditional beauty: five feet eleven, red-haired with features admittedly a touch too large, and flesh a touch too vivid. Designed for viewing in the Celtic Crepuscule, she looked, in more radiant lights, flammable' (p. 12). As she consciously constructs a narrative intended to correct what she sees as her Irish deficiencies—social, intellectual, and sexual—she finds that exercises in correction serve only to reinforce her Irishness. They transplant her, despite her relocation to a transnational social space and her efforts at cosmopolitanism, within colonial and precolonial Irish narratives. Furthermore, her use of status signifiers such as Hermès boots, particularly as juxtaposed with the pathos of Shevawn's Donegal tweed, correlates globalism and accelerated development. Sally's financial troubles at the novel's end—her future is dependent on a bailout that will set the terms of her future existence—mirror the arc of the Irish economy in the past two decades. Both the novel and recent history serve as cautionary tales about the consequences of cultural acceleration and correction, processes that are rarely emancipatory.

Attempts among O'Faolain's Irish characters to rewrite cultural narratives—through artistic expression, exogamy, and exile—are threatened, aborted, or silenced, and transnational subjects are regulated and managed even when they defy the containment of national boundaries. While the characters can temporarily escape the limitations imposed by Ireland and experience a superficial dilution of national identity abroad, their culturally ingrained identities—sexual, political, and national—remain more powerful than the ability to traverse physical space and rewrite cultural experience. Sally's unfinished narrative leaves readers uncertain of the extent to which her Irishness will intrude, and the longevity of collective nationalist fears in post-recession Ireland is equally uncertain. The limitations of cosmopolitanism as an antidote to provincialism—and the insidious ways in which the former can promote a return to the latter—have prompted Irish legislators, activists, and writers to consider new ways of responding to the effects of globalism. Whether Irish identity will ever adjust to its belated development remains to be seen, in both its history and its literature.

Becoming *Contrahecho*: An Irish-Irelander in Argentina

AMANDA TUCKER

William Bulfin provides an excellent example of the complexities and contradictions of Irish transnationalism in the nineteenth century. A minor figure in the Irish-Irelander movement,[1] Bulfin embraced the Gaelic Catholic monolith as the heart of Ireland and considered the rural Catholic class to be the only true representatives of the nation.[2] Bulfin's narrow version of nationalism, however, downplays the impact of his immigrant life in Argentina. His first success as a writer came in Buenos Aires, and his short-story collection, *Tales of the Pampas* (1900) offers a rare first-hand account of the Irish in Argentina. In his writing, Bulfin's amalgamation of Argentinean sensibilities with a deeply conservative Irish nationalism creates unsolvable contradictions about individual and collective identities. Ultimately, Bulfin demonstrates the difficulty of developing a cross-cultural orientation in an age of ethno-nationalism. In *Tales of the Pampas*, his attempt to integrate wildly different racial and national ideologies into a cohesive whole results in a type of multicultural schizophrenia, in which his genuine desires to engage with cultural difference are thwarted by his own ethno-racial assumptions.

In the nineteenth-century, the Irish increasingly were seen—and saw themselves—as a raced community. The Gaelic Celts were typically placed in the shifting middle space in Euro-American models of racial taxonomy: Steve Garner points out that 'theorists like Robert Knox (*The Races of Man*, 1850), and Gobineau (*Essai sur l'inégalité des races humaines*, 1853) saw the Celt as a less-developed element of the 'white race'. 'In America, "race" commentators in the mid nineteenth century tended to place Celts well below Anglo-Saxons, in a no man's land between Europeans and Africans'.[3] As Abby Palko demonstrates in her earlier chapter, at times this racial variance allowed the Irish abroad to make connections to individuals coded as black.[4] Within Ireland, however, the emphasis was on the Gaelic Celt as a white race. The idea of the Irish (i.e. the Gaelic Celt) as a distinct race from the English (the Anglo-Saxon) was a productive way of building national solidarity. Moreover, the Irish as a different but nonetheless 'white' race became a way to justify Home Rule: Garner suggests that 'what was at stake was the right to assume nationhood, and the key was whiteness at a political moment in which this term denoted superiority and aptitude for self-rule' and cites John Dillon's 1889 argument that Ireland deserved political independence because 'we are white men'.[5] Thus racial ideologies led to the construction of ethno-nationalism: in Bulfin's time, Ireland's nation-building project was inextricably linked with race.

RACE AND NATION IN ARGENTINA

Race and nation were also connected in Argentina, but in very different ways from those in Ireland. To begin with, Argentina had written a national constitution and won its War of Independence by the early nineteenth century. From its beginnings, the Argentine Republic reflected the ethnic diversity of Latin American nations, and multiple groups had claim to the new nation. *Criollos* (more often referred to as creoles in Latin America) were Spanish peoples born in Latin America; this group played a pivotal role—and often profited the most—in gaining independence. In contrast, the indigenous Indian population in Latin America continued to be neglected and discriminated against after independence. People who had both Spanish and Indian or African ancestry were known as *mestizos* or *mulattos*. The diverse cultures, traditions, and practices of these racialised communities often led to anxieties about creating a cohesive nation.

Domingo Faustino Sarmiento, the most influential nineteenth-century Argentine thinker and one-time president, sums up these apprehensions:

> Perhaps this is the first time we are going to ask ourselves who we are when they called us Americans, and who we are when we call ourselves Argentines. Are we Europeans? So many copper-coloured faces disprove this to us! Are we indigenous? Scornful smiles from our light-skinned women give us perhaps the only response. Mixed? No one wants to be that, and there are thousands who want to be called neither Americans nor Argentineans. Are we a nation? A nation without an amalgam of accumulated materials, with neither adaptation nor foundation? Argentines? It would be good to know on what basis and since when.[6]

For Sarmiento, questions of nationhood are intimately connected to issues of race and ethnicity. This conversation is one-sided: the only answers he needs are visual images of Argentines, which suggest the multitude of ethnicities contained in Argentina. The existence of both 'copper-coloured faces' and 'light-skinned women' makes it impossible for Argentina to identify as exclusively one or the other—that is, it makes it impossible to create an ethno-nationalism. But Sarmiento also presents the idea of 'mixing'—a vague reference that includes both individuals and collectivities—as repugnant. How, then, was Argentina to solve its identity crisis?

In nineteenth-century Argentina, two philosophies of nation-building, each completely contradictory of the other, proposed to answer the question. The first, advocated by Sarmiento and a Buenos Aires liberal *criollo* elite, wanted to differentiate Argentina from the rest of Latin America by aligning the nation with Europe. As the century progressed, Argentina had an increasingly neocolonial relationship with Britain, one that created huge disparities between the Buenos Aires region and the rest of the country. As Juan Corradi asserts, Buenos Aires was 'a dependency of Europe and it satellised—when it did not altogether ignore—the rest of the nation'.[7] Nineteenth-century Argentina was an oligarchy, and the *criollo* elite in Buenos Aires enjoyed wealth and privileges far beyond those in the more remote provinces. Britain also exerted social and cultural influence over Buenos Aires: as Edmundo Murray explains, the *criollo* elite were 'notoriously anglophile … they admired the British imperial structure and organisation, they imitated English fashion and they wished the *English way* could be adopted in Argentina'.[8]

European ideas about race were particularly important in discussions of the country's future: Amy K. Kaminsky argues that 'the differences of nations and (therefore) among races that predominated in late nineteenth-century European thought fueled Argentina's project of racial self-construction'.[9] Sarmiento in particular, and the Buenos Aires elite in general, sought to lighten 'the copper-coloured faces' through European migration. And they largely succeeded, as Corradi notes: 'the magnitude and impact of European immigration after 1853 have been so great as to literally remake the ethnic composition of the country'.[10] During the last half of the century, immigration rose astronomically: 'in the 1850s, the annual balance of immigrant arrivals over departures was under 5,000; by the 1880s the annual average was 50,000, and at its nineteenth-century peak in 1889 net immigration exceeded 200,000'.[11] Immigrants from Italy were the largest migrant group and Spanish migrants the second largest. This wave of immigration was also one way to marginalise and even eliminate citizens who were considered racially undesirable. For Sarmiento and other important liberal leaders, Indians had no place in the construction of a strong nation. Nicholas Shumway argues that while this group 'spoke grandly of civilising the Indians, but the programme Sarmiento actually followed came to little more than a policy of deliberate dislocation and extermination'.[12] Over several decades, the Patagonian Indians were pushed further and further into remote lands but the construction of railways suddenly made these lands more accessible—and therefore more desirable as fields for livestock grazing. A series of genocidal wars—most notably the 'Conquest of the Desert'—virtually eliminated the indigenous population, to clear the way for both a whiter Argentine society and Buenos Aires's economic interest.[13] What was best for Buenos Aires and its *criollo* elite came to stand for the nation.

In opposition to this nineteenth-century liberal ideology in Argentina, which favoured a Europeanised future for the country, is what Shumway describes as a 'messy, ill-defined, often contradictory tendency' that he identifies as nationalism.[14] Argentine nationalism repudiated Buenos Aires's aspirations of becoming a European country and was 'first and foremost natavistic', embracing the indigenous as embodying the true spirit of Argentina.[15] The figure of the *gaucho*, a nomadic cowboy who travelled and worked in the Pampas outside of Buenos Aires, most frequently represented in indigenous national culture, and the development of gauchoesque literature, in the middle of the nineteenth century, has proven to be one of the most lasting cultural influences in Argentina. This genre is characterised by its first-person narrative and close attention to the customs, manners, and speeches of the gaucho. Credited as the father of *literatura gauchesca*, Bartolomé Hidalgo uses the gaucho as a metaphor for 'an adolescent nation that arrogantly defies European pretense and asserts a new identity'.[16]

In its role within Argentine nationalism, the gaucho presents a much different racial model for the nation than Sarmiento's desire to whiten the ethnic demographic in Argentina. The gaucho typically has mixed Spanish and Amerindian ancestry, and thus offered the possibility of representing and valuing marginalised and silenced components of Argentina's population. This ambiguous ancestry creates a constantly shifting racialised understanding of the gaucho that was not wholly unlike the Gaelic Celt. On the one hand, the gaucho was *not* white and *not* European; indeed, that was part of his appeal for those who conceived him as the embodiment of the nation. He shared similar characteristics to the Indians, such as a significant attachment to the land, but was not considered (completely) barbaric and therefore was not the target of genocide. On the other, the gaucho was already, by the last half of the nineteenth century, a figure of the past rather than an indication of the future—and the modernisation of the country depended upon his disappearance. José Hernández's *Martín Fierro* (1872), often considered Argentina's national epic, readily demonstrates the gaucho's ambiguous matrix of cultural and racial affiliations. The eponymous gaucho, Martín Fierro, is at once a victim and perpetuator of racialised violence. In writing about his work, Hernández asserts in a letter that the purpose behind *Martín Fierro* is to show 'the abuses and denigrations endured by this disinherited class ... the hardship, misfortune, and haphazardness of gaucho life'.[17] Yet Fierro also participates, however briefly and reluctantly, in the campaigns against the Indians. And in one of the poem's most significant passages, he kills another gaucho for no other reason than he is black. Both as character and as signifier for the nation, Fierro cannot escape the racialised violence of the nineteenth century.

Thus in the nineteenth-century, race and nation-building were closely linked in Argentina, as in Ireland. But Argentina vacillated between two influential, but completely contradictory, racialised models of creating a nation: a 'whitening' of the country through European immigration—most commonly advocated by a liberal *criollo* elite located in Buenos Aires—and a natavistic embrace of the gaucho as the embodiment of the nation. These two versions of national identity obviously oppose one another, creating in Kaminsky's words, 'an internal gash that bleeds the nation'.[18] In a similar manner, Bulfin's stories in *Tales of the Pampas* move back and forth between these two understandings of Argentine nation-building: on the one hand, Bulfin feels racially superior to *criollos*, *mestizos*, and other immigrants in the stories, even when he has a lower economic or social status. On the other, Bulfin clearly feels the attraction of the pampas lifestyle and desires to make connections with the gauchos he works alongside. His contradictory impulses do not just suggest a struggle between assimilation and exile, for this binary reduces the complexities of race, migration, and national belonging in Argentina. In other words, Bulfin does not simply compartmentalise his experiences as an Irish nationalist and an Argentine immigrant. Instead, Bulfin's writing—even at the height of his Irish-Irelander fervour—demonstrates what is possibly the most unique quality of Argentinean life—the *contrahecho* quality of being at war with oneself.

IRISH AND *INGLESES* IN ARGENTINA

The Irish-Argentine community illustrates the flaws in Sarmiento's plan to Europeanise Argentina, for this group generally had no desire to assimilate to their adopted country. As Bulfin represents in his story collection, *Tales of the Pampas*, the Irish-Argentine population (estimated between 40–50,000) was large enough for it to be an insular, if not isolated, community. Many, though not all, Irish-Argentines shared common goals and origins. In contrast to their Irish-American counterparts, Irish-Argentine immigrants frequently came from middle-class families: often they were farmers' sons wanting to enlarge their fortunes or daughters hoping to increase their marriage prospects.[19] Moreover, migration to Argentina came primarily from the midlands. Following what R. F. Foster calls chain migration,[20] Irish citizens would immigrate to Argentina based on the reports of friends and acquaintances already established there. Peadar Kirby mentions an extreme example in which nearly the entire population around Ballymore emigrated to Buenos Aires during the 1860s.[21] As a result, community alliances and networks within the Irish-Argentine population often predated their migration.

The insularity of the Irish-Argentine community was further supported by their physical proximity to one another: the majority of Irish immigrants ended up in Buenos Aires or the surrounding countryside, known as the River Plate region. Directed by Father Fahy and other Irish clergy members, the Irish community in Argentina created their own professional and personal community, independent of their adopted country. Eventually they developed an entire infrastructure so that all of their needs—educational, religious, medical, and social—were handled within the Irish population.[22] As it grew, the Irish in Argentina deliberately resisted becoming Argentine: often they had no need to learn Spanish, and even second-generation emigrants frequently did not learn the language.[23]

Bulfin's *Tales of the Pampas* portrays this insularity, for the unnamed, first-person Irish-Argentine narrator (who we can assume to be a stand-in for Bulfin) differs greatly from the rest of his community in his desire to associate with the gauchos and with other (non-Irish) migrants in Argentina. This difference is most clearly demonstrated at the end of the story 'Campeando', when the narrator is chastised for associating with Castro, a gaucho colleague. His friend Mike warns him that he is 'gettin' too much of the country into you, me boy'.[24] In both content and form—for instance, the story's Spanish-language title—the story emphasises the narrator's assimilation into gaucho culture. When he is confronted by Mike, however, the narrator minimises his Argentine associations, weakly protesting that he was assigned to work with Castro. Mike replies:

> That's all collywest. Of course they sent you. If you're always stuck with the natives behind the *galpon* [shed] instead of attendin' to your good name, you'll be sent with them, and you'll get into their ways, and the day will come when the dickens a decent man in the country will have anything to say or do with you. (p. 110)

Mike's warning makes clear the general prejudice of the Irish immigrants: 'decent' men, by which he obviously means *Irish*men, do not interact with their gaucho co-workers. The narrator has transgressed this social boundary by being on friendly terms with Castro and other gaucho *peons*, thereby endangering his position within the Irish-Argentine community. But even as Mike's statement attests to the insularity of this immigrant community, it also indicates the precariousness of Irishness as an ethnicity when placed in contact with other racialised groups: Mike fears that, by agreeing to work with Castro, the narrator is in danger of 'going native' and losing his Irish identity as well as his good name.

While Mike's rebuke reveals the insularity of the Irish Argentine community, it fails to understand how ethnic and cultural affiliations work in nineteenth-century Argentina. Outside their community, Irish immigrants in Argentina were usually not recognised as 'Irish'. Instead, they were known as *Ingleses* because they spoke English. Although English and Irish identities were entirely distinct in Ireland, they were not mutually exclusive in Buenos Aires. The designation of *Ingleses* also brought with it distinct advantages: as residents of Northern Europe, English immigrants were considered the most racially superior, and therefore the most desirable in terms of national culture and demography, by the *criollo* elite.[25] Being Ingleses thus offered considerable commercial and social advantages in Buenos Aires. This sort of racial privilege is best demonstrated in the most 'Irish' of the stories in *Tales of the Pampas*, 'The Course of True Love'. The title, with its reference to Shakespeare, reinforces the narrator's (and his audience's) English-language affiliations and therefore stands in stark contrast to the earlier stories with Spanish-language titles such as 'Campeando' or 'El High-Life'. Moreover, the reference to Shakespeare emphasises the narrator's—and indeed, the entire Irish-Argentine community's British—as opposed to Irish—racialised affiliations. If the title thus implicitly acknowledges the racial privilege that Irish-Argentines enjoy as *Ingleses*, it also indicates the closed nature of the Irish-Argentine population. This insularity is further communicated through its style and tone. Although it is the final tale in the collection, 'The Course of True Love' gives the English translation of words like *estancia* and *puesto*, which have been used regularly and without definition in earlier stories. On the other hand, Gaelic words such as *garrahalya* are used without explanation. These details indicate Bulfin's desire to construct a monolithic Irish-Argentine community: indeed, the narrator insists early on in the story that all are 'Irish in thought, in sympathy, and in character' (p. 136).

However, this description erases important differences in the Irish-Argentine community[26] and ignores the particularly contradictory position of the middle-class Irish Catholic group in Argentina—of which Bulfin was a central figure. Buenos Aires could be considered what Mary Louise Pratt has famously termed a 'contact zone', in which 'disparate cultures meet, clash, and grapple with one another, often in highly asymmetrical relations of domination and subordination'.[27] For this group of Irish-Argentines, the contact zone produced a matrix of shifting affiliations and attachments with the region's native and immigrant populations. Their Catholic faith linked them to Italian and Spanish immigrants in Buenos Aires. Although they shared a common language with the English expatriate community, being known as *Ingleses* was undoubtedly uncomfortable for a fervent Irish-Irelander. And in the city, Irish-Argentines may have enjoyed an elevated social status because they spoke English, but in the countryside it was necessary for some to learn Spanish because they often worked alongside or in subordinate positions to the gauchos on the large *estancias* (cattle ranches). Irish-Argentines who, like Bulfin, were very strongly anti-British probably felt more of a kinship with the gauchos. Not only were the gauchos, like middle-class Irish Catholics, thought to be representatives of their national character, but they also were victims of European scientific racism. *Literatura gauchesca* perhaps even provided a model for politically-minded Irish-Argentines by suggesting a successful way to develop cultural nationalism, prefiguring Ireland's own literary renaissance in the late nineteenth and early twentieth centuries.

What we know of Bulfin's life in Argentina suggests that he may have embraced these varying positions. After arriving in Argentina, Bulfin worked as a *peon* on an Irish-owned cattle estate, where he learned Spanish, presumably from the gauchos with whom he worked. After working on the Pampas for a few years, he moved to Buenos Aires and took up white-collar jobs: teaching English, working for a furniture maker, and writing for various newspapers. Though Bulfin's actual contact with gauchos was brief, this part of his life was clearly pivotal, and Bulfin returns to this period again and again in his writing. *Tales of the Pampas* reflects Bulfin's multiple, sometimes contradictory alliances. Some of the tales trace Irish immigrants' process of absorption into Argentinean society, but in others, the narrator accentuates his outsider viewpoint by turning Argentine life into mere spectacle. As a result, this text is much less cohesive than most story collections—partly due to the fact that Bulfin wrote these stories individually for newspapers and only compiled them later, but also because of the narrator's fluctuating and contradictory responses to the Argentine natives. This incohesiveness signifies the complex web of relationships among racialised communities in Argentina under the nation's conflicting racial ideologies. Moreover, *Tales of the Pampas* provides a counter-example to facile, institutionalised versions of contemporary multiculturalism, best signified in the image of people from different races and cultures holding hands under a rainbow. Multiculturalism on the Argentine plains happens from below, through individual engagement and interaction.

NATIVE AND MIGRANT COMMUNITIES IN THE PAMPAS

As illustrated in the first story in *Tales of the Pampas*, 'A Bad Character', race relations in the Pampas are continually in a state of negotiation. The central conflict is between the community at large and Sailor John, whom the narrator describes as a 'camp *atorrante*—that is, a tramp on horseback who begs, borrows or plunders his way through life' (p. 19). After pleading with Mike Horan, an Irish-Argentine landowner, for room and board in exchange for labour, the sailor robs his benefactor. He then sells these stolen goods to a series of men, promising each one to leave these items at the local *pulpería* (camp-store).[28] After the narrator's frame, Mike (who, as discussed above, also appears in 'Campeando') directly tells the rest of the story. As the men gather one-by-one at the store, they realise that Sailor John has deceived them. Although these events clearly are enough to inspire hostility between the sailor and the others, ethnic tensions underlie this situation. Most of the men deceived are Irish—Mike Horan, Tommy Hennessy, Ned Rafferty, Larry McGowan—as is the unnamed, and uninvolved, narrator. As with most of the characters in *Tales of the Pampas*, Sailor John's ethnicity is never directly stated, but Bulfin gives enough information to ascertain his English identity: the sailor is 'a deserter from the crew of a British merchant vessel', and his choice of songs during his drunken spree, 'Tom Bowling' and 'Trafalgar Bay', further indicate his Englishness.[29] For the Irish-Argentine characters, who seem, like Bulfin, to be nationalist-minded, the fact that Sailor John is English increases their hostility. Moreover, Bulfin's portrayal of Sailor John as a drunken, idle thief, offers ironic commentary on the popular racialised perception of English immigrants in Argentina, who with their work ethic were supposed to help modernise the country.

The antagonistic relationship between Sailor John and the Irish-Argentine characters creates a temporary alliance between the latter and Domingo, a gaucho who has also been deceived by the sailor. Sailor John himself suggestively links the Irish and the Argentine populations as marginalised cultures through a series of ethnic-based insults: He first calls Larry McGowan an 'H-H-Hirish hass' (he has a stuttering problem) and later deems Domingo a 'black swipe' (pp. 32–33). In his indignant description of Sailor John, the narrator more explicitly indicates the collusion between the gauchos and the Irish. Drawing up a litany of the sailor's negative characteristics, the narrator states that '[h]e was dishonest. He stuttered. He despised the Irish and the Gauchos. He was a liar. He was quarrelsome' (p. 19). It is telling that the narrator considers the sailor's dislike of both Irish immigrants and Argentine natives indicative of his nature, for it suggests the narrator's esteem for these two groups. The parallel syntax of this statement further indicates an assumed equivalence between them. However, this moment of cross-ethnic solidarity is short-lived. The Irish immigrants may include Domingo in their dispute with Sailor John, but they also treat him less favourably than they do one another. Even while Domingo is sympathising with the other deceived men, Mike thinks that it doesn't much matter if the Sailor did trick Domingo because the latter is a 'cliver rogue' (p. 24, sic). And while both the Irish and Domingo drown their troubles with drink, the narrator pointedly states that Domingo takes 'a drop too much' and must go to sleep it off (p. 28). These details indicate an implicit disapproval of Domingo that the narrator and Mike—indeed all the Irish characters—share. Their disapproval can be partially attributed to the liberal rhetoric that favoured English-speaking immigrants and rejected gauchos within modernised Argentina.

But another mutual enemy, this time the Spanish store owner Francisco, once again establishes a tenuous link between Mike and Domingo. Although Francisco commiserates with the men congregating at his store, Mike imagines the shopkeeper 'laughin' to himself the whole time' at their misfortune (p. 23). Mike's impressions are strengthened at the end of the story, when Francisco does not send for the police but sets Sailor John free after he has slept off his drunken stupor. The sailor therefore goes unpunished for his crimes, to the irritation of both Mike and Domingo. Mike indicates that the Irish and Gaucho alike have been mistreated by the English and secretly mocked by the Spanish, who form their own covert alliance. Rather than building from Argentine racial thought, this moment suggests cross-ethnic solidarity based on a shared status as victims of colonisation. Depending on the mode of Argentine political rhetoric—either a liberal elite or natavistic stance—either the Irish as immigrant or the gaucho lies outside of 'true' nation. However, this scene indicates that, regardless of their geopolitical location or racial affiliations, both the Irish and the gaucho are victims of European imperialism. As Edmundo Murray states, '[i]n Bulfin's logic, both the gauchos and the Irish shared similar circumstances. The spaces colonised by the English and the Spanish belonged to the Irish and the gauchos respectively'.[30] It is in this moment of shared oppression, then, that Mike feels the closest to Domingo. But this moment too is ephemeral and by no means implies that Mike has embraced this multi-ethnic, multicultural environment in the Pampas.

AN IRISH GAUCHO?

In one of the fullest and most astute discussions of *Tales of the Pampas*, Edmundo Murray argues that Bulfin separates himself from other Irish-Argentine writers by offering 'a positive reading' of the gauchos: 'Bulfin uses the gaucho as a symbol of Argentiness … [while] previous descriptions of the natives in general and the gauchos in particular were frequently derogatory, and recorded the feeling of superiority of the Irish immigrants in Argentina'.[31] This sense of separation is mirrored in the collection itself, for the narrator is often the only immigrant present in the tales that prominently feature gaucho characters. Consequently, the most genuine and long-lasting moments of cross-cultural engagement in the story collection occur outside the Irish-Argentine community. Within the collection itself, three stories—'Castro Telleth of Tavalonghi's Horse', 'The Defeat of Barragan', and 'Campeando'—constitute a novella of sorts that offers Bulfin's most extended example of cross-cultural engagement. The focus is on the narrator's developing friendship with the gaucho Castro. These tales are told consecutively, with each picking up directly where its predecessor left off. On one hand, these stories indicate the narrator's admiration for the gaucho community, an admiration built upon his natavistic understanding of both Argentine and Irish nationalism. On the other, the stories also reveal the narrator's unthinking reproduction of racial prejudice and condescension with which Buenos Aires often viewed gauchos.

This novella begins with 'Castro Telleth of Tavalonghi's Horse', the first tale in which a gaucho character plays a substantial role in Bulfin's narrative. At the start of the story, the narrator sets off on a quest with Castro, for both men have been charged with the task of tracking down cattle that have wandered away because the fences of their ranch have been destroyed. Castro informs the narrator that the ranch's fences are perpetually being cut by gauchos on their way to town because the ranch is situated on the path of three different camp-stores. The narrator adds his own commentary to Castro's explanation: 'To him no more than to his fellows did a wire fence convey any idea of the right of property: it merely constituted an impediment. There had been no wires long ago and festive gauchos could gallop for miles unchecked. Those were ideal times!' (p. 70). This appreciative remark locates gauchos within a fading past, rather than in the country's future. Nonetheless, he admires Castro and laments that they are 'almost strangers as yet'. He hopes this journey might be a first step in 'getting within the inner circle of his [Castro's] friendship and learning something of the world thereby' (p. 71). The statement suggests the narrator's cross-cultural orientation: he will separate himself from his own (Irish-Argentine) community, in order to join Castro's.

However, the narrator's physical description of Castro complicates this cross-cultural potential. Castro is described as '[a] good-looking fellow, despite his swarthy skin, white-toothed, slim, somewhat bow-legged while on the ground but a living and superb picture when on horseback … What more of him? A good deal more, but let his character grow upon you as it did on me. Mount, if you like, and come with us' (p. 71). This sketch, which immediately follows the narrator's wish to befriend Castro, shows his desire to know Castro as a stock character rather than as a unique individual. In addition to the underlying racial prejudice hinted by the reference to his 'swarthy skin', the narrator indicates that Castro's individual attributes are less interesting than the 'superb picture' he presents.[32] The imperative statement at the end mimics a journalistic style, as though he were presenting Castro as a case study to curious readers. The power dynamic here is explicit and in keeping with liberal Argentine racial ideology. The beginning of 'Castro Telleth of Tavalonghi's Horse' therefore illustrates the narrator's ambivalence about the native Argentines: in his wish to join Castro's inner circle (which we can logically assume to be composed of other gaucho workers), the narrator begins the process of integrating himself into Argentine society. But what is his purpose in doing so? Perhaps it is a genuine attempt at cross-cultural engagement; perhaps it is so that Bulfin may have fodder for future writing projects. Bulfin appears to recognise and pursue both options simultaneously.

The next story 'The Defeat of Barragan' further demonstrates this ambivalence. The narrator and Castro continue their quest for the missing cattle, but when Castro suggests that they attend a gaucho-planned horse race to inquire after the livestock, the narrator questions his motivations. He asks his companion 'honour bright' if he just wants to see the races, in the process attempting and bungling a gaucho proverb, *Entre bueyes no hay cornadas* (p. 81).[33] The narrator's use of Argentine Spanish suggests his eagerness to befriend Castro, and he is inordinately pleased about attending the race with his colleague: 'I had long been wishing to see a first-class camp race and, although I kept this thought to myself, it gave me more satisfaction than the probability of hearing something about our missing cattle' (p. 83). He experiences plenty of excitement after Castro races against Barragan, a villainous character, and beats him.

Yet as he literally rides off into the sunset with his new friend, the narrator expresses a radically different sentiment than he does at the beginning of the story. He now believes that he and Castro have 'disgraced themselves' by attending the races and were 'scamps of the deepest dye' (p. 100). Even though the narrator has repeatedly expressed his desire to participate in gaucho culture, he now implies that it has led him astray. Although he labels both himself and Castro 'scamps', the narrator actually distances himself from his coworker here, for his anxiety about their day's labour implies that he is ethical and hard-working and that Castro, who laughs in response to his companion's concern, is shiftless and lazy. At this moment, more than any other in the story, the narrator invokes his racial privilege as an *Ingles*, for he transposes the English colonial view of the Irish onto Castro, who becomes the feckless native.[34] Importantly, the narrator only expresses this regret after the day's activities are over, which allows him to experience the excitement that he craves yet feel smugly superior to Castro. This ambivalence demonstrates the narrator's conflicting attitudes towards Castro in particular and gauchos in general. Unlike the rest of the Irish-Argentine community, who are represented as having whole-heartedly adopted the racial ideology of the Buenos Aires liberal elite, he enjoys being in the company of gauchos. However, the narrator also deliberately creates moments of rupture between himself and Castro, which indicates the tenuous nature of their relationship.

The narrator reinstates his imperial and racialised gaze in the next story, 'Campeando'. He and Castro stop their hunt for the missing cattle and take a meal at Castro's friends' home. Since Castro is the godfather of the couple's son, he is asked to bless the children. Observing this scene, the narrator suddenly reflects of gaucho culture, 'Ages of twisted theology and warped religious tradition are behind them. Around them, in the pampa air, are the freedom, the romance, the poetry, the heroism, the squalor, the viciousness, the empty monotony, the fatalism from which they cannot escape—of which they are the product' (p. 106). What is a touching scene of family connection and cultural tradition becomes, for Bulfin, representative of gaucho 'backwardness'. Ironically, in suggesting 'twisted theology' as the predominant element of gaucho culture, the narrator once again reproduces the English view of the Irish, particularly their view of Catholicism. The narrator links this credulity to the gauchos' inevitable downfall, claiming that 'before them is a future which belongs to others, not them and theirs' (p. 106). Ironically, this same statement could have been written—indeed, was written—about the Irish, though obviously Bulfin felt that the future of Ireland was more hopeful than the gloomy portrait he presents of the gauchos.

In contrast with the narrator's internal judgements about Gaucho culture, Castro's reception by others during their adventure complicates the way that gaucho identity is viewed. On the pampas, away from the

Irish-owned *estancia* where he works, Castro occupies a socially privileged position that is further enhanced after he defeats Barragan. As they ride through the pampas countryside looking for their lost cattle, the narrator and Castro enjoy a 'pleasant word with some of Castro's many friends—and peradventure a cup of *mate* from some of the many girls that smiled upon his compliments' (p. 107). The narrator is clearly thought of as an outsider during these exchanges; nonetheless, he is generally treated politely and kindly because of his connection to Castro. However, during a conversation with a fellow gaucho, the narrator is viewed with suspicion and disdain; though he has knowledge of the lost cattle, the gaucho refuses to pass on this information with the narrator there. He 'spoke at first in a cautious, formal, wooden and non-committal way, and fastened his eyes especially on me … therefore did I dutifully swallow my pride and diffidently keep in the background' (p. 108). Yet the gaucho still distrusts Castro because of his working relationship with the immigrant narrator. Only after he finds out that Castro is the victor over Barragan does he finally provide the necessary information. This scene, brief as it is, indicates the narrator recognises the shifting and contradictory nature of racial and social privilege in Argentina: while in Buenos Aires, his racial status as 'white' affords him certain social and economic benefits, but it is a disadvantage in the pampas. That the narrator acknowledges this disadvantage without much protest—he says cheerfully that he 'swallow[ed] large imaginary helpings of humble-pie'—reflects his ability in perspective taking. Rather than disgust at working with someone he views as inferior, he feels pride at being known as a 'compadre' of Castro's (the fact that Castro has defeated a notorious villain undoubtedly helps). He is willing to be viewed as an outsider in order to forge a friendship with Castro, and this willingness to be vulnerable, to alter one's views and social position, is essential in developing a cross-cultural orientation.

Therefore, although later passages in 'Campeando' indicate the narrator's condescending attitude towards gaucho culture, the opening of the story demonstrates his celebration of the gaucho way of life. In recalling the most pleasurable moments of his life, he includes memories closely associated with Argentina, such as 'a night by a campfire' (p. 103). More particularly, the narrator's recollections stem from his friendship with Castro: 'I have my share of such memories, thank God, and none is brighter than the recollection of a certain summer's day spent with Castro galloping over the rich clover and skirting the clumps of flowering cardos which stretched for leagues and leagues around us' (p. 103). This overwhelmingly positive description demonstrates that the narrator does not view Castro merely as a symbol of a downtrodden race. Nor is the yoke of colonisation, which the narrator uses elsewhere to create a political alliance between Irish and the gauchos, mentioned. In spite of whatever assumptions these men have about the other's ethnic group, they become friendly towards one another after becoming acquainted on an individual basis. This is not to suggest that Castro and/or the narrator have learned to become 'colour-blind' in their responses to one another; rather, their interpersonal relationship momentarily transcends the racial and cultural ideologies that have often shaped it.

TOWARDS A MULTICULTURE IN THE PAMPAS

The next tale, 'The Fall of Don José', takes multiculture one step further by suggesting the possibility of creating a hybrid community, composed of immigrants and natives alike. The story's action takes place around a campfire (perhaps the very one that the narrator favourably remembers in 'Campeando'), and as the ranch-hands are eating their supper, the well-liked gaucho, Domingo, tells them of a snobby cook's comeuppance. The narrative structure mirrors that of 'A Bad Character', as the narrator relinquishes control over the story shortly after it begins, turning the reigns over to Domingo. Previously the stories have been told by Irish narrators such as Mike Horan, who in fact chastises the narrator for his friendship with Castro. This is the first and only time in the collection that we hear (in)directly from a gaucho perspective. Before the narrator reproduces Domingo's story, he laments his sad art of reproduction:

> I cannot give it to you as it fell from him in his graceful Spanish, so full of quaint conceits, word-play, droll humour, and subtle irony. And alas, too, for the art of the gaucho storyteller!—who can hope to emulate it? Who can aspire, above all, to catch even a gleam of it in any other language than Argentine Spanish? Let me therefore ask you to be indulgent with me while I try to give you the story of Don José as Domingo told it while we swallowed the roast. (p. 116)

In this passage we learn not only of the narrator's admiration for gaucho culture, but also his progression in that culture: clearly he knows Argentine Spanish well enough to translate it into English, and he acknowledges the linguistic beauty of the hybrid language, which cannot be translated. He attempts, nonetheless, to replicate the story as closely as possible in English, which he indicates with the quotation marks he places around the entirety of Domingo's tale. In 'The Fall of Don José', the narrator provides an uncensored view of Argentine life and, through his silent endorsement of it, suggests its inherent value.

The content of Domingo's story is as significant as the way in which it is told. Domingo's tale centres on the conflict between the cook José and the other gauchos working on an *estancia*. The cook, originally from the city, feels superior to the other workers and appears to delight in making their hard life even more difficult: for instance, he refuses to reopen the kitchen to feed the men who have worked late and missed supper. In order to teach the cook a lesson, Domingo pairs with Don Tomás, an *Ingles* book-keeper, and they work secretly together in order to bring about Don José's defeat. As Domingo tells the story, he expresses his admiration for Tomás over and over again, and largely attributes their success to him. When we focus on this aspect of the story, it seems that cooperation rather than conflict is the central theme, for Domingo's tale focuses on the successful relationship between an *Ingles* (how both Bulfin and the narrator would have been identified) and a gaucho.

Murray argues, however, that 'the use of two narrators suggests the aim of the author to assign greater omniscience to the Irish one. He is a foreign person, well educated, who appreciates the customs of the gauchos but does not belong to their class'.[35] His remark harkens back to the earlier stories in which the narrator displayed an ambivalent attitude toward the gauchos offering both praise and condescension in his descriptions of their culture. Certainly we get indications of this patronising tone, such as when the narrator describes the 'picturesque rag' of the gaucho's chosen clothing (p. 114). But since the story also includes Domingo's point-of-view, we get a dual perspective here: that is, we get to see how both the English and Irish are viewed from a gaucho perspective. For example, when Domingo provides his audience with explanation about who Don Tomás was, he explains 'he was an *Ingles*. Macintosh was his name, and he always swore at us because we called him an Englishman—but it was all the same to us' (p. 120–1). This description suggests that Don Tomás, given his name and his intense dislike of Englishness, might be a Scottish nationalist. However, he is never described as such by the gauchos, nor is the affiliation of Irishness ever mentioned from a gaucho perspective. Instead, Don Tomás is well liked because he 'could speak Spanish real well, and was, for a *gringo*, a good horseman. He was young and full of fun' (p. 121). The qualifying phrase 'for a *gringo*' indicates that Domingo shares with the narrator a condescending ethnocentrism.

It is easy, in this story and others, to focus on the cross-cultural failings of the characters. But rather than reading this story as another example of the narrator's feelings of superiority, I suggest that it is a culmination of his evolving feelings towards the Argentine natives. In 'The Fall of Don José', we have two examples of successful cohabitation between the *Ingleses* and the Argentine: Domingo and the Scottish bookkeeper Tomás, from Domingo's story, and equally important, the actual group of *peons* who listen to that story. The possibility of a hybrid community, composed of immigrants and Argentine natives, emerges through these simultaneous tales. This moment of harmony does not mean that the Irish narrator will completely assimilate into Argentine culture. As Castro and the narrator are repeatedly reminded during their adventures, despite their friendship, each man has a different culture, tradition and, values. Neither the Irish immigrant nor the Argentine native feels as highly about the other's culture. Nonetheless, the stories from 'Castro Telleth' to 'The Fall of Don José' chart the narrator's remarkable progression within gaucho culture: he has finally joined Castro's 'inner circle' (p. 71).

During the nineteenth-century, Argentine thinkers were preoccupied with figuring out how to create an ideal nation through racialised models of identity. But Bulfin and others had to live in the Argentina that already existed—a country created by diverse racialised communities, some native and some migrant, and divided by its contradictory attitudes towards race and culture. It is telling, therefore, that *Tales of the Pampas* doesn't end with 'The Fall of Don José'. If it did, the collection as a whole might indicate the narrator's progression within, and perhaps assimilation to, the multiculture created on the pampas. However, several of the other stories—most notably, 'The Course of True Love'—break and belie the tenuous cross-cultural orientation constructed in this three-story arc. Ultimately, the narrator refuses to embrace either exile, as most of the Irish-Argentine community did, or assimilation, through becoming absorbed into gaucho culture. Neither can he embrace the notion of multiculturalism that stories like 'The Fall of Don José' advocate: such moments of cross-cultural engagement are always rewarding but also ephemeral. Like Argentina itself, Bulfin is conflicted about what matters most—the affiliations we are born with or those we choose to make. Throughout his prolific writing about Argentina and Ireland, Bulfin favours one and then the other but never resolves the question.

The politics of comparison: Romance at the edges of Europe

KATARZYNA BARTOSZYŃSKA

Irish Studies has long had an implicitly comparative dimension, often seeing its cultural output in relation to, and in terms set by, that of its nearest neighbour, Great Britain. Recent years have seen an increased interest in different forms of comparison: in examining Irish writing alongside that of other cultures, be they other colonies, other islands, or other predominantly Catholic nations. New geographical coordinates have the potential to highlight aspects of the tradition that have heretofore received less attention. Following suit, this piece sketches out a possible comparison to Poland, whose socio-historical conditions in the eighteenth and nineteenth centuries bore a marked similarity to that of Ireland. I focus specifically on the early novel in both traditions, examining how a comparison between the literary works of both places illuminates the ways in which their reception has linked aesthetic form to historical circumstances. In particular, I examine the romantic elements of nineteenth-century novels from Poland and Ireland, and critical responses to them. Simultaneously, I consider how such a comparison is constructed: both its benefits, and the assumptions that ground it, as a way of questioning the nature of transnational studies and how they function in practice. Although a comparison between Poland and Ireland serves to contest the apparent anomalousness of certain features of the nineteenth-century Irish novel (particularly its apparent inability to produce realist works), it also risks reinforcing the sense of these traditions as peripheral in damaging ways.

Irish literary criticism has a long-standing sense of shame or inadequacy about the nineteenth-century Irish novel. As Joe Cleary writes, 'Studies of the nineteenth century Irish novel have long been conditioned by the search for the Irish *Middlemarch* and by the attempt to explain why there is not one'.[1] David Lloyd clarifies that this is not simply a sense of inadequacy in comparison with England—it is not only that Irish literature produced no *Middlemarch*, he writes, 'it also produced no *Pére Goriot* or *Sentimental Education*, no *Effi Briest*, no *Moby Dick*, no *War and Peace*, *Crime and Punishment* or *Fathers and Sons*'.[2] The implied criticism is clear: Irish literature contains no masterpieces of realism, which is considered to be the most important trend of nineteenth-century writing.

The idea that realism is a natural or obvious outgrowth of any novelistic tradition is not unique to Irish critics; it is a notion arguably as old as the novel itself. Alongside the development of modern prose fiction, we find the rise of a literary criticism that trumpets the view that the novel is a genre that emerges out of the death of the comparatively more crude and simplistic romance.[3] There is a political dimension in these accounts. Socio-historical accounts of the novel's development have linked the rise of realism to the emergence of a strong (Protestant) middle class and the emergence of capitalism.[4] Moreover, in the early nineteenth century, romance was not only considered an older form of writing, it also developed a strong association with the exotic and the pre-modern. Writing in 1824, for instance, Walter Scott explained that a romance was

> a fictitious narrative in prose or verse; the interest of which turns upon marvelous and uncommon incidents; being thus opposed to the kindred form of the *Novel*, which (...) we would rather define as a fictitious narrative, differing from the romance, because the events are accommodated to the ordinary train of human events, and the modern state of society.[5]

Realistic fiction is not only associated with everyday occurrences in such an account, but also with modern society, thus implicitly aligning the romantic or marvellous with less developed cultures.

This view persists, to a surprising extent, even today, as recent critiques by Nicholas Paige and Srinivas Aravamudan make clear.[6] In 'On Fictionality', Catherine Gallagher writes that '[p]lausible stories are thus the real test for the progress of fictional sophistication in a culture',[7] and ponders 'what it was about early modernity in the first capitalist nation that propagated not just *realist* fiction but realist *fiction*'.[8] There is a problematic slippage in such accounts, from a correlation between the development of capitalist society and that of the realist novel (and an understandable interest in the dynamics underlying such a correlation), to a sense that realist fiction is a sign that a given culture has achieved 'sophistication'. This paradigm has implications for theories of the novel's developments in 'minor' or 'peripheral' European traditions as well. In Franco Moretti's 'Conjectures on World Literature', for instance, we find an account of realist fiction developing in the 'centre' and being imported, with difficulty, into the 'periphery'.[9] Though it is accurate to note that realism became the dominant mode of fiction in many places during the nineteenth century, the sense of an opposition between the 'romantic' and the 'novelistic' is overstated,[10] and often has a dangerously teleological slant that dismisses 'romance' as a crude and outmoded form of writing.

In his classic *Remembrance and Imagination*, Joep Leerssen explores the romance-realism dichotomy and its applications to Irish fiction, noting that 'the early novel in Ireland appears uncomfortably hybrid if viewed against the background of this genre distinction'.[11] The problem, he argues, is that what is specifically Irish about nineteenth-century Ireland is increasingly seen as its picturesque but antiquated Gaelic roots; the more modern, cosmopolitan side is essentially indistinguishable from England. In other words, to write an 'Irish' novel requires utilising archaic materials, which are fundamentally incompatible with the conventions of the novel, be it realistic or historical, as a form, thus making the 'Irish novel' as such impossible.

This is a fairly typical account of nineteenth-century Irish writing. Ireland, it is suggested, presents a unique problem for novelists, because its particularities are only appropriate for romance, and cannot be accommodated in the realist mode.[12] The result is that authors are forced to compromise between the two, producing bizarre, unbalanced texts. Thus, for example, Leerssen writes that Lady Morgan 'found herself unable to write a historical or realistic novel, and her failure becomes paradigmatic for the century as a whole'.[13] Considered from a perspective that sees the development of the novel as tending towards realism, these novels are perceived as flawed, struggling to strike an impossible balance, and this problem is generalised to encompass the majority of nineteenth-century Irish writing. As Jacqueline Belanger and James Murphy have both pointed out, however, the blame for this is perhaps more rightly attributed to critics who will not consider a novel 'Irish' unless it explicitly announces itself as such, precisely by including such archaic materials.[14]

This is where a more transnational perspective is of clear value, as a way of questioning assumptions of what constitutes 'Irish' material, as well as teleologies of the novel's rise. Accordingly, in an effort to ameliorate this image of a failed nineteenth-century tradition, Joe Cleary suggests that the problem is that Irish writing is typically read in relation to that of its nearest neighbour, Britain, and that it might instead be more fruitful to compare it to other 'colonial and agrarian peripheries, such as South America or Eastern Europe, which may in fact offer closer parallels to the Irish situation'.[15] Cleary suggests that Irish fiction will appear less anomalous when compared to that of places with similar historical experiences, with the result that the works of its authors will come to seem more typical of their time period, and therefore, more respectable.

Indeed, in a recent essay on comparative history, Peter Baldwin suggests that this is precisely the benefit that comparative studies can offer. 'Comparative history', he writes, 'serves primarily to separate the important from the incidental and thus to point the way towards causal explanations'.[16] By examining two environments with distinct similarities, he suggests, we are better able to track which events play a meaningful causal role by determining whether they produced the same effects in both.

Polish literature indeed proves itself a rich site of comparison with Irish writing, particularly in the eighteenth and nineteenth centuries. It offers a similar trajectory of Romantic nationalism with a martyrological bent, a tradition of the poet as national bard, an impressively robust national theatre, and a notable lack of realist masterpieces.[17] In fact, comparisons between Poland and Ireland were apparently a commonplace in the nineteenth century, as Ireland struggled against Great Britain, and the Polish-Lithuanian Commonwealth experienced partition at the hands of the Prussian, Russian, and Austrian Empires.[18] Looking more closely at early works of the novelistic tradition in both places allows us to examine and evaluate some of these critical claims about the links between culture and history with greater specificity. We indeed find similar patterns of representation, but the comparative perspective allows us to reassess their broader function and how they fit into larger claims about the development of the novel in both places.

In what follows, I look at two early works from the Polish and Irish novelistic traditions, Lady Morgan's *Wild Irish Girl* and Maria Wirtemberska's *Malvina, or the Heart's Intuition*, and consider how we make sense of the similarities between them. On a superficial level, the resemblances between these novels seem to support the view that political struggles generate generic hybridity and render straightforward realism impossible, but a closer look reveals that such accounts rely on anachronistic assumptions about the status of romance. What is more, such readings have a tendency to collapse different aspects of the works into one large cluster rather than considering them separately, conflating very different narrative concerns into an undifferentiated collection of features seemingly opposed to realism. A perspective that privileges realism has a tendency to see anything outside its confines as aberrational or irrelevant: it does not ask what purpose these features serve. As the realism-focused storyline of the novel's development gradually gives way, however, new perspectives on early nineteenth-century texts open up, allowing for a re-evaluation of their complexity, and a more nuanced sense of what they seek to do.

The Wild Irish Girl by Lady Morgan (Sydney Owenson) is emblematic of the kinds of problems that Leerssen perceives in nineteenth-century fiction. In his words, '*The Wild Irish Girl* is a very uneasy blend of fictional narrative and referential discourse'.[19] The novel's plot appears to be a rather convoluted process of uniting its lovers. Horatio, the hero, is a somewhat dissipated young man who is sent to Ireland by his father, with the hope that this temporary banishment will cure him of his indolence. Aware that his family's land was won in the Cromwellian wars, he learns that the former owners, an old Prince and his daughter, Glorvina, are still alive and living nearby. Spying on them one night, he is so mesmerised by Glorvina's singing that he falls from his hiding place and loses consciousness. He awakens in their castle, and is nursed back to health by Glorvina herself. Aware that he would hardly be welcomed if they knew his true identity, he pretends to be an itinerant artist named Henry Mortimer. During his convalescence, he gradually falls in love with Glorvina, and the novel ends with their marriage, preceded by the revelation of his true identity, and the death of her father. Thus, it appears to be a somewhat 'stock' and occasionally overwrought love story, resolved in a cross-cultural marriage meant to symbolise the reconciliation of Britain and Ireland.

But the novel also has an extensive didactic element, which contributes to the sense of generic hybridity of the whole. The process of courtship is simultaneously one of education, for Horatio must not only learn to love Glorvina, he must also shed his prejudices about Ireland. During his recovery, he (and in the process, the reader) receives many lengthy lectures on Irish history and culture, which serve to correct his sense of it as a wild and barbaric place by detailing its venerable ancient roots. This educational element is bolstered by a massive array of footnotes that serves to document, or simply reaffirm, the claims of these lectures for the potentially sceptical reader. This paratext is so extensive, however, as to create the sense of an independent work alongside the main story. Thus, for instance, when the priest complains that 'in [England] it is usual to attach to that class of society in [Ireland] a ferocious disposition amounting to barbarity; but this, with other calumnies, of national indolence, and obstinate ignorance, of want of principle, and want of faith, is unfounded and illiberal', the reader is immediately directed to a lengthy footnote:

> When nature is wounded through all her dearest ties, she must turn on the hand that stabs, and endeavour to wrest the poignard from the grasp that aims at the lifepulse of her heart. And this she will do in obedience to that immutable law, which blends the instinct of self-preservation with every atom of human existence. And for this, in less felicitous times, when oppression and sedition succeeded alternately to each other, was the name of Irishman, blended with the horrible epithet of cruel.[20]

The footnote continues on for nearly an entire page, discussing Wexford, and arguing that the violence committed there can actually be attributed to the fact that the area was so thoroughly colonised by the British that all contact with Irish culture was lost. It is the British, in other words, who are barbaric and cruel, not the Irish. But this is a message for the reader alone; Horatio, it seems, can be persuaded by simple assertions, whereas Lady Morgan must supplement the priest's arguments in order to reach a broader audience.

The extended nature of these kinds of footnotes is why a critic such as Leerssen sees the novel as unbalanced and flawed. Ina Ferris has argued that the effect is intentional, serving precisely to disrupt the standard form of the Irish tour common to British fiction of the time. In her reading, the footnotes create 'a dynamic of contestation',[21] destabilising any sense of a single authoritative perspective. Thus, what one critic sees as a failing, another perceives as an intentional technique serving a specific purpose; not an inability to conform, but a willful decision not to.

For Leerssen, what is most worthwhile about the book is its more 'realistic' elements, the detailing of Irish life and culture. These are often found in the less polemical footnotes, such as one that explains a casual aside of Glorvina's with a fuller account of the tradition she makes reference to:

> On St. Bridget's day it is usual for the young people to make a long girdle rope of straw, which they carry about to the neighbouring houses, and through it all those persons who have faith in the charm pass nine times, uttering at each time a certain form of prayer in Irish, which they thus conclude: 'If I enter this thrice-blessed girdle well, may I come out of it nine times better'. (p. 89)

This is the sort of description that one might think ought to be integrated into the text as part of its tapestry of daily life, but that, in Leerssen's view, is the kind of detail pushed out by the attachment to the romantic mode, which seemingly cannot accommodate it. The romance is mere distraction, an archaic throwback to an older form of writing. 'But in the midst of all this passion', he writes, 'there is also a discursive element which offers observations on Irish life and antiquity, matters of curiosity and political relevance. These discursive digressions from the fictional storyline obviously represent the novel's real interest.'[22] The obviousness here is highly questionable: if it were indeed the novel's 'real' interest, why include the romance plot at all?

For Ina Ferris, the lover's plot matters because of the way it serves to articulate and explore a set of political issues, 'mobilising the old romance trope of encounter on behalf of very contemporary and civic concerns'.[23] Claire Connolly offers a similar account, noting, for instance, that 'a scene that seems to enact a retreat from reality into the modes of clichéd sentimental fiction (…) is also the occasion of an explicit mention of the recent history of the 1798 rebellion'.[24] In other words, these critics argue that the romantic elements of the plot are not 'mere' sentiment, but are doing complex work in the text, serving to encode political meanings and historical problems.[25]

While such readings are compelling and persuasive, it should be noted that they also play into a sense that romance is a form that requires validation, implicitly suggesting that it is of worth or interest primarily as an allegory of something else that is of greater importance. Rarely do we find a critical account willing to argue that romance is, quite simply, a worthwhile form that readers enjoyed, or a mode with aesthetic strengths and pleasures of its own. In other words, we remain within the orbit of a perspective that concedes a realist teleology to the novel, overlooking the persistence of romantic tropes even into the present day. This is where a more global perspective can be of service. Becoming aware of romance's strong hold on literary traditions all over the world helps to normalise it, and question the disparaging treatment it receives in many critical histories. Rather than being the product of a specifically Irish nostalgia, we see it as a more widespread form, and one that was considered not only valid, but even noble.

In her opening to *Malwina, czyli domyślność serca—Malvina, or the Heart's Intuition* (1816), Polish author Maria Wirtemberska makes an explicit claim about the merits of romance as a form, arguing that it is an effective way to convey moral lessons. Although she acknowledges that '*wiele innych gatunków pism byłyby nad romans użyteczniejszymi*' / 'many other literary genres might be more socially useful', she asserts that the lessons found '*pod pokrywk zabawy*' / 'beneath the mantle of entertainment' of romantic works '*więcej nieraz przekonywają niżeli suche morały, obnażone z ponęt ciekawość wzbudzających, a do czytania których mało kto się nawet porywa*'[26] / 'often do more to persuade than do dry moral precepts, stripped bare of the allurements that arouse curiosity and which few feel inspired even to read'.[27] That romances are entertaining and enjoyable to readers is taken for granted; Wirtemberska feels the need to defend only their potential social benefits.

Indeed, this way of framing the romance/novel (or romantic/realistic) divide is far more in keeping with the critical debates of the late eighteenth and early nineteenth centuries. The problem with romances was less that they were unsophisticated as that they were potentially damaging, deluding their readers by presenting unreal situations. In her defence of the romance form, *The Progress of Romance* (1785), Clara Reeve acknowledged that they had a clear potential for harm, and that 'if read indiscriminately they are at best unprofitable, frequently productive of absurdities in manners and sentiments, sometimes hurtful to good morals', but also argued that the best examples were 'truly respectable, works of genius, taste, and utility, capable of improving the manners and morals of mankind'.[28] This should remind us that aesthetic standards are historically contingent and mutable. What is at stake for these authors is demonstrating the social benefits of romance, rather than its sophistication. This realisation changes the way we conceptualise the complex negotiations of these works. It suggests that what appears to be an effort to find a way to integrate details of everyday life is part of a different dynamic entirely, namely, an effort to show that prose fiction can be morally beneficial, rather than mere light entertainment. Thus, for instance, footnotes documenting the text's claims can be seen, not as providing otherwise absent realistic detail, but as reiterating its assertions in a non-fictional mode, or anchoring the descriptions in a more established and reputable discourse. This dilemma was not limited to romance, but was a concern for authors of fiction more broadly. In other words, it was not specific claims about Ireland or Poland that required validation per se, but fiction itself. Realism was not necessarily equated with moral edification; as Wirtemberska's quote demonstrates, there was a competing sense that romance could potentially be *more* effective in conveying moral lessons than more realistic works.

Indeed, it is clear from Wirtemberska's writing that romance is in no way considered an archaic or outmoded form detached from everyday life, but a wholly respectable and even admirable mode of writing. *Malwina* opens with a Dedicatory Preface from the author in which she writes that the book '*przypomni, że nie ma tego rodzaju pisma, do którego język polski nie byłby zdolnym*' / 'may serve to remind reader … that there is no genre of writing of which the Polish language might not be capable' (p. 3/p. 3). She also explains that whereas earlier romantic works attested to the mores of their own time, *Malwina* would be the first to portray the society of the present day, thus destabilising the apparent pre/modern dichotomy between the romantic and the novelistic; although romances depicted earlier times, this does not mean they are unable to portray the present effectively. The novel offers the very sort of hybridity that is criticised by Leerssen in his account of nineteenth-century Irish writing, combining a somewhat far-fetched romantic story with lengthy digressions written in a more realistic vein. Examining the specific form of this hybridity helps us rethink assumptions made about nineteenth-century Irish writing as well, particularly the ways in which we make sense of how the different aspects of the texts work together.

Malwina is a love story complicated by a somewhat bizarre plot of mistaken identity, which is resolved by the discovery that what had appeared to be one highly erratic man is in fact two, twin brothers who were separated in their youth when one was kidnapped by gypsies. Unlike *The Wild Irish Girl*, the romance does not serve as a political allegory, but neither is it entirely gratuitous. The vagaries of the plot are underpinned by a broader philosophical question, that of the 'knowledge of the heart', or the nature of love. Malwina is perplexed by the apparent inconstancy of her lover, and her own shifting feelings towards him. The circuitous plot of misplaced twins not only provides intrigue; it also accounts for why her love for one man is apparently mutable, ultimately demonstrating that '*serce się nigdy nie omyla*' / 'the heart never errs' (p. 143/p. 191). Here too, in other words, the romantic elements of the plot are being mobilised towards a more complex philosophical inquiry, not unlike the kinds of deliberations found in *The Princess of Cléves*, *The Man of Feeling*, *The Sorrows of Young Werther*, and other works of the sentimental tradition that examine the status of emotion and the dilemmas of the heart.

At the same time, the narrator does not uncritically accept tropes from romance writing. For instance, she critiques the trope of the supposedly fated chance encounters of lovers, explaining that it is in fact unsurprising that two people who are thinking of each other may be drawn to the same locations (p. 28/p. 36). At other moments, the narrator is winkingly obtuse, pretending to be blind to the attraction the characters feel for each other: '*Wtem dochodzili do batu, i na te jego słowa Malwina mimowolnie chwyciła go za rękę, jak żeby się bała, że ją chce porzucić. Ale to zapewne z przezorności było, żeby w wodę nie wpaść; ja przynajmniej tak rozumiem.*' / 'They were just getting into the boat, but at these words Malvina involuntarily seized Ludomir's hand as if afraid he was about to forsake her. But this was no doubt merely from caution, lest she fall into the water; at least that is how I understand it' (p. 28/p. 36). Narratorial intrusions regularly question the story, debating whether Malwina has fallen in love, or requesting the reader's indulgence for what appear to be her flaws. Often, this is prefaced with the claim that Malwina is not a romance heroine, but a real person. Indeed, at the most bizarre moments in the story, the ones that seem most obviously indebted to the whimsical turns of romantic fiction, we often find a comment from Malwina's aunt, who is confused because she has never heard of such things happening in the romances she has read. In other words, the novel simultaneously revels in romance and its inherent appeal, and shows itself aware of its shortcomings or indulgences (and gently pokes fun at its fans). Using a curiously ironic narrative voice that balances precariously between satire and sentiment, Wirtemberska manages to have it both ways. But she finds a way to do so while keeping a plotline that is thoroughly romantic in nature.

Though less extensive than what we see in *The Wild Irish Girl*, *Malwina* also offers glimpses of nineteenth-century Polish life, some of which are detailed enough to seem tangential to the narrative. For example, when Malwina goes from house to house collecting money for charity, we are given surprisingly protracted accounts of the various homes she visits, which are clearly meant to offer a cross-section of society. Even more noticeable is a lengthy aside about the specificities of the Polish war-time experience:

> *Och, nie takie u nas wojny bywają jak po innych krajach, gdzie wola jednego mocarza wysyła w dalekie okolice płatne roty swoje, ażeby małą, a najczęściej niepotrzebną cząstkę kraju jakiego nabyły (…) U nas wojsko z ojców, braci, synów, kochanków, przyjaciół złożone, bije się blisko nas, pod naszymi*

> *oczyma, bije się o swoją własność, o swoje schronienie, za żony, dzieci, prawa, język i byt swój!* (p. 105)
>
> Oh, our wars were not like those of other countries, where the will of one powerful ruler might pack off his mercenaries to distant outposts in order to acquire some tiny, and often quite unnecessary, share of some other country (…) with us the army consists of our own fathers, brothers, sons, lover, friends. They fight close to home, before our very eyes. They fight for their own property, for their own place of refuge, for their own wives, children, rights, language, for their very existence! (p. 140)

Though this type of detail in Irish fiction is seen as evidence that the books are written with an English readership in mind, Wirtemberska repeatedly makes clear that she is writing for Polish readers. Indeed, she even notes that some of her descriptions are therefore superfluous: '*Ale na cóż mam tu powtarzać rozmowę, którą czytelnik łatwo sobie wystawi będąc Polakiem*' / 'But what is the sense of repeating a conversation which the Reader, being Polish, may easily imagine' (p. 109/p. 144). This pushes back against the sense that the ethnographic detail in Irish writing is always auto-exotic or insistently portraying the home as Other. The detail here is not fraught with the baggage of self-commodification for a foreign audience, but rather, comes across as the author dilating on matters close to her heart, and fostering a sense of community with her readers.

Certainly, these moments demonstrate the author's effort to think through the ways in which the novel as a form can integrate an awareness of the concerns of its contemporary moment. One of the specific challenges Wirtemberska faces is finding a way to acknowledge the political trauma of the present in an otherwise seemingly light-hearted tale. We find a similar dynamic at work in *The Wild Irish Girl*, which vacillates from the swoons and sighs of the lovers to grim reckonings with Irish history. Although this palpable sense of suffering is seen as an obstacle to realism, it should be noted that it is not exactly 'native' to romance, either. Although the plotlines of romance would seem more amenable to the heightened drama of war, or melancholic portrayals of ruin, both of these authors pause the action, or step outside the narrative frame (as in Lady Morgan's footnote on Wexford discussed earlier, or Wirtemberska's digression above) in order to give voice to the sufferings of their compatriots. To these two authors at least, then, these moments arguably do *not* naturally fit comfortably into a work of romance: the hybridity of these scenes is not a clash of realism and romance, but is of a different nature entirely.

In both works, we find two different kinds of material that initially register as tangential or disruptive: expanded ethnographic description or detail, and discussions of historical turbulence, which shift the mood into a tragic (or melodramatic) register. The typical critical response has been to collapse these two aspects into a broader account of how these works fail to achieve realism: they cannot integrate everyday detail properly into the narrative, and political upheaval bars them from achieving normalcy or equanimity. The heterogeneity of these texts is thus used to attest to claims that their political contexts are hostile to realism. But we should be careful about the ways in which we make sense of the various kinds of hybridity that we find in these works, and how those different aspects are related to each other. It is tempting to map the melange of romantic and quotidian elements onto the question of how the novel as a genre manages political turmoil. A closer investigation reveals that these elements are related to entirely different problems. What is more, this perspective relies on assumptions about the status of romance that emerged in the wake of realism's ascendance, projecting certain perspectives back onto the texts. Thus, for instance, it construes romance as an archaic and comparatively unsophisticated mode. Both authors, however, use romance plots as a way to engage deeper underlying problematics of their own time. It is true that both authors perceive limitations to the romantic mode, but they also seem invested in finding solutions to those shortcomings by working within the romance mode, rather than abandoning it.

It is notable, for instance, that while both novels have happy endings, neither is completely unambiguous. In *The Wild Irish Girl*, the narrative's inexorable progression towards the union of Glorvina and Horatio is suddenly forestalled, a mere thirty pages before the ending, by the revelation that she has been promised to someone else. The other man turns out, astonishingly, to be Horatio's own father. When the truth is revealed, the shock proves too much for Glorvina's father, who is much weakened by illness, and he dies, which in turn sends Glorvina spiraling into madness. The pandemonium is quickly resolved, first between Horatio and his father, and then between the young pair, but when we last see Glorvina, she is on the road to recovery, rather than the picture of a blissful bride: she is 'the interesting invalid, whose flushing colour and animated eyes spoke the return of health and happiness; not indeed confirmed—but fed by sanguine hope; such hope as the heart of a mourning child could give to the object of her heart's first passion' (p. 203). Similarly, *Malwina*'s joyful conclusion is interrupted, on the final page, by a minor threat, when Ludomir wonders if perhaps his wife does in fact prefer his twin (who, conveniently, has married her sister). Her reassurance, a particular term uttered already at several key moments in the story, satisfies him completely, and the novel's closing lines assure us that all is now well: '*To słowo (…) odtąd na zawsze moc miało serce jego zupełnie uspokoić napełniając go najprawdzisz i wygasnąć niezdolną szczęśliwości*.' / 'That word (…) now for the third time—and forever after—was to have the power to reassure his heart completely, filling it with the truest happiness which nothing further could extinguish' (p. 152/p. 201). But why raise this doubt at all, when the reader was already fairly well assured that all was well? Similarly, why does *The Wild Irish Girl* need to digress into utter pandemonium and madness before the desired marriage can take place? This hesitancy about happy endings again calls into question the apparent obviousness of romance as a choice for these authors. It also demonstrates that both women clearly register the challenges romance faces, and gesture towards its limitations. But they nonetheless do progress to those joyful resolutions, rather than breaking with the form completely.

Literary criticism has retrospectively decreed that realism offers the best solutions to the aesthetic problems attendant on the rise of modernity, and thus assumes that nineteenth-century authors dissatisfied with romance were groping towards realism. But this is hardly a foregone conclusion. Rather than seeing Lady Morgan or Wirtemberska as having only made it part of the way towards realism, we should instead consider these works on their own terms, and try to tease out what they perceive as the weaknesses of romance, and how they strive to address them. Instead of assuming that both authors fall back upon romantic plots as the only option, we should take seriously the possibility that both saw that type of writing as offering the greatest pleasures to its readers, and that they valued the form and consciously chose it. By doing so, we can also become better readers of those forms, which in turn makes us better able to take seriously and appreciate other works of their time.

Ultimately, part of this process is moving outside the narrow confines of the national comparison. Because the original impetus of considering

Polish and Irish works alongside each other is their socio-political resemblances, a comparative reading of two novels from Poland and Ireland will tend to focus on aspects of the text that speak to their political conditions. Because of the strong interest in considering how historical turmoil shaped aesthetic production, the emphasis will be on symptoms of suffering first and foremost. But there are other ways in which we can read the influence of their particular contexts on these works. Given the links between the romantic and the pastoral, for instance, and the fact that both Poland and Ireland were largely agrarian economies, we could also consider how rural life is represented in both texts. It is unsurprising that the peasantry features more prominently in these novels than in, say, Goethe's *Sorrows of Young Werther*. Although Werther appreciates the simple life of the folk, he also repeatedly registers his difference from them, even when looking to bridge the gap: '*Ich weiß wohl, daß wir nicht gleich sind, noch sein können; aber ich halte dafür, daß der, der nötig zu haben glaubt, vom so genannten Pöbel sich zu entfernen, um den Respekt zu erhalten, ebenso tadelhaft ist als ein Feiger, der sich vor seinem Feinde verbirgt, weil er zu unterliegen fürchtet.*'[29] / 'I well know that we are not equal, nor can be; but I maintain that he who supposes he must keep his distance from what they call the rabble, to preserve the respect due to him, is as much to blame as a coward who hides from his enemy for fear of being beaten.'[30] Or later, '*Zwar weiß ich so gut als einer, wie nötig der Unterschied der Stände ist, wie viel Vorteile er mir selbst verschafft: nur soll er mir nicht eben gerade im Wege stehen, wo ich noch ein wenig Freude, einen Schimmer von Glück auf dieser Erde genießen könnte.*'[31] / 'Of course I know as well as anyone that differences of class are necessary, and that they work greatly to my own advantage: but I wish they would not place obstacles in my way when I might enjoy a little pleasure, some scrap of happiness in this world.'[32] In contrast, Glorvina 'will sit in a smoky cabin for hours together, to talk to the poor' and an old peasant man tells Horatio that 'many a time I carried her in these arms, and taught her to bless herself in Irish' (pp. 69–70). In *Malwina*, we similarly learn that Malwina has a strong attachment to a woman named Somorkowa, '*gdyż ta wie niaczka mlekiem ją swoim karmiła i od dziecińistwa jak własną kochała córkę*' / 'for the peasant woman had suckled her with her own milk and loved her as her own daughter since she was a little girl' (p. 7/p. 11). This is not to say that either of these two novels is a model of cross-class interactions; both texts can certainly be accused of sentimentalised portrayals of the peasantry, and the lower-class characters are clearly of a lesser status. In *The Wild Irish Girl*, the descriptions of these characters, which are delivered from Horatio's perspective, are often dripping with contempt, especially in the early portions of the text, and his father's injunctions to care for the people on the estate on the final pages partake of blatant cultural paternalism. Nonetheless, these people are part of the narrative, and not only do they often receive names, they also frequently step forward to speak for themselves, even if those moments are arguably presenting commodified versions of rural 'authenticity'. There is a greater visibility of rural life in these novels, in other words, which could be due to the socio-economic make-up of both Poland and Ireland, where the lack of a strong middle class made for a different kind of relationship between upper and lower classes, both of whom were dependent on agriculture.

Such a comparison could lead us even further towards a more strictly aesthetic inquiry: why not look for similarities to *Werther*, along with the differences? This could lead to considering, for instance, how the novels deal with minor characters overall, or how they deploy the epistolary form, in contrast to other authors from various parts of the world working in a similar mode. This would be a truly transnational account: moving beyond mapping formal features onto historical conditions, and considering their experiments in more strictly aesthetic terms. This is not to say that we should sever these works from their historical contexts; rather, it is to suggest that we not focus too narrowly on those contexts, so as not to lose sight of the authors' specific aims in producing these works.

A comparative reading of Polish and Irish literary history can very easily serve to both reiterate and reinforce their marginal positions vis-à-vis mainstream European writing. Finding similar conditions of political turmoil in both places, and a similar lack of realism, the answer seems clear: these exceptions prove the rule of socio-cultural explanations of realism's rise. The only redeeming aspect of this account, as James Murphy points out, is that it also paves the way for a celebration of twentieth-century Irish literature, when Irish writers become early innovators of fractured styles of post/modernism[33]—as indeed do Polish writers such as Witold Gombrowicz, Bruno Schulz, Witkacy, or Bruno Jasieński. The literature of the nineteenth century, however, is essentially consigned to the dust-bin of history, with only the occasional meek argument suggesting that it might have value as a precursor to these more interesting later developments. Moreover, the aesthetic aspects of these texts are yoked ever more firmly to historical developments, contributing to deterministic readings that view literature as a reflection of political conditions first and foremost, without examining its formal innovations.

But rather than uncritically adopting paradigms of the novel's development emerging from other literary traditions, we can use a comparative reading of these two literatures in order to decentre those accounts, and challenge their underlying assumptions. The assertive way in which Wirtemberska celebrates romance, for instance, provides a strong counter-argument against the sense that Irish authors turned to it as mere compensation, and brings to light more widespread anxieties about fiction's social benefits, rather than its ability to create realistic portrayals. Looking at these two works alongside each other gives us a more complex sense of the specific forms of their hybridity, and the different dilemmas they were grappling with. Rather than using a comparative reading to strengthen the perception of these traditions as anomalous, we can use the similarities between them to lend force to counter-arguments proposing alternative accounts of the novel's development, and a more nuanced perception of their aesthetic goals. This comparative reading, in turn, opens onto a broader transnational perspective on these works. A focus on the socio-political dimensions of the Irish literary tradition impels us towards comparisons to other similar contexts, but we rapidly find that many of the most rewarding insights from such research may instead emerge from a more attentive reading of the formal innovations of the works in question. This, in turn, encourages us to cast a wider net, and to seek out other texts from all over the world that share similar literary concerns. Thus, we arrive at a perspective that would situate nineteenth-century Irish writing, not only alongside works from similar socio-historical conditions, but together with other romantic or hybrid works they have a natural affinity with. Instead of considering Irish fiction in developmental terms, viewing these texts alongside others that dealt with similar formal challenges can help us see them as experiments in literary genre: as efforts to innovate the romance, rather than overcome it.

Imperial interrelations in Maria Edgeworth's *Essay on Irish Bulls* (1802)

SONJA LAWRENSON

Since 1904, when Emily Lawless first sought to rediscover 'the more purely Irish side of her writings, as well as the influence which those writings have exercised in Ireland itself',[1] numerous academics have devoted themselves to the task of examining and evaluating Maria Edgeworth's attitude towards Ireland and the Irish. However, the intense scrutiny placed upon Edgeworth's 'Irish' writing has often resulted in narrow critical disputes as to whether she should be regarded as the progenitor of the 'national' Irish novel or a mere apologist for Anglo-Irish Ascendancy. Hence, Edgeworth has customarily been enveloped in a critical discourse that wavers between commendations of her subversive radicalism and condemnations of her didactic conservatism.

Fortunately, recent scholarship has begun to transcend this longstanding division. For example, whilst acknowledging that 'critical commentary on Edgeworth … remains split on what are effectively national lines', Clíona Ó Gallchoir contests 'that Maria Edgeworth's position as an Anglo-Irish woman writer leads her to uphold the ideals of cosmopolitanism, rather than nationalism'.[2] Ó Gallchoir claims that Edgeworth's 'complex sense of identification with French women writers' such as Germaine de Staël and Stéphanie-Félicité de Genlis bespeaks a desire to transcend the limitations imposed on women writers by both British and Irish nationalisms.[3] As an avid reader of continental literature and philosophy, Edgeworth was both troubled and fascinated by the political and intellectual disputes that arose in the wake of France's spasmodic progression from *ancien régime* to revolutionary democracy. Over the last decade, Edgeworth scholarship has become increasingly attuned to the underlying significance of this broader European context within her fiction. Critics such as Miranda Burgess and Katie Brundan have endeavoured to trace the transnational dimensions of Edgeworth's fictional allusions to continental customs and cultural practices.[4]

At the same time, it is important to acknowledge that Edgeworth's cosmopolitan perspective reaches far beyond the geographical borders of mainland Europe. For, although French culture and politics maintain a persistent presence within her works, references to the wider imperial networks of both France and Britain are just as prevalent. From *Belinda*'s ardent yet tempestuous West Indian plantocrat, Mr Vincent, and his erstwhile slave, Juba, to the young men of *Ennui* (1809), *Patronage* (1814) and *Ormond* (1817) seeking East Indian appointments, Edgeworth's fiction never loses sight of the global transactions and interactions upon which both the national and the local depend, regardless of whether the main action is located on the Irish estate or within London polite society. And yet, here, as elsewhere in Edgeworth scholarship, division is rife. Kathryn Kirkpatrick's description of Edgeworth as 'neither plantation owner nor slave, [yet] possessed [of] a dual vision which saw both'[5] is piquantly counterpoised by George Boulukos's condemnatory inquiry: 'were African slaves and Irish tenants interchangeable to her?'[6] Ultimately, more wide-ranging and far-reaching exploration of Edgeworth's oeuvre is essential if we are to appreciate fully the complexities, intricacies and, indeed, problematics of her global-political vision.

The exigency of attending to the complexity and breadth of Edgeworth's worldview is encapsulated in a letter Edgeworth wrote in 1834 to her youngest brother, Michael Pakenham Edgeworth, who was then stationed in Uttar Pradesh as an East India Company soldier.[7] This letter has become somewhat of an ubiquity within Irish literary studies, as it contains one of the most striking testimonies of Anglo-Irish anxiety in relation to the political and economic instability of pre-famine Ireland:

> It is impossible to draw Ireland as she now is in a book of fiction—realities are too strong, party passions too violent to bear to see, or care to look at their faces in the looking-glass. The people would only break the glass, and curse the fool who held the mirror up to nature—distorted nature, in a fever.[8]

Written ten years after Daniel O'Connell's Catholic Association had first mobilised the Catholic masses of Ireland into a cogent political force, Edgeworth's statement has been widely interpreted as evidence of her 'angry resistance'[9] to the growing threat this populist movement posed to Protestant hegemony in Ireland. This letter has thus been engaged by many to support a postcolonial critique of Edgeworth's writing that presents it as 'grounded in a series of dyadic oppositions' between England and Ireland.[10] For Maria, however, the primary purpose of writing to her brother was to commend his 'good observations on the state of [his] part of India'.[11] Admiring Pakenham's 'generous indignation against oppression and wringing by 'any indirection from the poor peasant his vile trash',[12] she observes that 'many of [his] observations on India apply to Ireland; similarity of certain general causes operating on human nature even in countries most different'.[13] However, even as

Edgeworth extols her brother's professional achievements in India, it soon becomes clear that she is also disquieted by the obscuring complexity of Ireland's transnational ties:

> Sir Walter Scott once said to me, 'Do explain to the public why Pat, who gets forward so well in other countries, is so miserable in his own.' A very difficult question: I fear above my power. But I shall think of it continually, and listen, and look, and read.[14]

Despite the difficulty of this question, Edgeworth had in fact been ruminating upon it for at least thirty years. In her comic treatise of 1802, *An Essay on Irish Bulls*,[15] Edgeworth deals precisely with the question of Ireland's worldwide economic and political networks, and, in particular, Irish interconnections with an increasingly global British Empire. This essay traces the ways in which Edgeworth capitalised on the essay's generic hybridity and formal flexibility to re-conceptualise both Irish nationhood and British imperialism within this wider transnational framework. Just like the aforementioned letter, *An Essay on Irish Bulls* has often served as a textual base for critical examinations of Anglo-Irish attitudes towards both Britain and Ireland, yet the transnational dimensions of its comedic framework have been largely overlooked. Hence, though *An Essay on Irish Bulls* draws on a global range of cultural texts and topographical milieux, critical controversy has once again centred upon a narrowly circumscribed view of Anglo-Irish cultural and political relations.

It is only by exploring the multifarious interconnections and interactions between Ireland, Britain and its global colonies that the true political import of Edgeworth's cosmopolitan defence of Irish bulls is fully appreciated. Focusing particularly upon 'Little Dominick', an inset story that relates the Eastern adventures of an impoverished Irish youth, this essay examines Edgeworth's attempts to integrate a discussion of British India's colonial history into the transnational imaginary of *An Essay on Irish Bulls*. By this means, she not only illustrates the significance of Britain's global empire within her political and cultural geography but also reveals her desire to re-envisage the relationship between Britain and Ireland as a global partnership as opposed to a domestic union. At the same time, Edgeworth refuses to shy away from the difficult questions that this imperial alliance raises. This essay draws upon the concept of 'minor transnationalism' developed by Françoise

Lionnet and Shu-mei Shih to illuminate the complex cartography of transnational exchanges that Edgeworth's fiction charts. Defining the transnational as 'a space of exchange and participation wherever processes of hybridisation occur and where it is still possible for cultures to be produced and performed without necessary mediation from the centre', Lionnet and Shih argue that 'minor transnationality points towards and makes visible the multiple relations between the national and transnational', including a 'varied terrain of minority interactions with both majority cultures and other minorities'.[16] Although Lionnet and Shih specifically locate their critique within the late capitalist era of globalisation, Edgeworth's 'Little Dominick' proves the equal relevance of their concept of minor transnationalism to a study of British imperialism in the early nineteenth century. Exploring the myriad relations, negotiations and confrontations between various marginal and dominant spaces within the British Empire, 'Little Dominick' participates wholeheartedly in the kinds of lateral cultural engagements that Lionnet and Shih identify as the hallmark of minor transnationalism. Hence, by infusing the eclectic and referential comedy of this narrative with a composite of regional, national and imperial identities, Edgeworth deliberately fractures and destabilises the surface coherence of 'Little Dominick's' imperial success story.

Although these narrative cracks and fissures are not heavily pronounced, it is worth remembering that 'Little Dominick' is but the single component of a larger text that repeatedly deploys such radical narrative strategies to pursue its foundational claims. Indeed, in order to comprehend the full scope of this brief tale's political agenda, it is first necessary to explore the allusive and elusive frame text in which it is located. Proclaiming that the Irish propensity to commit verbal blunders, otherwise known as 'bulls', 'is a subject which dilates the heart of every true Briton',[17] the parodic introduction to *An Essay on Irish Bulls* states that its object is to uncover 'what it is that constitutes a bull' (p. 4):

> The essence of an Irish bull must be of the most ethereal nature, for notwithstanding the most indefatigable research, it has hitherto escaped from analysis … it must be determined in what an Irish bull essentially differs from a blunder, or in what Irish blunders specifically differ from English blunders, and from those of all other nations. (pp. 5–6)

Drawing upon a diverse range of stylistic forms and generic modes, including linguistic analysis, anecdotal reportage, philosophical dialogue and prose fiction, *An Essay on Irish Bulls* enumerates a global range of verbal, written and practical blunders. However, instead of accomplishing their purported objective of differentiating these from the Irish bull, the *Essay*'s narrators wryly confess that 'notwithstanding our utmost diligence, we have not yet been able to point out the distinguishing character of an Irish bull' (p. 53). On the contrary, they 'find bévues [blunders] French, English, Italian, German, Latin and Greek, of theologians, historians, antiquarians, poets, critics and translators, without end' (p. 25). From the governors of Munich who forbade the reading of a catalogue of forbidden books to bear-hunters in Canada who bargain for the skin of a bear before it is caught (pp. 18, 50), *An Essay on Irish Bulls* stresses the universality of such verbal and practical blundering and thereby situates the Irish bull alongside those of 'other nations' (p. 48). Via this comic cosmopolitanism, Edgeworth posits a serious challenge to the 'practice of ridiculing the blunders, whether real or imaginary, of Irishmen' (p. 22).

And yet, whilst we might admire both the humour and the liberality of the *Essay*'s broad-minded and pluralistic approach to Irish national identity, the political dynamics underpinning this cosmopolitan worldview require further scrutiny. Indeed, as the text's concluding paragraph makes clear, the shifting constitutional relationship between Ireland and England lies at the heart of the *Essay*'s political agenda:

> One of the Czars of Russia used to take his cap and bells from his fool, and place it on the head of any of his subjects whom he wished to disgrace. The idea of extending such a punishment to a whole nation was ingenious and magnanimous; but England cannot now put it into execution towards Ireland. Would it not be a practical bull to place the bells upon her own imperial head? (p. 123)

Succeeded only by a date mark of 1801, this final paragraph serves to remind the reader of the radically evolving political context from which the *Essay* emerged. Only a year earlier, Irish and British parliamentarians had passed twin Acts of Union that abolished the Irish parliament and subsumed Ireland into the United Kingdom of Great Britain and Ireland. Although Richard Lovell Edgeworth was initially enthusiastic regarding the prospects of free trade and Catholic Emancipation that the Union appeared to promise Ireland, he ultimately voted against the act in protest at British attempts to pressure and even bribe Irish parliamentarians to vote in favour of the Union. Nevertheless, the *Essay* appears to retain something of his earlier political optimism, declaring that '[w]hatever might have been the policy of the English nation towards Ireland whilst she was a separate kingdom, since the union it can no longer be her wish to depreciate the talents or ridicule the language of Hibernians' (p. 123).

Consequently, scholars ranging from Terry Eagleton to Jacqueline Belanger have been sceptical of the political implications of the *Essay*'s sympathetic yet conciliatory portraits of Irish national character. Belanger, for example, argues that the *Essay* offers 'an imaginative attempt at a cultural union to match that in the political sphere'.[18] From this perspective, Edgeworth's defence of the Irish nation actually serves to reinforce an economy of power that underwrites British hegemony in Ireland, as the granting of Catholic Emancipation within the Union would render Irish Catholics a minority within the political framework of the United Kingdom. In contrast, this essay contends that the complexity of the *Essay*'s national politics can only be appreciated fully when situated in the wider transnational framework of the British Empire. For, as the *Essay*'s concluding reference to Britain's 'imperial head' signals, the Irish Act of Union was but one in a long series of events that transformed the geo-political landscape of Romantic-era Britain. Furthermore, while the comparison between this 'imperial head' and the Russian Czar's fool may initially appear comically incongruent, in actual fact this reference to Czar Paul I (1754–1801), a notorious and fanatical admirer of Napoleon Bonaparte, alerts the reader to the wider transnational nexus through which the text's satire operates. With the loss of the American colonies in 1783, the onset of Anglo-French warfare in the wake of the French revolution of 1789, the expansion and consolidation of colonial administrative control in India subsequent to Warren Hastings' unsuccessful yet controversial impeachment of 1788 to 1795, and, of course, the failed Irish rebellion of 1798, the final decades of the eighteenth century saw Britain increasingly conceptualise its remaining territories in Ireland, the West Indies and the East in relation to one another.

Thus, for the flourishing novelist and her contemporaries, the transformations taking place across Britain's global empire were no less topical and contentious than Ireland's new constitutional status. In fact, the two were intricately intertwined in the political discourse of the period. Within both the Irish and British parliaments, the pressing question of Ireland's constitutional relationship with Britain was primarily configured in terms of its position within the British Empire. Over the course of the eighteenth century, British sanctions on Irish commerce had specifically targeted Ireland's transnational trade networks, both colonial and foreign. From Jonathan Swift's *Proposal for the Universal Use of Irish Manufacture* in 1720 to the United Irishman Thomas Russell's lobbying on behalf of Irish merchants wishing to participate in the East India trade in 1791,[19] eighteenth-century Irish patriots of every hue regarded British restrictions on Ireland's transnational commerce as a particularly acute source of resentment. However, in the final few years of the eighteenth century, both British and Irish supporters of the Union endeavoured to promote it as an 'imperial connexion which [sic] makes Ireland a member of the noblest Empire of the globe'.[20] Alarmed by the United Irishmen's recent alliance with revolutionary France and facing renewed French imperial aggression overseas, the British government was anxious to promote the idea of a 'Union of Empire'.[21] For example, the former Irish Chief Secretary, Sylvester Douglas, argued that 'Ireland, by an Union, no more becomes a province in any offensive sense of the word, than Great Britain: they both become provinces, or component parts of one whole and integrated Empire'.[22] As Edgeworth was undoubtedly aware, though Irish Catholics were formally prohibited from enlisting as British soldiers, from the Seven Years War of 1756–63 onwards,[23] the British army covertly recruited Irish Catholics, particularly those from low socio-economic backgrounds. In fact, by the 1770s up to fifty per cent of soldiers in the East India Company Army were Irish.[24] Therefore, although the Union might place Irish Catholics in the minority within the United Kingdom, it also offered the opportunity to formalise and advance Catholic Ireland's pre-existing imperial connections. As was to become apparent throughout the course of the nineteenth century, Irish Catholics were also eager to take advantage of the professional, educational, economic and social advancements that participation in Britain's global empire appeared to offer.[25]

This context indicates that, whilst the *Essay*'s witty, light-hearted and playful allusions to a dizzying array of national characters and contexts may underscore the universalising impulse of its cosmopolitanism, its oblique yet persistent references to British imperial politics simultaneously situates the text within a specifically imperial context.

The following anecdote concerning Hyder Ali (1721–1782), Sultan of the Kingdom of Mysore in southern India, provides a salient example of the hidden political connotations of Edgeworth's seemingly jovial relation of foreign bulls:

> There are other persons, as well as the Irish, who do not always understand their own interests where their passions are concerned. That great warrior, Hyder Ali, once lost a battle by a practical bull. Being encamped within sight of the British, he resolved to give them a high idea of his forces and of his artillery; for this purpose, before the engagement, he ordered his army to march early, and … caused all his artillery, even the very smallest pieces, to be drawn up the hill for the purpose of making a vain parade … The English, presently after this farce was over, obliged Hyder Ali to come down from labour-in-vain hill, and to give them battle in earnest. (p. 49)

The incident to which Edgeworth refers took place during the First Anglo-Mysore War of 1767–69, in which Hyder Ali had resisted the military advances of the British East India Company. Pertinently, in the Second Anglo-Mysore War of 1779–84, Hyder allied with the French against the British after the latter captured the French colonial port of Mahé as part of a concerted effort to seize all French outposts following France's entry into the American Revolutionary War in 1778. On Hyder Ali's death, his son Tipu became Sultan of Mysore and continued to challenge the East India Company's rule in India. He was, however, defeated in both the Third Anglo-Mysore War of 1789–92 and the Fourth Anglo-Mysore war of 1798–99. By the early years of the nineteenth century, British accounts of this complex colonial history repeatedly recast the Company's humiliating defeat in the second Anglo-Mysore war, and its rather discomforting settlement of the third, in the light of its jubilant victory in the fourth.[26] Arguably, by selecting to portray Hyder Ali as a stereotypically childish and capricious Eastern despot, Edgeworth participates in the reinscription of the colonial historical record and is thus complicit in furthering the narrower political agenda of a pre-established colonial discourse.

Admittedly, the *Essay*'s portrait of Hyder Ali thus appears to substantiate the widespread view of Edgeworth as a supporter of British colonial interests, whether in Ireland, India or elsewhere. It also accords with Julia M. Wright's analysis of the *Essay*'s short instructive story,

'Little Dominick'. Describing *An Essay on Irish Bulls* as a text that 'follow[s] British imperial interests [by] praising the Irish for their proximity to and value within *English* culture', Wright argues that 'Dominick synecdochically figures the Irish; they will be good loyal servants of the empire if properly anglicised'.[27] Purportedly reflecting Richard Lovell's own doleful experiences as a brogue-laden youngster attending boarding-school in England, 'Little Dominick' is the story of a young Irish boy who is bullied by his Welsh schoolmaster on account of his use of Irish vernacular. Having later secured his reputation and fortune in British India, Dominick returns from service with the East India Company in order to present this classroom tormentor with his comeuppance. Like many of the other Hibernian bunglers that crowd the *Essay*'s broad canvas, Dominick rarely perpetrates the linguistic and social blunders of which he is accused. Yet, even when he does commit genuine 'Irish bulls', they only ever serve to emphasise the fact that 'Irish blunders are never blunders of the heart' (p. 89).

At this basic level of narrative cogency, the story of Dominick arguably colludes with its frame text to form a warm-hearted if piquant satire on the cultural and linguistic conceit of the English. In fact, Dominick and his creator seem disposed to evade the crucial political contexts out of which his 'accumulated misfortunes' arise (p. 71). For a start, Dominick's taunting schoolmaster and jeering peers are not actually English but Welsh. This fact immediately undercuts any preliminary attempts to read this story as a straightforward allegory of colonial oppression. Similarly, the overweening national pride of the Welsh schoolmaster is repeatedly pitted against the enlightened paternalism of Dominick's defender, young Edwards. The son of a landed gentleman, Edwards protects and provides for Dominick by convincing his father to flex his established legal and economic might over this unsanctioned Welsh despot. By this means, the narrative manages to castigate the 'practice of ridiculing the blunders of Irishmen' without having to posit a direct challenge to British hegemony in Ireland (p. 59).

This reading is further borne out by the dramatic denouement of the plot, in which an older and more eloquent Dominick returns from service with the East India Company only to discover that his old schoolmaster has consigned an impoverished Edwards to prison for debts that his father incurred exploring a Welsh mine. Dominick uses the fortune he has made in India to settle 'the rascal's demand' (p. 83), an act of munificence which he insists is 'justly due to [Edwards] for my education' (p. 86). The enlightened upper-class gentleman is compensated for his earlier investment in the young Irish boy—not only in regards to the pecuniary assistance that Dominick provides but in his continued support and maintenance of British colonial interests in India. From this perspective, the story of 'Little Dominick' appears to offer a harmonious resolution to the question of Ireland's position within the United Kingdom. Both the personal bonds and economic ties between England and Ireland are seen to acquire a perfect circularity of flow under the wider auspices of the British Empire.

Decidedly, any measured critical reading of this tale must acknowledge its didactic functions. Nevertheless, the following section of this essay demonstrates how Edgeworth's particularised treatment of regional, national and global axes of power simultaneously complicates and disrupts a cohesive surface narrative that appears to uphold both race and class hierarchies. By subtly linking metropolitan constructions of regional identities within the British archipelago to the increasing essentialism of colonial identity politics across the British Empire, Edgeworth suggests that Ireland's transnational affiliations may not operate simply or solely within the sanctioned economic and political networks of a 'Union of Empire'. Though by no means claiming a radical cross-colonial intersubjectivity for 'Little Dominick', this essay nonetheless argues for a careful and considered reassessment of the destabilising potential of its minor transnationalism. For, once we become alert to the subtle yet profound complexities of Edgeworth's transnational vision; we discern a somewhat more ambiguous and rather less celebratory tenor to the *Essay*'s evocations of colonial India. And, even if Edgeworth was not entirely willing to extend her critique of British policy in Ireland to the Empire's more distant territories, her fiction does, at the very least, allow for an exploration of potential identifications amongst the disenfranchised and disempowered via its intersecting portraits of lateral cultural engagements between imperial, colonial and regional spaces.

Indeed, the potential significances and implications of this tale's national and political allusions deserve further qualification. As stated above, the main thrust of the plot definitely inclines towards a more conservative and authoritarian agenda than the rest of the *Essay*. Yet, the interpretative import of this broader narrative structure becomes harder to assess once the tale's underlying gaps and contradictions begin to emerge. Most notably, the details of Dominick's family background and personal history are repeatedly alluded to yet perpetually evaded. This is evident from the very outset of the tale, where we are dubiously informed that 'Little Dominick was born at Fort-Reilly and bred nowhere until his tenth year when he was sent to Wales' (p. 68). This humorous reference to a child 'bred nowhere' is typically Edgeworthian in its pointed emphasis on the importance of the early instruction of children. However, when placed immediately after a reference to the Gaelic estate of Fort Reilly, this comic aside assumes graver political connotations. As a descendant of a Gaelic aristocracy who, by the end of the eighteenth century, were almost wholly dispossessed of their Irish estates by an incumbent Anglo-Protestant Ascendancy, Dominick no longer possesses any legal claim to his primogeniture.

From this point onwards, the tale's surface affirmation of Ireland's imperial role is continuously compromised by its own dissonant specificities. At one crucial moment the narrative confidently asserts that Dominick's 'utmost ambition was to return to his native country with a fortune that should enable him to live independently of all the world' (p. 81). Consequently, he is overcome with 'inexpressible joy' to discover 'the estate of Fort-Reilly advertised to be sold—the very estate which had formerly belonged to his own family' (p. 81). However, beyond the text's earlier declaration that Dominick was raised 'nowhere', very little indication is given as to when or how his family first lost possession of the O'Reilly estate. Yet, renowned for her systematic and coded nomenclature,[28] it seems unlikely that Edgeworth wrote this story without a full knowledge of the political significations designated by her protagonist's Gaelic patronym and lost primogeniture. Certainly, for an Irish audience of the early nineteenth century, the political and religious reasons for this mysterious dispossession would require no further elaboration.

The narrative is equally vague in its relation of Dominick's experiences in India as private secretary to a British 'commander in chief' (p. 80):

> How he got into this situation, or by what gradations he rose in the world, we are not exactly informed: we know only that he was the reputed author of a much-admired pamphlet on India affairs; that the despatches of the general to whom he was secretary were remarkably well written, and that Dominick returned to England after several years absence, not miraculously rich, but with a fortune equal to his wishes. (pp. 80–81)

The final line of the above quotation, in which Edgeworth comments obliquely on Dominick's lack of pecuniary desire, can thus be read as a veiled effort to appease earlier imperial anxieties and reinforce the operational logic of a new imperial epoch. In the aftermath of the Hastings impeachment trial where both the late Governor-General and his colonial administration had been accused of 'extirpat[ing a] whole nation or tribe for ... extortions and peculations',[29] many powerful interests laboured tirelessly to redefine the imperial project in India as a worthy, altruistic and humane endeavour. In a period when many East India Company officials had been accused of exploiting native labour and resources in India for pecuniary gain, Edgeworth tacitly disassociates Dominick from the stereotypical English 'nabob'.

Hence, the elision of details regarding Dominick's career in India may appear expedient both in terms of the tale's narrative structure and in relation to its ideological framework. On one level, this ambiguity permits Edgeworth to address the practical demands and political concerns of an expanding British Empire without having to comment upon the ethical implications of specific imperial policies such as the territorial dispossession of Gaelic Ireland or the colonial exploitation of India. On the other hand, though only ever expressed cautiously and obliquely, the veiled allusion to Britain's colonial exploitation of India deranges the story's surface trajectory. Whilst the overarching plot celebrates Dominick's material and professional gains in India, the textual interstices regarding Dominick's colonial career hint at the rapacious underbelly of Britain's eastern imperial venture.

Moreover, as Marilyn Butler points out, Edgeworth's representation of Ireland and the Irish is 'consistently and deliberately historical, but in an idiosyncratic mode that relies on quotation, the naming of authors and books, and allusions to familiar thoughts and ideas'.[30] Celebrating the *Essay* as 'the most elaborate of Edgeworth's imagined Irelands', she supports her claims by reference to the following excerpt:

> 'You Irish plockit!' continued the relentless grammarian, 'will you never learn the difference between 'shall' and 'will'? ... The welsh boys all grinned, except Edwards who hummed, loud enough to be heard, two lines of the good old English song,
>
> 'And will I see him once again?'
> 'And will I hear him speak?'

> Many of the boys were fortunately too ignorant to feel the force of the quotation; but Mr Owen ap Jones understood it, turned upon his heel and walked off. (pp. 74–75)

On first appraisal, this passage merely reasserts the *Essay*'s wider vindication of Hiberno-English. According to Butler, however, this relatively innocuous endeavour assumes an added political dimension when we consider that the tune Edwards hums to support Dominick is a Jacobite song.[31] As she and Desmarais note in the most recent edition of the *Essay*, the aforementioned song commemorates Prince Charles Edwards' 1745 defeat at Culloden and ensuing escape from Skye.[32] This fact provides a possible explanation as to why Butler mistakenly identifies Edwards as 'a bigger Scottish boy' (p. 279). After all, a tendency to burst into Jacobite song is hardly the mark of a loyal English Protestant of the early nineteenth century. Most intriguingly, Edgeworth appears astutely aware of the discrepancies within her national categorisations. In fact, in the second edition of this text, she further emphasises the historical and narratival incongruity of this scenario by permitting Owen ap Jones to reflect upon the political origins of this song whilst darkly fulminating that 'the scotch are as bad as the Irish!' (p. 75). In this way, the 'good old English song' that Dominick's cultural and intellectual superior intones is revealed to be no less than a seditious 'scotch ballad' (p. 75). Rather than present a homogenised Celtic periphery that must either oppose or assimilate to the British metropole, Edgeworth's tale reminds us of the multiple and, at times, fraught transnational interactions that occur across the margins. Such subtle details quietly alert us to the kind of conflicted and fragmentary national identifications with which this narrative undermines the seemingly clichéd and formulaic representation of its central protagonists.

Indeed, the general identification of Edwards with an English colonial agency is not easily accounted for once the precise details of the story are fully contemplated. Although Edwards states that his home is in England and the narrator correspondingly distinguishes his father as Dominick's 'English protector' (p. 80), he is first introduced to us as 'the son of a neighbouring Welsh gentleman' (p. 72). This fact alone suggests the difficulty of reading this character in simplistic terms of a powerful colonising and anglicising agency. Rather, such syntactic inconsistencies, factual hiatuses, and discursive ellipses interrupt the rigorous ethnographical mapping performed by the text's surface narrative and open up an alternative space for interpreting its ideological content. In fact, the three central characters of this story, namely the young Irish boy Little Dominick, the Anglo-Welsh young gentleman Edwards and the Welsh schoolmaster Owen ap Jones all display the sort of 'colonial mimicry' famously outlined by the postcolonial theorist Homi Bhabha. Just as the mimic man of Bhabha's formulation reveals 'the effect of a flawed colonial mimesis', the characters of this story certify that, 'to be Anglicised, is emphatically not to be English'.[33] Regardless of either Owen ap Jones' relentless insistence upon the rules of 'enclish crammer' or Dominick's successful integration into the British imperial system, both characters retain the linguistic and ethnic markers of their Celtic origins. Moreover, whilst Edgeworth's representation of the Welsh schoolteacher might appear to serve the metropolitan desire for a colonial subject incapable of either full assimilation or effectual resistance, Dominick's professed talent for mimicry arguably presents a more subversive and profound threat:

> ... it is certain that our hero sometimes ventured with sly Irish humour to revenge himself upon his most powerful tyrant by mimicking the Welsh accent, in which Mr. Owen ap Jones said to him, 'Cot pless me, you plockit, and shall I never 'learn' you 'Enclish crammer?' (p. 52)

Here, Dominick deploys mimicry as a weapon against his Welsh schoolmaster, yet it arguably serves a much greater purpose in the tale. Although Dominick eventually adapts to English cultural norms and professes his allegiance to the imperial episteme of 'reform, regulation and discipline' through his military service in India (p. 122), his underlying intention is to buy back the O'Reilly estate. As Fort-Reilly's dispossessed heir, Dominick's retrieval of this land enables him not only to restore this 'old ruin' but to rehabilitate its displaced Gaelic aristocracy (p. 82).[34] In this way, the narrative covertly engenders Dominick with the sly civility that Homi Bhabha regards as the mimic man's latent weapon against colonial rule. From this perspective, 'Little Dominick' 'displays the continual slippage between civil inscription and colonial address' that Bhabha regards as intrinsic to British colonial discourse (p. 141). Of course, the question of whether or not this latent equivocality ever succeeds in fully displacing the didactic aspirations of the surface narrative remains hitherto unanswered.[35] Furthermore, we would do well to query the extent to which Dominick's reclamation augurs the possibility of a sweeping Gaelic renaissance in Ireland. Rather, through her portrait of the overweening Welsh schoolmaster who takes no less pride in his Celtic roots than his (supposed) assimilation of English culture, Edgeworth's tale satirically exposes what Lionnet and Shih describe as 'a politics of retrieval [that] presupposes a desire to recapture a lost purity … [and] can lead to problematic forms of cultural essentialisms and mythical views of authenticity':[36]

> This gentleman had reason to think himself the greatest of men; for he had over his chimney-piece a well-smoked genealogy, duly attested, tracing his ancestry in a direct line up to Noah; and moreover he was nearly related to the learned etymologist, who, in the time of Queen Elizabeth, wrote a folio to prove that the language of Adam and Eve in Paradise was pure Welsh. With such causes to be proud, Mr. Owen ap Davies ap Jenkins ap Jones was excusable for sometimes seeming to forget that a schoolmaster is but a man. (p. 71)

As an anglicised Gael untrammelled by Owen ap Jones' atavistic Celtic nationalism, Dominick shares in the cultural hybridity of the Anglo-Irish and is therefore as closely akin to the existing elite of Ireland as the 'mere Irish' nobility of a hundred years previous. We might thus speculate that Dominick's triumphant return to his former domain represents an effort to integrate Gaelic culture and tradition into Anglo-Ireland rather than a direct challenge to its ascendancy. Whatever the case may be, it is undeniable that this oscillating and undulating narrative belies any attempt to impose homogenous ethnic designations upon any of its characters.

In this regard, it is pertinent to note that Edgeworth explicitly and forcefully condemns such discursive practices within the pages of this very text:

> He slept little, ate less, and played not at all; indeed nobody would play with him upon equal terms, because he was nobody's equal; his schoolfellows continued to consider him as a being, if not of a different species, at least of a different 'caste' from themselves. (p. 71)

Here, Edgeworth deliberately invokes the alleged rigidity of the Indian caste system in order to express her distaste for the ethnic, racial and cultural hierarchies of colonial Britain.[37] Poised on a slightly more elevated gradation than Dominick, the Welsh boys relish the opportunity to flaunt their assumed superiority. And yet, as the eventual fate of the old schoolmaster might imply, their own position within this highly stratified society is extremely precarious. This forthright denunciation of caste boundaries conspires with the tale's unrelenting agitation of national classifications to disrupt the budding essentialist logic of early nineteenth-century identity politics. Moreover, it suggests that British imperial culture is no less atavistic in its social stratifications than India.

Conceding this, it becomes difficult to maintain any reading that seeks to locate the tale's central narrative dynamic within an uncomplicated colonial power structure. As the Jacobite-sympathising son of a Welsh gentleman, Edwards' moral and social authority is certainly not predicated upon his ambivalent association with English cultural norms. Even so, as the rightful possessor of the wealth, intellect, refinement and 'spirit of a gentleman' (p. 72), he is nonetheless portrayed as wholly warranting Dominick's devotion, fidelity and respect. Whilst Edgeworth denounces the divisive and exclusionary barriers of 'caste,' she salvages the ideal of enlightened paternalism by envisioning a malleable and permeable class system that allows for a certain degree of autonomy within the pre-existing social and economic networks of the British Empire. Once Dominick attains the social and material attributes of the landed classes, he too acquires the personal authority and command inherent to the benevolent patriarch. Ultimately, in this story, class mobility supersedes caste distinctions. Dominick succeeds in becoming a cosmopolitan gentleman without ever having to relinquish his former cultural allegiances nor, perhaps, his political ones.

Admittedly, despite Dominick's individual triumph, the wider political impact of this colonial *coup de langue* remains relatively slight. In its obscure allusions to Indian cultural practices, the text alluringly gestures towards a more expansive imperial critique. Yet, despite such abstruse and oblique referencing, India largely subsists within this narrative as a convenient nodal point in an abstracted economy of empire. If, by the end of this narrative, metropolitan standards become contorted and dislocated through continued interregional interaction, Western imperialism as a viable enlightenment project is preserved relatively intact. It survives, however, not as a vehicle for English cultural dominance but as a facilitator of Irish political acquisition. Overall,

'Little Dominick' contributes to a counter-narrative of empire that allusively draws on the history of British colonialism in the East, yet finally falls short of extending its critique beyond the borders of cosmopolitan Europe.

However, even if *An Essay on Irish Bulls* anticipates a new imperial centrality for Ireland, Edgeworth remains cognisant of the potential for an intra-imperial transnationalism that might circumvent the colonial hierarchies of metropolitan Britain. In this way, the tale's deceptively didactic prose unleashes a major interpretative dilemma for modern readers. Indeed, the fact that Edgeworth's fictions perform such elaborate narrative manoeuvres is amply documented and most often construed as evidence of her personal reluctance to come to terms with the stark realities of the British civilising mission.[38] It would be rather tendentious to argue that Edgeworth ever fully confronted the discord and duality of her own text, yet it seems equally presumptive to ascribe such complex textual negotiations to psychic entropy. Edgeworth's political subtexts exist not as a deluge of unsuccessful sublimations but as a tightly-controlled and richly-woven tapestry of historical, political and socio-cultural allusions. Most importantly, whether or not Edgeworth ever expected or intended either of these works to reach beyond a Western European readership (however varied that may be),[39] *An Essay on Irish Bulls* nonetheless seeks to encompass the remote colonial space of India within its overarching transnational dynamics. In fact, one might argue that the strategic positioning of a peripheral figure such as Dominick within this wider global context provides his creator with an opportunity to explore the potential for intra-imperial identifications that circumvent metropolitan classificatory systems. Hinting elusively at the parallels between the Indian caste system and British ethnic hierarchies, 'Little Dominick' vacillates between an earnest idealisation of a new imperial order and a sly articulation of its latent ironies. In the process of reconfiguring the British Isles to ensure a more prominent and secure position for the Irish, Edgeworth concomitantly provides a space for transnational interaction outside the discursive parameters of the British Empire. A tacit acknowledgement, perhaps, that Irish sympathies might justifiably rest closer to Britain's global peripheries than its metropolis.

Subverting the waves of global capital: Piracy and fiction in the wake of Union

ANDREW KINCAID

PIRACY, PRIVATEERING AND MUTINY IN THE YEARS BEFORE UNION

In November of 1765, Captain George Glas, a Scottish seaman, was sailing from the Canary Islands to London on his ship, *The Earl of Sandwich*, when four of his crew, led by an Irishman, Peter McKinlea, took over the ship, stabbed the captain to death, and threw his wife and daughter overboard.[1] Glas, at the time, was engaged in establishing a trading outpost on the Western Sahara seaboard to facilitate his triangulated trade between London, Africa and Brazil. The four mutineers steered the ship, laden with silk, gold dust, jewels and Spanish dollars, for Ireland. Before embarking on a wild spree in New Ross, they scuttled the ship and buried what loot they could carry ashore at the local beach at Duncannon. The next morning, as the debris of the *Sandwich* washed ashore, the pirates made for Dublin. Warrants having been sent from Wexford to the mayor of Dublin, all four were promptly arrested. They admitted their guilt and revealed the location of the buried treasure. All four were quickly hanged in Stephen's Green. Their bodies were then taken to Bull Wall in Ringsend to swing at the entrance to Dublin harbour. After two weeks, their smell and the sight of the local seagulls picking the skeletons led to complaints from the local walkers. The corpses were removed and hanged a third time on Muglins, a rocky outcrop just north of Dalkey Island.

Some years later, another Irish pirate, or privateer (one man's pirate is another man's privateer) converted his profitable smuggling and plundering operation into one of the most successful naval operations during the American War of Independence. Luke Ryan, of Rush, a smuggler of brandy, tea, and arms, operated between Dunkirk and Dublin. Captured by the British revenue in February 1779 aboard his ship, *The Friendship*, his crew subsequently broke out of Black Dog prison in Ringsend, retook their ship, and sailed for France to seek another nationality. There, with the mediation of a down-on-his-luck Boston sea captain, Stephen Marchant, Ryan and his partners received a letter of marque from Benjamin Franklin to attack British shipping on the Irish Sea.[2] Over the next three years, *The Friendship* was converted into the *Black Prince*, a fully gunned warship with a crew of sixty. Ryan claimed 114 prizes, as rewards for seized ships were called, and captured hundreds of British prisoners, who became objects of exchange for captured Americans. Ryan was eventually apprehended in the Firth of Forth, on the east coast of Scotland. During his years of plunder, insurance rates for merchant vessels operating on the Irish Sea soared, while up to forty Royal Navy frigates were diverted in pursuit of him. He was sentenced to death, and Marie Antoinette herself intervened for his pardon. The Admiralty, however, required that at least one of his crew be sacrificed, and settled on an Irish crew member to be caged: that is, to be partly strangulated, then lowered in a cage into the Thames at low tide to await drowning as the waters rose.

Clearly, in the years before the Act of Union, the waters around Ireland were a dangerous place, open to raiders, illicit commerce, and subversive international alliances. The sea was more barrier than highway. And piracy, symptomatic of territorial conflict on land, disrupted shipping routes and trade monopolies; reversed hierarchies, if temporarily; exposed the hypocrisy of state humanitarianism and challenged legal and national sovereignty. John de Courcy Ireland, Ireland's primary maritime historian, writes that as the waves of radical republic-anism spread from America to France and to Ireland, the United Irishmen found many adherents in the Royal Navy. In the large organised mutinies at Spithead and Nore in 1797, several delegates elected by the proto-anarchic crew of the seventeen rebellious ships were Irish, including Patrick Duggan of Waterford, a quartermaster's mate, who represented the *Glory*. Valentine Joyce, de Courcy claims, was the ablest delegate. Edmund Burke, by then a paranoid conservative, labelled Joyce a 'seditious Belfast clubist'.[3] Manwaring and Dobree, authors of *The Floating Republic*, a history of the mutinies, argue that an eighth of the Royal Navy at this time was Irish and that republicanism must have been pervasive, although they doubt, as Burke claims, that the United Irishmen led the mutiny.[4] Here we see perfect examples of the radical transnational connections that are forming at sea.

Insurrection, republicanism, piracy, smuggling, privateers, and invasion: the coastal waters around Ireland had provided scant comfort for English trade and security during the Revolutionary Wars with France. The Act of Union itself marked a major step by the British to address this. Union claimed expanded sovereignty and combined legislatures, maintained religious preferences, and regulated the flow of trade. In short, it attempted to convert what the English saw as resistant space into regulated territory. Article six of the Act of Union, which resonates uncannily today, abolished tariff protection for Irish produce, did away with the Irish exchequer and merged the currencies. 'From the first day of January one thousand eight hundred and one', the commercial section states, 'all prohibitions and bounties on the exports of articles, the growth, produce, or manufacture of either country, to the other, shall cease. All articles shall be imported free from duty.'[5] Autonomous Irish economic activity was subsumed by London's commercial weight.

Real, historical piracy would be on its way out as a strengthened imperial bond between England and Ireland made the seas a more lawful, protected, trafficked and surveyed surface. Interestingly, literary piracy, which I will examine in the coming pages, emerges concurrently, I argue, as a kind of compensation for that loss. If real piracy engaged the black market and subverted official state alliances and trade monopolies, then the pirates of fiction spoke to what was lost and to the messy hopes of a more local, unregulated, even internationally oriented future.

MOTIVATIONS FOR THE ACT OF UNION

The fantasy of security—military, political, economic and imperial—motivated Union. In the wake of the American, French and United Irishmen revolutions, William Pitt and his cabinet saw the opportunity to remove the Irish Parliament, which, the British upper class believed, could neither be trusted to govern the island nor to hold it against French contagion. Not only was Ireland the 'back door' into Britain, but 'it stood on the sea routes vital for trade and for access to regions which they controlled or coveted: the West Indies and the Americas, Africa, India, the Far East and the South Pacific'.[6] An enemy in control of Irish ports could cut the lifeline of British commerce. Just about every historian who has written about the Act of Union acknowledges this mixture of fear and imperial ambition that propelled Britain to permanently absorb Ireland within its sovereignty. Thomas Bartlett, for example, in *A Military History of Ireland*, argues that 'the worsening situation in Europe, most notably France', made Pitt, in the Prime Minister's own words, seek 'to connect all lovers of order and good government in a union of resistors to the abettors of anarchy and misrule'.[7] The Act of Union sought, by simple fiat, to annul the longstanding contradictions between Ireland and Britain, Protestant and Catholic, landlord and peasant, nation and Empire. Like all fantasies, the desire for Union, for security and order, remained impossible to fulfill.

The Act of Union attempted to create an expanded British territory, politically, economically and culturally centred in London, out of diverse regions and nations. It was born out of a host of transnational concerns, including fears of French Jacobinism, developing radical connections between Ireland and America, the deepening of laissez-faire ideology, and the need for Irish goods and labour to support the growing imperial and industrial market. Determined, indeed overdetermined, by the multiple threads of international commerce and diplomacy, along with internal English political manoeuvring, the Act of Union was, in essence, an effort to fortify borders, minimise threats and consolidate sovereignty.

TRANSNATIONALISM, MODERNITY, AND THE OCEANIC

The aspiration motivating Union was national security. What accounts for today's interest in transnational studies, the subject of this volume of essays? The answer, in brief, lies in the desire to disrupt borders and to no longer study nations as self-contained units inhabited by citizens loyal to accepted cultural, political and economic practices. No longer can scholars ignore 'the fact that ideologies, movements, people, or goods rarely stop at national borders'.[8] The transnational turn, as the phrase suggests, emerged out of studies of nationalism and out of the recognition that a range of identities, temporalities, and flows (ethnic, imperial, tribal, religious, etc.) could not be contained within a single field demanding transcendental loyalty. The desire for transnationalism, therefore, represents a broad range of concerns, from the cause of migrants to literary representations. All seek the possibility of an alternative mapping, of both space and time, that is better able to chart what seeps in and out of hegemonic discourses but that cannot be captured or adequately represented easily by them. But, at the same time, transnationalism does not mean giving up altogether on the nation, still a primal category. As Ronald Vegso puts it, '[t]ransnationalism differs from nationalism and internationalism in that it registers both the impossibility of consistently articulating nationalism and the impossibility of abandoning the idea of nation'.[9]

Moreover, to think through the term 'transnationalism' inevitably requires paying attention to those other terms, such as postcolonialism, modernism and globalisation, that hover around it, draw on its energies, but which foreground different aspects of modern cultural and political change. The postcolonial, for example, developed out of the specific historical context of decolonisation, and, as the prefix 'post' highlights, tends to theorise historiography and competing temporalities. Globalisation, as Tucker and Casey put it in the introduction to this volume, highlights the 'economic forces' that drive the cultural.[10] I see my own commitment to understanding the fluidity of migration and culture as falling under the rubrics of 'modernism' and 'modernity', terms that refuse to recede in face of other neologisms. Modernity draws our attention to the ways in which the new and the contemporary are forged out of opposition to the non-modern, the premodern, or postmodern. Modernity and modernism are flexible umbrella terms. They allow for a range of methodologies and disciplines invested in exploring disruptions in the lived practices and perceptions of those caught up in the collision of spatial scales, from the global to the local, the urban to the rural, from the collective to the individual, from the state to the domestic. But it is to yet another contemporary theoretical development in the study of cultural and political circulation that I wish to turn for the remainder of this essay, namely oceanic studies.

The ocean has long featured as a complex, rich and ambiguous symbol of modernity. When seeking to describe the emotions of fear and terror in *On the Sublime and the Beautiful* (1756), Edmund Burke conjures up the image of the ocean during the Age of Revolution, that can no longer serve as a protective barrier.[11] Published twenty years before the American Revolution and some thirty years before the French Revolution, *The Sublime* was written during the apogee of the Enlightenment worship of reason; it was prophetic in anticipating the return of the irrational that was the dark side of the aesthetic and political quest for beauty and order. A generation before the Terror, Burke analysed the sublime in terms of terror. The beautiful he described in terms of human scale and clarity. The sublime is the terrifyingly out-of-scale that crushes or overwhelms traditional notions of selfhood. The sublime is the unconscious, uncontrollable emotion, themes that found full expression in Romanticism and took their fullest political and violent form in the French Revolution. In the globalising world that the Jacobites inspired, allegiances were formed between Scotland, France, Haiti, Ireland and others. The sea made those allegiances possible. That is its force. Maritime borders become porous and flexible, no longer stable and reassuring. The French attempted to land in Ireland several times to support the United Irishmen. Piracy, too, both real and imagined, raised the question of what sort of power and order could be maintained at sea, an area neither settled by society nor carved into political units. Revolution, we might say, like piracy, is sublime, and the ocean becomes the means by which it can travel, to Ireland, to England, across the Empire.

One hundred and fifty years later, we find Freud, too, employing the same language to equate the romantic and unruly with the ungovernable sea. Freud opens *Civilization and its Discontents* with a discussion of the 'oceanic feeling'.[12] Bound to an understanding of religion and mysticism, the oceanic feeling refers to the moment of pre-Oedipal identity, to a time and space of the ever present, the eternal, in which one's ego is bound unconsciously to the collective. The oceanic feeling marks, too, adult nostalgia for a moment free from the constraints and demands of the reality principle. It's a hymn for a lost life. This modern longing for transcendence is a foil against which Freud can offset his own psychological version of history: the rise of heroic individualism, the personal and social maturation of the modern ego. But why does Freud conjure up the image of the ocean at all? For similar reasons to Burke: The sea is the opposite of reason; it is unknowable, feminine, unruly and elemental. Freud works with a romantic image of the sea as a realm of unspoiled nature and as a primal refuge from the threats of civilization.

Foucault is often accused of seeing a seamless grid of power in every social situation. In the essay, 'Of Other Spaces', however, he develops a concept of resistance, a way of reading counter-sites in culture that simultaneously 'represent, contest and invert' traditional practices of time, community and place. The ship is the heterotopia par excellence:

> If we think, after all, that the boat is a floating piece of space, a place without a place, that exists by itself, that is closed in on itself and at the same time is given over to the infinity of the sea and that, from port to port, from tack to tack, from brothel to brothel, it goes as far as the colonies in search of the most precious treasures they conceal in their gardens, you will understand why the boat has not only been for our civilization, from the sixteenth century until the present, the great instrument of economic development ... but has been simultaneously the greatest reserve of the imagination. In civilizations without boats, dreams dry up, espionage takes the place of adventure, and the police take the place of pirates.[13]

The ship, then, is often a trope for inventing new identities, for throwing together disparate populations and forcing upon them self-reliance, co-existence, nationhood and economics writ small. The ship is a laboratory of social relations. What unites all these thinkers is the idea that the ocean and modern life are both spaces of irreconcilable confusion. All deal in the same contradictions: the familiar and the strange, the rhythmic and the unpredictable, the terror-inducing and the peaceful, the natural and the socially constructed, the fertile and the fallow.

LITERATURE AND THE OCEANIC

Modern literature, too of course, picks up on and runs with the idea that landed identities and relations are often best illuminated at sea. In the nineteenth century, the sea narrative changes in part from having focused on what is at the end of the journey, i.e. the island, to the journey itself. *Moby Dick*, *Heart of Darkness*, 'The Secret Sharer', and *The Narrative of Arthur Gordon Pym* place the stress on the relationships between and among characters as they voyage toward a destination, rather than on the destination per se. On these journeys, characters become suspicious of those unlike themselves, and question their own motivations. Life aboard the ship is revealed in all of its economy of power—its disciplinary mechanisms, racial conflicts, nationalist chauvin-isms, gendered roles, sexual desires and homophobic anxieties, and the strict organisation of space. Violent doubts and insecurities lurk, as modernist literature becomes homologous with modernism's focus on consciousness and societal mistrust. Then, too, there is the corollary to the pervasive sense of fear and restlessness that are endemic to modern life; there is the profound boredom and ennui that is the chaff to the wheat of modernity's improvements. Nineteenth-century representations of the sea frequently, then, turn the ocean into a reflector of subjective consciousness, often equating the sea voyage with psychological catharsis and metaphysical brooding.

At first glance, Irish literature appears neither to contribute much to the tradition of maritime writing nor to reflect a culture mindful of the country's island status. 'We have seen ourselves as saints, scholars, farmers, but not as fishermen, mariners or explorers', Kevin Whelan has stated. 'The national question', he continues, 'intensified the land focus and turned the culture inwards',[14] With all due respect to Whelan's analysis, I seek to complicate his perspective. Writing about, or upon, the ocean, with all of the attendant themes of globalisation and trade, hierarchies and mutinies, boredom and drift, crews and social cohesion, does appear once one moves beyond the Irish canon. Saint Brendan's sixth-century narrative of crossing the Atlantic in search of the Garden of Eden is not just a pre-modern fable, but has become a modern text spawning symphonies, re-enactments, and science fiction novels. Brendan's epic is an historic, vast quest that reworks the Celtic Otherworldly voyage for emerging Christian audiences. No account of maritime fiction can be complete without *Gulliver's Travels*, of course: a text that sits between the onset of a new rationalism (being created through navigation and science) and the retreat of outmoded political and religious views. Conrad, the great maritime writer, became close friends with the Dubliner, Roger Casement, who wrote his own accounts of charting the Amazon and the Congo rivers.

Irish literature, therefore, is not lacking in its engagement with maritime themes. In each Irish text, just as with maritime fiction in general, the ocean is not simply an object to be described or traversed, or a setting for heroic and romantic adventure; it emerges as a social and cultural space upon which broader contemporary national and ethical questions can be re-imagined, rethought, and revisited away from the constraints of land. Each generation, each country, indeed each writer, therefore, shapes the sea anew in order to take up the concerns of their own epoch. Not only is the sea a volatile object, but the topic of sea literature would seem to cover a range of genres and works as well. If we include voyage narratives, poems reflecting on the sea, essays on the experience of seafaring, invented voyages to utopia, geographical and scientific accounts of discovery, diaries and autobiographies of passengers and captains, legends, chanteys and ballads, we end up with a topic that lacks cohesion. Within the emerging field of oceanic studies, it is the figure of the pirate who interests me here. Maritime figures such as the sailor, the adventurer, the castaway, the explorer, the traveller, the pirate help us, writes Hester Blum, 'move beyond methodologies imported from existing discourses' and establish a 'proprioceptive point of inquiry. Freedom from national belonging can make possible other ways of understanding affiliation, citizenship, mobility, rights, and sovereignty'.[15]

PIRACY: HISTORICAL AND LITERARY

The word pirate shares the same root as ex*per*iment, ex*per*t and ex*per*ience. Peira means an attempt, trial or attack. *Peirates*, a brigand or a pirate, meant, literally, one who attacked or put to the test. Ancient piracy referred not just to maritime attacks, but to both landed and seafaring communities that refused to submit to authority. Pirates, in their earliest origins, as with today's cyber and music piracy, or as with Grace O'Malley, Ireland's most famous pirate in the sixteenth century during the reign of Elizabeth I, pushed the boundaries, tested the limits of the sovereign, and broke away from norms, laws and official trade practices. Produced by the state and the corporation as those institutions expand their reach into unchartered territories, pirates have often subsequently been absorbed by the hegemon. The Pentagon and IBM hire hackers. Commercial stations absorb pirate radio DJs; Tony Blackburn, who began on Radio Caroline, became the first voice to speak on BBC Radio One. Queen Elizabeth I bestows a knighthood on the privateer and slaver, Francis Drake, who gains command of the English fleet.[16]

Pirates blur the boundaries between society and its outside in other ways too. As England grew outward to become Britannia during the eighteenth and nineteenth centuries, the life of a sea pirate tested the loyalty of a Royal Navy sailor and a merchant seaman, a loyalty that reached breaking point, as I suggested earlier, at Spithead and Nore. Marcus Rediker, in *Villains of all Nations: Atlantic Pirates in the Golden Age*, argues that seafaring European men, the majority of whom were working class or displaced rural poor, knew that the world was carved greedily among three or four nations.[17] A typical sailor knew he faced war, knew he defended the riches of others, knew that thousands of others like him were subject to violent discipline. And he knew that his labour made the ship sail. A rebellious sailor was also keenly aware that there were potential riches to be made in piracy, by deserting, and that life aboard ship flying a flag of no nation could be more prosperous, egalitarian, and provide better food and conditions. Piracy, as my opening anecdote about piracy off the Wexford coast reveals, tested the monopoly of trade routes, as ships returning from the New World ventured London-ward via Ireland's southern coasts. As Luke Ryan's shifting national allegiances make evident, piracy and privateering challenged and mocked the depth of national allegiances. As the mutinying Irish in Royal Navy ships illustrate, the strict hierarchies at sea could be overthrown and renegotiated.

If England and Ireland were to be more than symbolically united, if trade were to flow seamlessly, as the Act of Union desired, from one nation to the other, and if one hundred per cent of trade flowed by ship, then the Irish Sea would need to be protected, its hidden locales made visible, sovereign waters restored. If piracy persisted, it testified to disharmony at sea and on land.

Thus far, I have been claiming that several historical events are converging at the end of the eighteenth century on Irish coastal waters: the spread of republicanism, the failures of French invasion, the persistence of piracy and privateering, and the claims of imperial Union. Oceanic Studies, specifically the examination of piracy, is one lens through which to view this emerging constellation of territorial, legal, and economic forces, for it poses basic questions. We can ask, for example, who owns the sea, as we would later ask in the 1960s and 1970s, who owns the airwaves, or as we currently deliberate, who owns the internet, and as we may argue in the future, who owns our DNA? Piracy blurs the lines between commerce and theft, law and might, citizen and renegade. John de Courcy Ireland's chapter on piracy and privateers in *Ireland and the Irish in Maritime History* begins with Grace O'Malley in the late 1500s and ends by recounting the various Algerian pirate incursions to Ireland in the 1630s, most notably the sack of Baltimore in 1631 when 109 Protestant planters were captured for ransom. Michael Carroll's book, *Irish Pirates and Privateers*, details the major players involved in Irish piracy between 1530 and 1760.[18] While neither author explains his reasoning for these cut-off dates, it's safe to assume that increased action by the British admiralty would be one significant cause. Several high profile accounts of piracy and privateering around Ireland appear in the late eighteenth century. Luke Ryan's trial for piracy and treason began at the Old Bailey in 1782. Gustavus Conyngham, a Donegal emigrant to America also obtained a letter of marque from the Continental Congress in 1777, proceeded to Dunkirk aboard the *Surprise* and sank or captured a British ship every three days during his first two-month stint in the North Sea, earning him the nickname, 'The Dunkirk Pirate', Patrick Dowlin, a Dublin smuggler, cruised the Irish Sea attacking the regular mail service from Holyhead to Dublin. The US government issued 1,697 letters of marque during the Revolutionary War. Ben Franklin in Paris issued orders mainly to Irish smugglers and adventurers. The uses and abuses of piracy and privateering in years before the Union reflected a decade of revolutionary republicanism marked by the 'greening of the Atlantic', the republican nexus that linked not just France, Ireland and the United States, but Haiti, Botany Bay (transportation), and South America (William Brown from Mayo becoming Admiral of the Argentinian navy during its War of Independence in the early 1800s).

While piracy is not hard to find in Ireland before 1800, little historical trace of it can be found in the years after the Act of Union. The naval defeat of Napoleon's fleet at Trafalgar left Britain, despite the losses in North America, the most powerful nation on the planet. After 1827, no major battle at sea took place until World War I. *Pax Britannica* relied upon a fleet larger than all rivals combined in order to defend its global routes. As troops returned from Europe, the numbers of soldiers billeted in Ireland increased rapidly. By the time of the famine, more troops were stationed there than in India. Naval ships ploughing back and forth across the Irish sea, the move of tactics away from deep water battles to protecting close-to-shore installations, and the convoying of commercial vessels with naval protection all played their part in the diminishment of violent crimes at sea at the beginning of the nineteenth century.

In *The Pirate Organization: Lessons from the Fringes of Capitalism*, Rodolphe Durand and Jean-Phillippe Vergne maintain that piracy arises at pivotal moments, for example when capitalism spreads to the Caribbean in the sixteenth century. Pirates navigate the grey areas of an expanding world. Like their historical counterparts, fictional pirates often act at the fringes or margins of a text. In literature pirates are numerous but rarely are they the main actors. In *Hamlet*, for example, they occupy little room but function as a major plot twist: rescuing the prince from the vessel taking him to his death in England and returning him to Denmark.[19] In *Robinson Crusoe*, pirates take up just one or two scenes but allow for moments of ideological clarity. Early in the novel, when Robinson is captured by Moorish pirates, he laments having 'nobody to communicate' with, 'no Englishman, Irishman or Scotsman'. Piracy propels Crusoe's imagining of a United Kingdom.

IRISH PIRATE FICTION

No obvious contender exists amidst the canon of Irish fiction for the great Irish pirate, nor a recognised epic novel or poem along the lines of Walter Scott's *The Pirate* or Defoe's *Captain Singleton*. What does emerge, surprisingly, is a significant number of novels, less lasting in the national or popular memory, which deal directly and indirectly with piracy in Ireland at the end of the eighteenth and throughout the nineteenth century. Using Rolf and Magda Loeber's *Guide to Irish Fiction*, Google Books, and the National Library of Ireland's online database, I located thirty-five novels published between 1800 and 1900 whose plots contain significant passages involving piracy, pirates and smuggling.[20] Of these thirty-five, fourteen appear in the years between Union and the outbreak of the Famine. Fifteen were published between the beginnings of the Celtic Revival in 1885 and 1900. Seven were printed between the 1850s and the early 1880s.

I am arguing here that as real piracy diminishes, literary piracy emerges as a symptom of that decline. Literacy piracy comes to perform a range of cultural functions. Fictional pirates, for example, can be nostalgic, championing outmoded forms of custom or economics, such as smuggling, wrecking (drawing ships onto rocks), or collecting tolls at sea. Literary piracy can be prefigurative, in that it promotes a more equitable distribution of spoils and promotes fairer treatment of sailors, moves that would be addressed in subsequent decades. Symbolic piracy can navigate international allegiances that are, in reality, threatening, for example between Ireland and France, Spain and Scotland. Piracy, too, relies upon bypassing the imperial economy, avoiding taxes and revenue. And piracy can merely be a defiant act of rage by the dispossessed and the evicted.

After 1800, piracy novels set in and around Ireland begin to appear. There is little evidence of piracy in Irish fiction before this date. *The life and extraordinary adventures of C. Netterville with the various hardships and vicissitudes that he encountered both by sea and land, until his safe return to Ireland, his native country*, was published in Dublin in 1806 and charts the adventures of a Carlow peasant from England to the East Indies and Madagascar. In 1832, Frederick Dunne, a customs officer, published *The Pirate of Bofine*, a historical romance set during the time of Henry VIII amidst the ruins of a western island. A subset of these maritime and pirate novels, many of which are multi-volume, concerns plots that revolve around Grace O'Malley, with two appearing in the 1820s and then four alone between 1895 and 1900, the later increase perhaps explained by the rise of juvenile fiction, which itself is tied to the fortunes of civic, bourgeois nationalism.

Let me now turn to a few of these novels and point to a couple of the ways that the liminal figure of the pirate operates as a resonant symbol of economic, political and geographic desires at the beginning of the nineteenth century. 1825 saw the second Dublin edition of *The Life and Adventures of Jack Connor, commonly called Jack the Bachelor: The Famous Irish Bucker*, originally published in the 1785.[21] Written by an anonymous author, it reads more as a seventy-page, swashbuckling ballad, a prose shanty to the spirit of romantic, libertine, and populist escapades rather than a literary bildungsroman or morality tale. The novel is a fictional account of the historical figure, John Connor, a smuggler and pirate who operated between Loughshinny and Skerries. The Skerries Historical Society website contains a number of tales that still circulate in the region about his cave, including one that has a large green serpent guarding his treasure.[22] Born in Wexford and taken to Rush as a child, John, according to the plot, runs pirate ships between north County Dublin and the Isle of Man, until the 1765 Isle of Man Purchase Act by England. Forced to shift his operations to Dunkirk, he fits out a number of cannoned vessels, as 'the king's ships had full power over them in the open seas' (p. 10). Running rum, laces, brandy and tea between France and Balbriggan, Dunboyne and Ringsend, the high points of the drama involve his escape from various attempts by the army recruiters, the navy, the police, and Revenue officials to apprehend him. He is never reluctant to murder British sailors. Bawdy scenes in the tone of *Tom Jones* have Jack moving between his various mistresses. He redistributes his wealth, 'relieving every person in distress ... by which humane disposition, he acquired an universal esteem of the poor; so that when enquiries were made by any of the Revenue Officers' spies, they always received false information' (p. 9). In order to evade the law, he dresses as a tinker, in the process saving a sixteen-year-old from transportation, and as woman, in the process saving a fallen rural girl. Jack dies of a fever at the age of thirty-six, and his funeral is 'attended by thousands of mourners' (p. 76). Nowhere throughout the novel is Jack identified as Irish, although his enemies are either all British agents or native scoundrels, particularly those who mistreat women and children.

As one popular instance of piracy, *Jack Connor*, published in the aftermath of the Union, clearly, simplistically perhaps, raises a series of themes designed to test the law and British sovereignty. Most evidently, the story asks, 'Who owns the seas?' Who has the right to sail them and not be boarded or harassed? Unable to trade with France or America without government approval, Jack Connor tests the free trade pact recently signed between England and Ireland. Distributing, like Robin Hood, justice and wealth to the poor, pirate Connor questions the validity and power of official welfare and rights. His system of spies (which the novel implies is the entire population of Dublin) evades and tricks all branches of the British military, in a liminal network that is half landed and half afloat. His universal popularity is a political wish fulfillment for a sympathetic, powerful and effective, though not necessarily national, leader. His refusal to marry and settle down speaks to the larger reluctance to adopt social norms. His caves full of smuggled brandy, tea, lace, and rum suggest not only indulgence but also a natural inclination not to pay taxes to Empire. His local knowledge of small harbours, currents and tides promotes a resistant geography. The intimate system of lanes, fields, safe houses, and back roads creates a space ungovernable by state officials. But the vessels and safe harbours of piracy are not lawless. The social and personal codes of O'Connor, his partner and shipmate, Jack Field, and their crew assert loyalty, friendship, fair distribution of spoils, investment in the upkeep of their ships, and the solicitation of community opinion.

It would also be easy to read the moral of the tale as one of indigenous private enterprise. For example, Jack's first voyage, at the age of fifteen, to the Isle of Man yielded forty shillings. A year later, having taken in 'brandy, laces, and silk stockings', he earned 'two thousand pounds' and 'established a line of credit with the merchants of Dunkirk' (p. 19). The narrative of Connor's maritime exploits circulating around the Act of Union preserves and proclaims a counter economy in the face of British regulation. British ships constantly harass the Irish seafarers. On one journey back to Rush in north County Dublin, 'they perceived Captain L, bearing down on them … [who] fired a broadside at them, which Jack and his men returned with the utmost vivacity', The skirmish won, 'the British barge sailed off greatly shattered, after having three officers killed and several wounded' (p. 20). Defending a monopoly on the Irish sea is a violent business.

The movement of goods, smugglers and pirates between Portrane and Paris, Donabate and Dunkirk, not only maintains a shadow, unregulated economy but also facilitates the spread of emerging radical ideas. During one stay in France, Jack Connor is 'determined to go to Paris, to make interest for a naval commission, his great abilities being well known throughout France, where he was deemed a second Thurot for intrepidity, and a perfect knowledge of the Irish coast' (p. 22).

Francois Thurot, a French privateer, terrorised British shipping during the Seven Years War (1756–63). Clearly our protagonist's interests lie with breaking British control of the seas between Ireland and the Continent. Another chapter of the novel reveals its interest in promoting the emerging transnational ideologies of working class solidarity. During bad weather, Jack is forced to hold up at the English port of Bristol, where his own story, we learn, is legend. Jack and his partner Field spend a night drinking at a workingman's club. 'The chamber was filled with the servants of dukes, lords, bishops and 'squires' (p. 64). A structurally awkward chapter in the novel then unfolds: the complete, lengthy reproduction of the workers' charter that is being debated and voted upon in the presence of the Irish sea-rebels. The demands of the workers, Bakhtinian in their mix of political high-mindedness and comic satire, reveal the narrator's sympathies with the brewing discontent of the English working class. 'Resolved: That each member, when out of place, shall receive 2s. per week, for the space of six months. Resolved: That no member, when attending his master or mistress in their visits, shall attempt to open or hold the coach door, or assist them on coming out of it. Resolved: That in attending our masters or mistresses to the play-house, or any other public place or entertainment, where we are admitted, we will endeavour to mimic their conduct, but doing our utmost to disturb the audience; this will demonstrate our power' (p. 62). From unionising English servants to the emulation of French privateers, John Connor, Irish buccaneer, finds himself immersed in a world of transnational ideas and spaces, a realm that is committed to the local (not the national, but the towns of north County Dublin) while simultaneously searching out the foreign and international (France and North America). Not capable of remaining in either place (Dunkirk or Skerries) too long, the ship and the sea become the liminal places that make the possibility of avoiding more solid and landed identities possible. Oral and folkloric in structure, rebellious and free-spirited in tone, subversive and liminal in theme, *Jack the Bachelor* speaks to the populist desire for freedom of movement, independence from government oversight, and resistance to heavy-handed militarism.

The Hermit of Glenconella (1820) is one of several novels that appear in the 1820s and 1830s whose plots depend upon the figure of Grace O'Malley, Ireland's most mythical and renowned pirate.[23] The author, Eneas MacDonnell, studied law at Maynooth before pursuing the cause of Catholic Emancipation. He became a London agent for Daniel

O'Connell's Catholic Association. The tale opens with Charles O'Mahony, an Irish chieftain, who had taken up arms reluctantly during the Desmond rebellion. His wife kidnapped, his children murdered, and his lands granted to Colonel Sylvester, an English adventurer, the despondent hero wanders north and west to a remote valley in Mayo to become a hermit. Amidst romantic depictions of the scenery, digressions on Irish history, and homages to native custom and hospitality, the peasants of the valley welcome the hermit. He becomes the parish teacher, dedicating his life to literary, moral and political instruction.

One night, a storm causes a shipwreck, from which a child is saved. The hermit educates and raises the boy, Harry. He teaches him about proper conduct, fair taxation, the virtues of caution, and the evils of vanity. 'Never receive any political power over others', the hermit preaches, 'until you shall have, previously, examined into your own qualifications to exercise it for their benefit' (p. 196). Midway through the story, Grace O'Malley rides to the valley with her heiress, Isabel, having heard of O'Mahony's mysterious reputation. Toward the end of the novel, we learn that Harry, the hermit's adopted son, is the biological child of Col. Sylvester, the mercenary who had confiscated the hermit's lands some twenty years earlier. The colonel had died in the shipwreck. Isabel, O'Malley's constant companion, turns out to be the hermit's own daughter, whom he thought had died, but who, in actuality, had been rescued by O'Malley's pirates many years earlier, in the wake of the failed rebellion. Meanwhile, the hermit's kidnapped wife has also been found alive and rescued by smugglers off Cork. As the reunited party and Harry and Isabel, his new bride, retreat, 'cottagers, old and young, crowd towards them, cheering and exulting' (p. 284).

Jack the Bachelor, the pre-Act of Union buccaneer, spends his life at sea being harassed by British agents, but Jack never describes himself as Irish, nor his country as Ireland. Loyalty remains to friends, family and immediate acquaintances. By contrast, coming after the Union, written during the age of Daniel O'Connell and the rise of Catholic Emancipation, *The Hermit of Glenconella* projects an emerging national, Irish and Catholic tone. The folk, lyrical, bawdy and unruly voice of Jack makes way for an earnest, pedantic and moralising narrator. At the opening of the novel, '[t]he insurrection of Desmond had, for a long period, held that province in a state of agitation' (p. 2). Despite the violence raging around him, the novel's hero, Charles O'Mahony, expresses moderation and balance. He 'abstained from participation' in the uprising and 'declined to give any aid to the persecutions of the chief' (p. 2). Playing the role of mediator, he 'confided in the occasional parental assurances of [the Queen's] Deputy … hoping to soften down the asperities on either side' (p. 2). Taking advantage of his own neutral image, he managed to save 'twelve followers of the queen's party, who had been consigned by the insurgents to an ignoble death' (p. 2). British officials read his 'humane interposition', however, as 'abundant proof' of his 'secret correspondence' with the plotters of revolution. His lands confiscated and given to an English soldier, O'Mahony and his sons only reluctantly enter the insurrection. Even after his sons are murdered, he decides to walk away from the battlefield. 'No, no', he says, 'I will not seek revenge; it would not become a Christian or a generous soldier' (p. 22). Rather than pursuing military glory and vengeance, he resolves 'to pass the remainder of life in some remote part of the country, where his person and misfortunes would be unknown' (p. 23). Internal character, moderation, self-confidence, individualism, all the traits of the modern bourgeois citizen are on full display. All that's missing is a national space in which these values can find full, unhindered expression.

Travelling north through Connemara, he makes his way inland. What emerges as he encounters, walks and dines with the peasantry is a national vision, stereotypical in its romanticism. The word 'Irish' begins to appear frequently. Witnessing the rebellion in Munster that he is forced to flee, O'Mahony laments the war that vilifies 'the brave, generous, warm-hearted, good-humoured Irish peasant' (p. 28). On his northward migration, the English language becomes more rare. A woman tells him, she had 'but bad English', and on speaking to her in Irish, she becomes more at ease (p. 34). Landing in Mayo, he offers to pay the boatman, but 'the generous Irish peasant' rejects the offer (p. 41). Contrasting the 'society he had abandoned' with the 'provision' and 'comfort' he finds in the secluded glen, he mourns the broken bonds that attach an Irishman to his native land' (p. 61). One discussion between the Hermit and the local priest extols the traits of native character: generosity and affection, warmth of friendship, diligence, happiness, quick intelligence, good-humour, patience, kindness and chastity (p. 88). A national community is being imagined here, one that is homogenous and idealised. Located in the heart of the Gaelic west, it's a mythic vision that has persisted in Irish culture to the present day. The novel, and the rise of the myth, also represents a literary turn from the celebratory values of transnationalism (hybridity and flux) to the pedagogical principles of nationalism (stasis and order) associated with the rise of nineteenth-century Catholic parliamentarianism. We can read *The Hermit of Glenconella* as an example of an early moment in the production of the myth.

The Hermit's expedition into exile maps essential Irish character traits. It also surveys and documents Irish assets in a move that connects sovereignty to modernisation. The Hermit's journey not only charts Irish culture and history (lengthy passages fill in the presumably forgotten gaps of Irish folklore), but also records national resources. 'The neighbouring mountains on each side abound with the rich ores of copper, lead and iron … an active industry could search out silver' (p. 39). 'Joyce country has an abundance of coal' (p. 38). As the nation emerges, so too does the dream of industrialisation. In this early nineteenth-century stage of political dreaming, however, the exploitation of resources exists in harmony with the evolution of national character.

The plot of *The Hermit of Glenconella* is, for much of the midsection of the book, straightforward and harmonious—frankly not much of a page-turner. As Charles O'Mahony settles into a twenty-year stint as the local schoolteacher, the novel takes place in the Gaelic utopia of the vale of Glenconella. Money, for example, is useless: The Hermit 'brought with him a little, which he wished to place at disposal [of the village]. He handed the purse to Dermo'd, who told him that he could get all required without any money' (p. 46). In the valley, there was no 'swearing, cursing, lying, or gambling' (p. 98). At a local festival, 'there were none of those lascivious gestures, embraces, or decorations of the person, or studied distortions of the eyes, which modern civilization, as we must so call it, approves' (p. 228). As with many utopian novels (Thomas More's *Utopia* or Edward Bellamy's *Looking Backward*), the plot has a hard time propelling itself forward: tensions have been reconciled, progress reached, happiness attained.

The vast injustice committed against O'Mahony (a symbol for Ireland) in the past cannot be left unaddressed, however. But the Hermit is in exile. He refuses to return. He cuts an isolated figure. How, then to avenge the past? Innate political leadership, in the figure of Charles O'Mahony, has been dispossessed. Families have been ripped apart. Daughters have been abandoned and left unmarried. Sons have been killed in war, and lineage broken. Property has been transferred illegally by force of arms.

I mentioned earlier that pirates have rarely played the role of central protagonist in modern fiction. From *Hamlet* to *Robinson Crusoe* to *Peter Pan*, pirates have, however, often played minor but significant roles, be that by providing formal tension (in *Peter Pan*) or supplying ideological content (Ragnar Danneskjöld in *Atlas Shrugged*). It is at this point in the novel that Grace O'Malley, that notorious historical Irish pirate, enters the scene. Knowing the whereabouts of O'Mahony and his young charge, Harry Sylvester, whom the Hermit had rescued from a shipwreck, she travels into Glenconella, bringing into that happy space ambiguity and the threat of violence. O'Mahony is informed of a 'bold and enterprising woman, more devoted to the cares that generally occupy the other sex' and that 'she was a woman of sudden and strong resentments'. While 'she was generous to the poor and kind to the afflicted', she also 'exercised a princely control along the coast, levying imposts and committing piracy', Not coincidentally to this theme of otherness, 'her features were masculine' (p. 150). Not loyal to any Irish chieftain, she adhered generally, out of self-preservation, to 'English interests', for they, out of a policy of divide and conquer, 'suffered her to pursue her course unmolested' (p. 150). O'Mahony learns that it would be wise to avoid her 'hostility or intimacy' (p. 150). Her dress, he comments, 'was of a strange fashion' (p. 151). And yet we learn, too, that she moved with 'conscious majesty' (p. 15). From this point forward, the Pirate Queen becomes the agent of change and restoration.

As I have mentioned, her own adopted daughter, Isabel, whom she had rescued from a remote island many years earlier during a piracy raid off Cork, turns out to be O'Mahony's own child. In seeking out the reluctant Hermit and arranging the marriage between his adopted son and her adopted daughter, Grace unwittingly brings about a union between the exiled Irish nobleman, O'Mahony, and the English settler who had been granted his lands by Queen Elizabeth. The action moves toward Grace O'Malley's home on Clare Island and toward the marriage of Harry Sylvester and Isabel. Unbeknownst to the reader until the denouement, she sends emissaries and smugglers to various parts of the country to gather up the Hermit's wife and extended family. She also undertakes a visit to London, returning with a full pardon for the former Irish rebel, who, Grace promised Elizabeth had 'abandoned all pretentions to the restoration of his estates' (p. 279). His land now fell to his new son-in-law. The marriage solemnised, families reunited, all pour 'forth their affections' not for the pirate but for 'Lady Grace' (p. 282).

Grace O'Malley is initially portrayed in *The Hermit of Glenconella* as a pirate and menacing figure. Increasingly toward the end, she is depicted as a queen. An allegory through which contemporary, contradictory, and competing political desires resonate, she stands for order and stability amidst social and economic displacement. In her actual historical time, these upheavals were the Elizabethan plantations. When the novel, and others involving a fictionalised version of her, was published two centuries later, the context was the aftermath of the United Irishmen and the Act of Union. She is a pirate who represents atavistic Gaelic culture: regional, strong, heroic and indefatigable. Masculine and feminine, national and local, queen and rebel, mother to a child not her own, plunderer and legitimate trader, she is a character who sits between nostalgia for Celtic feudalism, opposition to British governance, and, due to her military strength, an ability to negotiate with Empire itself. She accomplishes all of this, while offering genuine leadership and peaceful compromise.

As these and other novels attest, piracy emerges in fiction as it diminishes at sea.[24] It fades at sea due to a confluence of forces, including the end of the Napoleonic wars, the Act of Union, new legislation against piracy, the large number of troops based in Ireland, and the decreased wealth travelling around the Irish coast. Piracy rises in fiction as a trope as it allows for the literary preservation of indigenous economies and local customs that are being assaulted on land. Piracy is prefigurative, too, in that it embodies and implements what some hope will appear in reality in the future: equality, fairer distribution, an end to monopolies, and, at times, greater freedom for women. As I worked through these novels, I was forced to acknowledge that they are frequently not of the highest literary merit. Their plots are convoluted and their language often inelegant, but they are crucial literary and historical markers. The emergence of the pirate in popular fiction and folk tale speaks to the tensions between increasingly monopolistic trade policies of the 1800s represented by powerful interests and those pushed to the periphery. The 'problem' of piracy emerges at moments in history, from the first use of the term in Greece to demarcate those who lay outside the city-states through pirates on the Irish sea, to today's internet hackers, when official sovereignty seeks to expand into unchartered waters and territory. The twin desires known as the pirate and the transnational emerge from the same dialectical tension: the rejection of nation and the simultaneous recognition of its reality. So long as there are nations and the desire to supersede them, the pirate will appear to challenge, confront, and promote alternative public causes. As Shell Oil now brings natural gas on shore to Mayo and as more of our national assets (forests, water, wind) are being privatised to pay off debt, returning to the figure of the pirate allows us to theorise that tension between corporatism and populism, the modern and the traditional, statism and the enemies it produces. Piracy, as the etymology of the term suggests, experiments, tests, and pushes to the limit boundaries that the powerful wish to remain impermeable and natural.

Notes and References

Bibliography

Index

Notes and References

NATIONAL AND TRANSNATIONAL IRISH LITERATURES

1 Paul Gilroy, *Between Camps: Nations, Cultures and the Allure of Race* (London: Allen Lane, 2000), p. 13.

2 John Wilson Foster, *Fictions of the Irish Literary Revival: A Changeling Art* (Syracuse: Syracuse University Press, 1987), p. xvii.

3 Floya Anthias, 'Evaluating 'Diaspora': Beyond Ethnicity?', *Sociology*, 32.3, 1998, p. 558.

4 Breda Gray, 'The Irish Diaspora: Globalized Belonging(s)', *Irish Journal of Sociology*, 11.2, 2002, p. 130.

5 M. Mac an Ghaill, 'Beyond a black-white dualism: racialization and racism in the Republic of Ireland and the Irish diaspora experience', *Irish Journal of Sociology*, vol. 3.2, 2002, p. 100.

6 Carmen Kuhling and Kieran Keohane, *Cosmopolitan Ireland: Globalisation and Quality of Life* (London: Pluto Press, 2007), p. 51.

7 See, for instance, Cormac Ó Gráda, *Jewish Ireland in the Age of Joyce: A Socioeconomic History* (Princeton, New Jersey: Princeton University Press, 2006).

8 Bryan Fanning, *Racism and Social Change in Ireland* (Manchester: Manchester University Press, 2002), p. 152.

9 Kuhling and Keohane discuss this pre-recession; see pp. 51–75. For a more extensive overview, see Kevin Denny & Cormac Ó Gráda, 'Irish Attitudes To Immigration During and After the Boom,' Working Papers 201322, Geary Institute, University College Dublin, 2013.

10 Central Statistics Office, 'Profile 6: Migration and Diversity in Ireland' 2011 Census Report, October 2012.
<http://www.cso.ie/en/census/census2011reports/census2011profile6migrationanddiversity-aprofileofdiversityinireland/>

11 Ronit Lentin and Robbie McVeigh, *After Optimism?: Ireland, Racism and Globalisation* (Dublin: Metro Éireann Publications, 2006), p. 10. Under the law, children who are born in Ireland to non-nationals are no longer to be considered Irish citizens; they are now classified as 'Irish-born children' (IBCs) and are not entitled to many of their previous rights.

12 Alison Healy, 'Citizenship 'denied for penalty points', *The Irish Times*, 4 November 2010.

13 Jaime Smyth, 'Refugee Recognition Rate Draws Concern', *The Irish Times*, 25 May 2011.

14 See Bryan Fanning, *Taking Racism Seriously: Migrants' Experiences of Violence, Harassment and Anti-social Behaviour in the Dublin Area*. Immigrant Council of

Ireland, 2011. <http://www.immigrantcouncil.ie/images/stories/191680_Immigrant_council_report_Final_with_cover.pdf>

15 Sean Kay, *Celtic Revival? The Rise, Fall, and Renewal of Global Ireland* (New York: Rowman & Littlefield, 2011), p. 202.

16 Ninna Nyberg Sorenson (ed.), *Living Across Worlds: Diaspora, Development and Transnational Engagement* (International Organization for Migration, 2007), p. 2.

17 See the introduction in Ulf Hannerz's *Transnational Connections: Culture, People, Places* (New York: Routledge, 1996), pp. 1–16.

18 Inderpal Grewal, *Transnational America* (Durham: Duke University Press, 2005), pp. 34–35.

19 For the best discussion of Irish-Southern African connections during the Boer War, see Donald McCracken, *Forgotten Protest: Ireland and the Anglo-Boer Wars* (Belfast: Ulster Historical Foundation, 2003). Joseph Lennon offers an insightful look at the connections between India and Ireland in *Irish Orientalism: A Literary and Intellectual History* (Syracuse: Syracuse University Press, 2004).

20 See Arjun Appadurai, *Modernity at Large: Cultural Dimensions of Globalization* (Minneapolis: University of Minnesota, 1996).

21 Grewal, p. 36.

22 Kwame Anthony Appiah, *Cosmopolitanism: Ethics in a World of Strangers* (New York: WW Norton, 2006), p. 85.

23 Peter Hitchcock, *Imaginary States: Studies in Cultural Transnationalism* (Champaign: University of Illinois Press, 2003); p. 9.

24 Suman Gupta, *Globalization and Literature* (Cambridge: Polity Press, 2009); pp. 3–4.

25 Nina Schiller, Linda Glick, Basch, Christina Szanton-Blanc, 'From Immigrant to Transmigrant: Theorizing Transnational Migration', *Anthropological Quarterly*, vol. 68.1, 1995, p. 52.

26 Roland Robertson, *Globalization: Social Theory and Global Culture* (London: Sage Publications, 1992).

27 David Held, *Global Covenant* (Cambridge: Polity, 2004), p. 89.

28 Grewal, p. 27.

29 Paul Jay, *Global Matters: The Transnational Turn in Literary Studies* (Ithaca, New York, 2010), p. 20.

30 Inderpal Grewal and Caren Kaplan, 'Postcolonial Studies and Transnational Feminist Practices', *Jouvert: A Journal of Postcolonial Studies* vol. 5.1 (2000): paragraph 3.

31 Inderpal Grewal and Caren Kaplan, 'Global Identities, Theorizing Transnational Studies of Sexuality', *GLQ: A Journal of Lesbian & Gay Studies*, vol. 7.4, 2001, p. 664.

32 Cheryl Herr, 'Re-Imagining Ireland': Rethinking Irish Studies', *New Hibernia Review*, vol. 7.4, 2003, p. 130.

33 Although it is impossible to provide a comprehensive list here, some notable scholarly works include Anthony Bradley and Maryann Valiulis's edited collection, *Gender and Sexuality in Modern Ireland* (Amherst: U of Massachusetts P, 1997); Eliabeth Butler Cullingford's *Ireland's Others: Ethnicity and Gender in Irish Literature and Popular Culture* (University of Notre Dame Press, 1992); Kathryn Conrad's *Locked in the Family Cell: Gender, Sexuality, and Political Agency in Irish National Discourse* (University of Wisconsin Press, 2004); *Opening the Field: Irish Women, Texts and Contexts*, edited by Patricia Boyle Haberstroh and Christine St. Peter (Cork: Cork University Press, 2007), a collection that was designed as a direct response to the Field Day Anthology Volumes IV and V.

34 Steve Garner, *Racism in the Irish Experience* (London: Pluto Press, 2003).

35 Chan, Suzanna. '"Kiss My Royal Irish Ass" Contesting Identity: Visual Culture, Gender, Whiteness and Diaspora', *Journal Of Gender Studies*, 15.1, 2006, p. 6.

36 Recent global ACIS conference themes include 'Ireland and its Global Influence: Past, Present, Future' (Midwest Regional 2011); 'Erin At Home, Erin Abroad: Capturing the Irish Experience' (National Meeting 2012); 'Ireland and Globalization' (Western Regional 2011). Recent related IASIL themes include 'Varieties of Irishness' (2007); 'Home and Elsewhere: the Spaces of Irish Writing (2008); and 'Irish Literatures: World Perspectives' (2009). Recent EFACIS conference themes include 'Ireland: Arrivals and Departures' (2011) and 'Towards 2016: Old and New Irelands'.

37 See John Brannigan, *Race in Modern Irish Literature and Culture* (Edinburgh: Edinburgh University Press, 2010); Gerardine Meaney, *Gender, Ireland and Cultural Change: Race, Sex and Nation* (New York: Routledge, 2010), and Pilar Villar Argaiz's edited collection, *Celtic Others: Irish Literary Representations of the Migrant* (Manchester University Press, 2014).

38 Jason Deparle, 'Born Irish, But with Illegal Parents', *The New York Times*, 25 Feb 2008.

39 Declan Kiberd, *The Irish Writer and the World* (Cambridge: Cambridge University Press, 2005), p. 20.

40 Kiberd, p. 317.

41 Roddy Doyle, *The Deportees* (New York: Viking, 2007), p. 181. All subsequent references to this text will be given in parenthetical in-text references.

42 W. E. Du Bois, *The Souls of Black Folk* (New York: Penguin Books, 1996), p. 5.

43 Oliver Goldsmith, *The Citizen of the World* (University Press of the Pacific), p. 24.

44 In addition to Lennon, see Kate O'Malley, *Ireland, India, and Empire: Indo-Irish Radical Connections, 1919–1964* (Manchester University Press, 2010).

45 Arjun Appadurai, 'Putting Hierarchy in its Place', *Cultural Anthropology*, vol. 3.1, 1988, p. 36.

46 See Henry Louis Gates Jr., *The Signifying Monkey* (New York: Oxford University Press, 1988) and Eric Sundquist, *To Wake the Nations: Race in the Making of American Literature* (Cambridge, Massachusetts: Harvard University Press, 1993).

47 See Toporek, Rebecca L. 'Violence against Individuals and Communities: Reflecting on the Trayvon Martin Case – An Introduction to the Special Issue', *Journal For Social Action In Counseling & Psychology*, vol. 5.1, 2013, pp. 1–10.

48 See Amanda Tucker, 'Strangers in a Strange Land: The New Irish Multicultural Fiction' in Villar Argaiz, *Celtic Others: Irish Literary Representations of the Migrant*, pp. 50–63.

49 See also Ronit Lentin, *Migrant Activism and Integration from Below in Ireland* (New York: Palgrave McMillan, 2012).

TO ADAPT OR NOT TO ADAPT: THE QUESTION OF ORIGINALITY IN A NIGERIAN REWRITE OF AN IRISH CLASSIC

1 Quoted in Fintan O'Toole, 'A Gallous Story and a Dirty Deed: Druid's Synge,' in Colm Tóibín (ed.), *Synge: A Celebration* (Dublin: Carysfort Press), pp. 33–47.

2 'Animals and Adaptations' <www.learninghaven.com/science/articles/animals_and adaptations.htm.>, Access date 22 Mar. 2014.

3 Ali Bahaloo, 'Are We Still Evolving?" <http://blog.alibahaloo.com/2011/05/16/are-we-still-evolving>, Access date 22 Mar 2014.

4 Young Yun Kim, *Becoming Intercultural* (London: Sage Publications), p. 9.

5 Luke Gibbons, '"We Knew Their Plight Well": Race and Immigration in Some Recent Irish Films', *Third Text* vol. 19.5, 2005, pp. 557–568.

6 See, for instance, Ronit Lentin's 'Anti-Racist Responses to the Racialisation of Irishness: Disavowed Multiculturalism and its Discontent' in Ronit Lentin and Robbie McVeigh (eds.), *Racism and Anti-Racism* (Belfast: Beyond the Pale Publications, 2002), pp. 226–238.

7 The Dun Laoghaire Festival of World Cultures, in which I was involved, began in Summer 2000. The festival, which embodied multiculturalism in all its glory ran successfully and got bigger and better yearly until it was unexpectedly pulled after its tenth anniversary, ostensibly due to the economic downturn Ireland had begun to experience from around 2008.

8 Another actor was cast to play the part of Paul when *Limbo* was revived a year later. I simply could not find the energy to play the part all over again.

9 See Olabisi Adigun, 'An Irish Joke, A Nigerian Laughter', in Eric Weitz (ed.), *The Power of Laughter* (Dublin: Carysfort Press, 2005) for a detailed analysis of how I felt about the play and how I was perhaps the only member of the audience the night I saw the play who did not burst out into laughter when Rai comes on stage in cast and crutches after she has been racially assaulted.

10 It is a double standard, in my view, as I have argued in a various panel discussions, for Irish people and the Irish media to be referring to immigrants who do not have papers in Ireland as 'illegal' immigrants, while Irish people who have no papers in America, for instance, are referred to as 'undocumented' Irish.

11 Ironically, it was Ugandan playwright/actor George Seremba, who, having played the part of the first asylum seeker on the Abbey stage (Peacock Theatre) in Donal O'Kelly's play *Asylum Asylum!!*, in 1994, also played the part of Gabriel Udenze. Nigerian/Irish actor Mojisola Adebayo who played Rai in *The Buddhist of Castleknock*, played his wife.

12 In 2000, RTÉ (Radio Telefis Éireann – Ireland's National Public Broadcaster) commissioned *Mono*, its flagship television programme geared towards representing an increasingly diverse Ireland. I featured in the pilot programme as an African artist but I was subsequently auditioned as its presenter. Between 2000 and 2003, I worked as a co-presenter /reporter on the programme. According to Mairead Ní Nuadháin, the Commissioning Editor of the programme, the idea of the programme came to her when she saw a television documentary in which a black man is refused entry into an Irish pub. Her view was that while bad stories make good television, the good parts of diversity needed to be highlighted as well. Thus in making *Mono* we consciously adopted the principles of interculturalism in the sense that unlike multiculturalism, it acknowledges the fact that in a diverse society such as Ireland, inequality, imbalance of power and discrimination exist and these need to be addressed and no better way to address this than by highlighting the positive side of a diverse Ireland.

13 *The Cambria* tells the story of Frederick Douglass, an African American slave who escaped to Ireland from the US after writing his autobiography in 1845. Irish fellow actor, Donal O'Kelly, wrote and performed the play with Irish actor Sorcha Fox. Both played all the parts including that of Frederick Douglass.

14 Patrick Lonergan, 'Review of *The Cambria*', *Irish Theatre Magazine*, vol. 5.23, 2005, p. 63.

15 Jose Lanter, 'Cobwebs on your walls: The State of the Debate about Globalisation and Irish Drama', in Ondrej Pilny and Clare Wallace (eds.), *Global Ireland* (Prague: Literaria Pragensia, 2005), p. 34.

16 See <www.arambeproductions.com>

17 Augusto Boal, *Theatre of the Oppressed* (Pluto Press: London, 1979), p. 9.

18 I co-produced, co-directed and played the part of Odewale in *The Gods Are Not To Blame* for the 2003 Fringe Festival. This was Arambe's first production and to formally launch the company in 2004, I revived the production. For more details, readers are advised to see: Bisi Adigun, 'Arambe Productions: An African's Response to the Recent Portrayal of the Fear Gorm in Irish Drama' in Karen Fricker and Ronit Lentin (eds.), *Performing Global Networks* (Newcastle: Cambridge Scholars Publishing, 2007), pp. 52–66.

19 Peter Brook, *The Shifting Point* (London: Methuen Drama, 1994), p. 164.

20 See Bisi Adigun, 'Why + how = Wow', *Irish Times Magazine*, 1 November 2008.

21 Kim, *Becoming Intercultural*, p. 9.

22 Ahmed Yerima, *Basic Techniques in Playwriting* (Kraft Book Limited, 2003), p. 119.

23 Thomas Kilroy, 'Adaptation: a privileged conversation with a dead author', *The Irish Times*, 13 Feb. 2010, p. 9.

24 See Matthew Spangler, 'The New Irish in Irish Theatre: Arambe Productions and Irish/West African Performance' in *SIAR The Journal of the Western Institute of Irish Studies*, vol. 2.1, 2008, p. 41.

25 Ruth Kennedy, Review of the *The Kings of the Kilburn High Road*, *Irish Theatre Magazine.*

26 Wole Soyinka, *Conversations with Soyinka*, ed. Biodun Jeyifo (Jackson: University Press of Mississippi, 2001), p. 38.

27 See Patrick Murray, 'Introduction', *The Playboy of the Western World* (Dublin: Criterion Press Limited, 1986) and F.S. Lyons, *Ireland Since the Famine* (The Chaucer Press, 1973).

28 Murray, p. 1.

29 Bill Bryson, *Shakespeare: The Illustrated Edition* (London: Harper Press, 2009), p. 131.

30 J.M. Synge, *The Aran Islands* (London: Serif, 2008), p. 95.

31 Synge, p. 95.

32 A pestle is used for pounding yams in Nigeria, but it can also serve as a perfect murder weapon; it is about four times weightier than a baseball bat.

33 *The Playboy of the Western World* in a New Version by Bisi Adigun and Roddy Doyle. Unpublished script for the Premiere production, 2007, p. 17.

34 All subsequent citations are from the Preface in *The Playboy of the Western World*, J.M. Synge (Bloomsbury: Methuen Drama,1983), pp. 39–40.

35 The hour glass theoretical model, is postulated by Patrice Pavis for the critical analysis of intercultural exchange that involves a western appropriation of another cultural product. For more on this model, see Patrice Pavis *Theatre and Crossroads of Cultures*, (London: Routledge, 1992).

36 Melissa Sihra, 'Re-location and Re-locution: Adapting Synge' in Patrick Lonergan (ed.), *Synge and His Influences* (Dublin: Carysfort Press, 2011), pp. 225–243.

37 Brian Singleton, 'Performing Conflict Migration and Testimony', in Karen Fricker and Ronit Lentin (eds.), *Performing Global Networks*, (Cambridge: Cambridge Scholars Publishing, 2007), p. 25.

38 See Karen Fricker. Review of *Mixing it on the Mountains, Irish Theatre Magazine* 3.15, 2003, pp 74–76.

39 To mark Nigeria's fiftieth anniversary of Independence in 2010, I completely rewrote *The Kings*. In this new version entitled *Home Sweet Home*, five Nigerian immigrants who are living in London and happen to be old school mates have gathered to celebrate a friend's birthday and as the celebration progresses it becomes an opportunity for reflection on what it means to be an immigrant. At the time of writing this essay, it is Arambe's plan to present, in repertory, *The Kings and its Double* in the Autumn.

40 I am deeply honoured and humbled that Brian Friel, who, in my view, is the greatest living Irish dramatist, has given me his blessing to rewrite his play *Philadelphia Here I Come!* The proposed new version will be entitled *California, Here I Come!!* So watch this space.

'GREENGOS': IRISH CONSTRUCTIONS OF LATIN AMERICA BEFORE AND AFTER THE CELTIC TIGER

1 'Compare' would be the Italian equivalent to compadre, which is likely drawn from American Western films; bambino is Italian and gringo Spanish. Eejit is northside.

2 Roddy Doyle, *The Barrytown Trilogy* (New York: Penguin, 1995), p. 200.

3 *OED*: 'A person without qualifications who competes against established traders or operators, providing shoddy goods or services usu. at low (or inflated) prices; one who is recklessly unscrupulous in business.'

4 Eliabeth Butler Cullingford, *Ireland's Others: Ethnicity and Gender in Irish Literature and Popular Culture* (Notre Dame: University of Notre Dame Press, 2001), n1, p. 259.

5 Cullingford, p. 13.

6 Edward Said, *Orientalism* (New York: Random House, 1978), p. 1. Since the Spanish language is no more congruent with a single national identity than English, its deployment can comment in particular on the way that an imperial language falls short of articulating the subject positions of its speakers.

7 Michael Cronin, 'Inside Out: Time and Place in Global Ireland', *New Hibernia Review*, vol. 13.3 (2009), p. 78. It is a sign of the suffusion of the field of Irish Studies with strong scholarship that I am referencing two worthwhile and useful articles by two different Michael Cronins: Michael G. Cronin's specialty is twentieth-century literature in English, while Michael Cronin works in Translation Studies. I will refer to both by their full names throughout to diminish confusion.

8 In Ireland, the 'foreign-born share of the population … increased from seven per cent in 1995 to 12.8 per cent in 2010' (p. 3). Demetrios G. Papademetriou, 'Rethinking National Identity in the Age of Migration', Council Statement, Migration Policy Institute (Washington DC: MPI, February 2012).

9 I am grateful to Claire Bracken for helping me recognise connections between the two groups of novels.

10 Franco Moretti, *Atlas of the European Novel* (New York: Verso, 1999), p. 3.

11 Moretti, p. 58.

12 Managua is not technically a colonial outpost—the Nicaraguan cities of León and Granada would be better examples—but it does constitute a port of entry that marks the point of transition into the territory of the 'native'. The Nicaraguan revolution began in 1979 with the overthrow of longtime dictator, Anastasio Somoza García, by the socialist Sandinistas, who were themselves attacked by the American-backed counterrevolutionaries, the Contras, beginning in 1984.

13 Shawn O'Hare, 'Joseph O'Connor' in Robert Hogan, ed., *Dictionary of Irish Literature*, vol. II (Westport: Greenwood Press, 1996), p. 947.

14 Joe Cleary, *Literature, Partition and the Nation-State: Culture and Conflict in Ireland, Israel and Palestine*, (Cambridge: Cambridge University Press, 2002), p.113. Ironically, Cleary's argument about Northern Ireland contrasts novels set there with romances across the divide in Latin America, where, as read by Doris Sommer, they serve more readily as national allegories.

15 Colum McCann, *Songdogs* (New York: Picador, 1995), p. 7. All subsequent references to this text will be given in parenthetical in-text references.

16 In the final chapter of the novel, Michael Lyons appears to believe that Juanita may have committed suicide in the river—a revealing manner of eliminating a character stuck in the past. 'For all I know she could be in Timbuktu' (p. 208), he offers, still linking his wife with the exotic and the remote.

17 Anna Batista, 'An interview with Emer Martin', *Go Barcelona*. Date of access 23 Mar. 2014, Reprinted in <http://www.erasingclouds.com/04emer.html>.

18 Michael Cronin, p. 82.

19 To be fair, Keelin does have a sexual relationship with one Hispanic character when she recuperates from Montezuma's revenge in Cuba, taking a local lover in the process, but the interlude is peripheral to the plot and the man does not have any dialogue.

20 Said, p. 115.

21 *Songdogs* triangulates Ireland, Mexico, and the United States, but I argue that its third space is contained by Ireland since the narrative focalisation through Conor in the week he is in Mayo frames the Americas in much the same way that the novel's present frames its past. *Let the Great World Spin* is narrated via a radically different temporal and geographic structure.

22 Anne Enright, *The Pleasure of Eliza Lynch* (New York: Grove, 2002), p. 1. All subsequent references to this text will be given in parenthetical in-text references.

23 Enright says that 'I did think that Eliza was about the boom, when I was writing it, but nobody else noticed that' (p. 28). Claire Bracken and Susan Cahill, 'Interview with Anne Enright, August 2009' in Bracken and Cahill, (eds.), *Anne Enright*. (Dublin: Irish Academic Press, 2011), p. 28.

24 Patricia Coughlan makes a similar point in her essay '"Without a blink of her lovely eye": *The Pleasure of Eliza Lynch* and visionary scepticism', *Irish University Review*, vol. 35, 2, 2005, pp. 349–73.

25 Colum McCann, *Let the Great World Spin* (New York: Random House, 2009), p. 167. All subsequent references to this text will be given in parenthetical, in-text references.

26 Fernando's melding of artistic inspiration and photojournalistic reportage challenges the esoteric, distanced, ultimately pretentious paintings and performance pieces created in the book's previous section by Lara and Blaine, trust fund babies who seek fame and artistic outlet in rejecting the present and painting with the style and technological limitations of the 1920s.

27 I count twelve distinct voices narrating the thirteen sections—the free indirect discourse telling the story of the wirewalker is the only one that repeats.

28 Joseph O'Connor, *Redemption Falls* (New York: Free Press, 2007), p. 451. All subsequent references to this text will be given in parenthetical, in-text references.

29 Mary McGlynn, 'Garth Brooks in Ireland, or, Play That Country Music, Whiteboys', in Diane Negra, ed., *The Irish in Us*, (Durham: Duke University Press, 2006), pp. 196–219.

30 Most of the migrants into Ireland are from other nations within the EU but statistics show increases in all categories. Migration Policy Institute, <http://www.migrationpolicy.org>, date of access 13 Mar. 2013, and Amanda Tucker and Moira Casey, 'National and Transnational Irish Literature,' p. 4.

TRIANGULATING IDENTITY: THE AFRO-IRISH CARIBBEAN ACT OF UNION IN *TESTIMONY OF AN IRISH SLAVE GIRL*

1 An earlier version of this paper was presented at the 2009 MLA convention, and benefited from the insightful commentary. I am also grateful to Amanda Tucker and Moira Casey, whose thoughtful engagement with my argument has proven invaluable in the revision process.

2 Kate McCafferty, *Testimony of an Irish Slave Girl* (New York: Penguin, 2003) p. 5. All subsequent references to this text will be given in parenthetical, in-text references.

3 On historical slave narratives from the Caribbean, see Nicole N. Aljoe, *Creole Testimonies: Slave Narratives from the British West Indies, 1709–1838* (New York: Palgrave Macmillan, 2012); on neo-slave narratives, see Ashraf H. Rushdy, 'The Politics of the Neo-Slave Narratives', in Judith Misrahi-Barak (ed.), *Revisiting Slave Narratives / Les avatars contemporains des récits d'esclaves*, (Montpellier: Presses universitaires de la Méditerranée, 2005), pp. 91-102.

4 See Michael Malouf, *Transatlantic Solidarities: Irish Nationalism and Caribbean Poetics*, (Charlottesville: University of Virginia Press, 2009) and Fionnghuala Sweeney, *Frederick Douglass and the Atlantic World* (Liverpool: Liverpool University Press, 2007).

5 Amanda Tucker and Moira Casey, 'National and Transnational Irish Literatures', p. 11.

6 Keating-Miller notes that McCafferty's narrative choices mean that Cot's testimony forecloses the possibility of 'creating substantial voices for various populations rendered silent' by slavery. Jennifer Keating-Miller, 'Explorations of affiliation: Irish indentured servitude in the English West Indies,' *Working Papers in Irish Studies*, Dept. of English, Winthrop University, vol. 8.3, 2008, p. 9.

7 Nini Rodgers, *Ireland, Slavery and Anti-Slavery: 1612–1865* (New York: Palgrave Macmillan, 2007), p. 44.

8 For a detailed discussion of the Irish experience of slavery in the New World, see Chapter 9 in Don Jordan and Michael Walsh, *White Cargo: The Forgotten History of Britain's White Slaves in America* (New York: New York University Press, 2008). This appeared after *Testimony's* publication.

9 Micheál Ó Siochrú, *God's Executioner: Oliver Cromwell and the Conquest of Ireland* (London: Faber and Faber Limited, 2008), pp. 232–233.

10 Seán O'Callaghan, *To Hell or Barbados: The Ethnic Cleansing of Ireland*, (Dingle: Brandon, 2000), p. 79.

11 Rodgers, p. 45.

12 For a cogent discussion of McCafferty's use of the term 'slave', see Evelyn O'Callaghan, 'Re-working the Slave Narrative? Fictions of White Indentured Servitude in the Caribbean', in Judith Misrahi-Barak, ed., *Revisiting Slave Narratives / Les avatars contemporains des récits d'esclaves* (Montpellier: Presses universitaires de la Méditerranée, 2005), pp. 400–18.

13 Hilary McD. Beckles, 'A "riotous and unruly lot": Irish Indentured Servants and Freemen in the English West Indies, 1644–1713', *The William and Mary Quarterly*, 3rd Ser. Vol. 47.4, October 1990, p. 513.

14 S. O'Callaghan, p. 75.

15 Beckles, 'A Riotous', p. 517.

16 Beckles, *White Servitude and Black Slavery in Barbados*, 1627–1715, (Knoxville: University of Tennessee Press, 1989), p. 3.

17 Beckles, *White Servitude*, p. 3.

18 Beckles, *White Servitude*, p. 6.

19 Eric Williams, *From Columbus to Castro: The History of the Caribbean 1492–1969* (New York: Vintage, 1984), pp. 103–4.

20 This complex imbrication of similar social positioning and competition also characterises the Irish and African experience in the US; see Hasia R. Diner, *Erin's Daughters in America: Irish Immigrant Women in the Nineteenth Century*, (Baltimore: Johns Hopkins University Press, 1983), and Bill Rolston and Michael Shannon, *How Racism Came to Ireland* (Belfast: Beyond the Pale Publications, 2002) for a discussion of their complicated relationship.

21 Rodgers, p. 38.

22 Rodgers, p. 38.

23 Rodgers, p. 44.

24 As Nicholas Draper asserts, the financial relationship between Ireland and the Caribbean was reciprocal, with Ireland both an essential supplier of provisions for Caribbean estates and a financial beneficiary, notably evidenced in the development of south-western Ireland (especially Cork) and Dublin and Belfast. Nicholas Draper, '"Dependent on precarious subsistences": Ireland's Slave-owners at the Time of Emancipation', *Britain and the World*, vol. 6.2, 2013, p. 222.

25 Rodgers, pp. 21–26.

26 Rolston and Shannon, p. 2.

27 Rodgers, pp. 9, 8.

28 Rodgers, p. 11.

29 Rodgers, p. 10.

30 For a discussion of the role the Irish have played in American identity politics since 9/11, see Diane Negra, 'Irishness, Innocence, and American Identity Politics before and after September 11', in Diane Negra, ed., *The Irish in Us: Irishness, Performativity, and Popular Culture* (Durham: Duke University Press, 2006), pp. 354–71.

31 William Talbott posits the necessity of developing empathetic understanding, which 'breaks down stereotypes and makes it possible to respond to the humanity of others' and depends on 'imaginative access to what their lives were like, from the inside', to the development of just relationships or solidarity between different groups of people. William Talbott, *Which Rights Should Be Universal?* (New York: Oxford University Press, 2005), p. 65.

32 McCafferty, 'Conversation', p. 6.

33 Maureen Reddy, 'Talking the Talk: Codes of Racialization', in Borbála Faragó and Moynagh Sullivan, eds., *Facing the Other* (Newcastle: Cambridge Scholars Publishing, 2008), pp. 221, 227–8.

34 Kathryn Conrad, *Locked in the Family Cell: Gender, Sexuality & Political Agency in Irish National Discourse* (Madison: University of Wisconsin Press, 2004), p. 70–116.

35 Conrad, p. 73.

36 Luke Gibbons, 'Ireland, Immigration, and the Ethics of Memory', in Julieann Veronica Ulin, Heather Edwards and Seán T. O'Brien, eds., *Race and Immigration in the New Ireland* (Notre Dame: University of Notre Dame Press, 2013), p. 206.

37 Sabaratnam Arulkumaran, 'Final Report: Investigation of Incident 50278 from time of patient's self referral to hospital on the 21st of October 2012 to the patient's death on the 28th of October, 2012', Dublin: Health Service Executive, June 2013, pp. 21, 33.

38 It is interesting to note that Afebwa uses herbal birth control rather than induced miscarriages, as is more typically ascribed to slave women, to control her fertility.

39 James L. Pethica and James C. Roy, 'Introduction' '*To the Land of the Free from this Island of Slaves': Henry Stratford Persse's Letters from Galway to America, 1821–1832* (Cork: Cork University Press, 1998), p. 7.

40 This is McCafferty's assertion; most historians suggest they would have been indentured until age 21.

41 McCafferty's claims are troubling given the paratextual structure in which she embeds them. While she cites Caribbean and Irish historians, she does not acknowledge African or Muslim scholars as sources for her research.

42 Michael Malouf, 'Feeling Éire(y): On Irish-Caribbean Popular Culture', in Diane Negra, ed., *The Irish in Us: Irishness, Performativity, and Popular Culture* (Durham: Duke University Press, 2006), pp. 321–2, 340.

43 Beckles, 'Historicizing Slavery in Western Indian Feminisms', *Feminist Review*, vol 59, Summer 1998, p. 35.

44 E. O'Callaghan 'Reworking the Slave Narrative', p. 421.

TRANSNATIONALISM, SEXUALITY, AND IRISH GAY POETRY: FRANK McGUINNESS, CATHAL Ó SEARCAIGH, PADRAIG ROONEY

1 Jahan Ramazani, *A Transnational Poetics* (University of Chicago Press, 2009), p. 39.

2 Ramazani, pp. 39–41.

3 Ramazani, pp. 63–68.

4 Ramazani, pp. 85–86.

5 I use the term *transnational* to denote, as Tucker and Casey suggest in the introduction, a 'sustained attention to the social, cultural, and political relationships [...] formed beyond national borders' (p. 3). Such relationships, real or imagined, are often critical to social and political identity formation for Irish lesbians and gays. I use the related term *transcultural* to suggest more clearly how cross-cultural relationships and discourses enable and sustain sexual identities and communities within and beyond the nation. (*Transcultural* may also suggest the layered, interstitial, or hybrid epistemologies and identities of the migrant.) I would note that although I open with a critique of Ramazani's *A Transnational Poetics*, my readings in this essay are deeply grounded in the insights and vocabulary of his work.

6 See Ed Madden, 'Queering the Irish Diaspora: David Rees and Padraig Rooney', *Éire-Ireland: A Journal of Irish Studies*, vol. 47.1–2, 2012, pp.172–200; see pp. 187–195.

7 Female homosexual sex was not criminalised under the laws of Ireland or Northern Ireland, though like male homosexuality was subject to stigma and social oppression, as well as a cultural suppression compounded by its legal invisibility.

8 Clodagh Boyd, et al. (Dublin Lesbian and Gay Men's Collective), *Out for Ourselves: The Lives of Irish Lesbians and Gay Men* (Dublin: Dublin Lesbian and Gay Men's Collective and Women's Community Press, 1986), p. 7.

9 Indeed, it is that inevitable recourse to foreign sources that prompted the publication of *Out for Ourselves*, the editors admitting, 'There have been many lesbian and gay books imported from abroad and helpful as they usually are, the Collectives felt it was vital to compile an entirely Irish book. *Out for Ourselves* is just one part of the struggle to reclaim our identity as Irish lesbians and gay men'. See Boyd, et al., p. 7.

10 Eoin Collins, 'Editors' Introduction', in Íde O'Carroll and Eoin Collins (eds.), *Lesbian and Gay Visions of Ireland: Towards the Twenty-First Century* (London: Cassell, 1995), p. 7.

11 Jeff Dudgeon, 'Gays and the Phoney War in Northern Ireland', *Gay Left*, winter 1978, p. 19.

12 For example, in a speech before the Irish Senate in June 1993, Norris relied on the fact that the criminal laws against homosexuality were British laws, arguing thus that legal reform was a way of 'effectively wiping the lingering shame of British imperial statute from the record of Irish law'. Similarly, Rose explicitly framed gay and lesbian politics as an anti-imperialist project and an extension of postcolonial struggles. He insisted that 'these changes stem from positive traditional Irish values arising from the anti-colonial struggle reinvigorated and amplified by the new social, cultural and economic influences of the 1960s onwards'. See Norris, Criminal Law (Sexual Offences) Bill, 1993: Second Stage, in *Seanad Éireann Debates*, vol. 137 no. 3 (Tuesday, 29 June 1993), p. 271; online at <http://oireachtasdebates.oireachtas.ie/Debates%20Authoring/DebatesWebPack.nsf/takes/seanad1993062900006#N64>, accessed 26 Jan 2014. See Kieran Rose, *Diverse Communities: The Evolution of Lesbian and Gay Politics in Ireland* (Cork University Press, 1994), p. 3.

13 Frank McGuinness, 'Hanover Place, July Eleventh', *Booterstown* (Oldcastle: Gallery Books, 1994), p. 85. All subsequent quotations of the poem are cited from this source, and references to this text will be given in parenthetical, in-text references.

14 See Anne Mulhall's 'Forms of Exile: Reading Cyphers', *Irish University Review*, vol 37.1, 2007, pp. 206–229. Mulhall notes the journal focus includes translations, minority languages and literatures, and transnational circuits of cultural exchange, migration, and exile.

15 The same year, 1994, saw the publication of Suzy Byrne and Junior Larkin's foundational *Coming Out* anthology; Carol Wardlaw's *One in Every Family: Dispelling the Myths About Lesbians and Gay Men*; Brian Finnegan's *Quare Fellas: New Irish Gay Writing*, the first collection of explicitly gay Irish short fiction; Emma Donoghue's *Stir-Fry*; and Kieran Rose's history of the gay movement in Ireland, *Diverse Communities: The Evolution of Lesbian and Gay Politics in Ireland*.

16 'Haunting', as Avery Gordon has argued, 'is an animated state in which a repressed or unresolved social violence is making itself known'; it is 'a very particular way of knowing what has happened or is happening', a 'structure of feeling of a reality that we come to experience'. See Gordon, *Ghostly Matters: Haunting and the Sociological Imagination*, 2nd edition with new introduction (Minneapolis: University of Minnesota Press, 2008), pp. xvi and xx.

17 Eugene O'Brien, '"*What Ish My Nation?*": Towards a Negative Definition of Identity', *Minerva: An Internet Journal of Philosophy*, vol. 2, Nov. 1998, online at <http://www.ul.ie/~philos/vol2/negation.html>, accessed 18 May 2013. See also Jacques Derrida, *Spectres of Marx: The State of the Debt, the Work of Mourning, and the New International*, trans. by Peggy Kamuf (New York: Routledge, 1994), p. 10.

18 In Northern Irish narratives, according to Cleary, 'the sexual embrace of lovers from different communities can generally be realised only if sexuality and politics are determinedly held apart; that is, if the lovers detach themselves from their communities and politics altogether to escape into an anti-political privacy where sexuality becomes the sole domain of authentic existential fulfillment'. See Cleary, *Literature, Partition and the Nation-State: Culture and Conflict in Ireland, Israel and Palestine* (Cambridge University Press, 2002), pp. 113–114.

19 Ramazani, p. 41.

20 Anne-Marie Fortier, 'Queer Diaspora', in Diane Richardson and Steven Seidman (eds.), *Handbook of Lesbian and Gay Studies* (Thousand Oaks, CA: Sage, 2002), pp. 183–197; see pp. 189–190.

21 To refigure the home is to reimagine the family. See Anne-Marie Fortier, 'Making home: queer migrations and motions of attachment' (Department of Sociology, Lancaster University, Lancaster UK), online at <http://www.lancs.ac.uk/fass/sociology/papers/fortier-making-home.pdf>, accessed 13 May 2013.

22 On this point, see Madden, pp. 176–178.

23 McGuinness, *Booterstown*, p. 40. The relation of love to language is critical to the book's tracing of transcultural encounter. In 'Hanover Place, July Eleventh', the Englishman does not understand the euphemistic 'water music' of the Unionist bonfires and drumming, that celebrates a political relationship with England, so the Irishman has to explain, translate, this cultural language that he understands but does not affirm for the Englishman he loves. Indeed, the relation of love to language in the poem intensifies disaffiliative impulses, beginning with the epigraph, which displays the poem's political and sexual politics: '*Mo grá thú, lá da bhfaca tú*', or 'My love you are, from the day I saw you', a statement of the primacy of love in a language associated, in this context, with political resistance.

24 Seamus Heaney, *North* (London: Faber and Faber, 1975), pp. 49–50.

25 Elizabeth Cullingford, *Ireland's Others: Gender and Ethnicity in Irish Literature and Popular Culture* (Cork: Cork University Press, 2002), pp. 64–66.

26 Cathal Ó Searcaigh, *Light on Distant Hills: A Memoir* (London: Simon and Schuster, 2009), p. 257.

27 Ramazani, p. 43.

28 Lillis Ó Laoire, 'Dearg Dobhogtha Cháin / The Indelible Mark of Cain: Sexual Dissidence in the Poetry of Cathal Ó Searcaigh', in Éibhear Walshe (ed.), *Sex, Nation, and Dissent in Irish Writing* (Cork: Cork University Press, 1997), pp. 221–234; and Frank Sewell, 'Between Staisiún Chaiseal na gCorr and Stantzia Zimá: the poetry of Cathal Ó Searcaigh' in James Doan and Frank Sewell (eds.), *'On the Side of Light': The Poetry of Cathal Ó Searcaigh* (Galway: Arlen House, 2002). For my understanding of Ó Searcaigh's work, I am deeply endebted to Lillis Ó Laoire's groundbreaking essay and to James Doan and Frank Sewell's collection, especially the essays therein by Sewell, Kieran Kennedy, and Brian Ó Conchubhair.

29 Kieran Kennedy, '"*Oirféas as gach orifice*": The Irish Language Question, Globalization and Homosexuality', in Doan and Sewell, pp. 107–132; see p. 112.

30 See Ó Searcaigh, *Light on Distant Hills*, p. 257. The term *flâneur*, of course, has a problematic history in relation to gender and sexuality, what Chris Jenks calls the 'difficult and continuous moral problem facing the *flâneur* in relation to gender'. Drawing on the work of Judith Walkowitz, Jenks notes that the *flâneur* was historically a male figure, usually a bourgeois male spectator visiting the 'bad' parts of the urban landscape, realms inhabited by the poor and by prostitutes, philanthropic motives masking more prurient and voyeuristic pleasures. Reinforcing a sexist hierarchy of male gaze and female object, the figure also depended on a gendered binary of mobility, the free male agent contrasted with the restricted female, who is limited to the domestic realm or to the urban zones of prostitution. See Jenks, 'Watching Your Step: The History and Practice of the *Flâneur*', in Jenks (ed.), *Visual Culture* (London: Routledge, 1995), pp. 142–160; see esp. pp. 150-151. See also Walkowitz, *City of Dreadful Delight: Narratives of Sexual Danger in Late-Victorian London* (University of Chicago Press, 1992). If Ó Searcaigh maintains the historical gendering of mobility, he does so, not by reinforcing the restricted status of women, but by contrasting his sexual and social mobility with the localised ethnic and (hetero)sexual allegiances of the migrant community: the contrast is more ethnic than gendered. Further, he reverses the class dynamics of the bourgeois man slumming through London's East End, claiming the position of spectatorship and mobility for the working-class migrant, wandering the more affluent West End in search of both commercial and sexual pleasures.

31 Ó Searcaigh, *Light on Distant Hills*, p. 180.

32 On this point, see Ó Laoire, 'Dearg', esp. p. 225, and Sewell, '*Between*', p. 63.

33 Kennedy, pp. 112, 124.

34 See Kennedy; and Brian Ó Conchubhair, 'Cathal Ó Searcaigh: Teip Agus Téagar na Teanga / Falling Down and Falling Back on Language', in Doan and Sewell (eds.), pp.167–204.

35 Cathal Ó Searcaigh, *Out in the Open*, trans. by Frank Sewell (Indreabhán, Conamara: Cló Iar-Chonnachta, 1997), pp. 134, 135. All subsequent references to this text will be given in parenthetical, in-text references.

36 Ó Conchubhair, pp. 195–196.

37 Kennedy, p.113.

38 Frank Sewell, 'Preface', in Ó Searcaigh, *Out in the Open*, pp. 13–15.

39 Ramazani, p. 58.

40 As Ramazani indicates, 'If sometimes the oscillating poem merges landscapes, at other times it plays ironically on the differences between the terrains it shoves together'. See Ramazani, p. 58. In this instance Ó Searcaigh ironically juxtaposes the 'modern' sexual freedom of one landscape with the older culture of the other.

41 Ó Conchubhair, p. 179.

42 Such linguistic borrowings might illustrate Ramazani's concept of 'translocal' poetics. As he writes, 'a *translocal poetics* highlights the dialogic intersections —sometimes tense and resistant, sometimes openly assimilative—of specific discourses, genres, techniques, and forms of diverse origins'. See Ramazani, p. 43.

43 Ó Conchubhair, p. 183.

44 In the introduction to *Quare Fellas*, the first collection of Irish gay short fiction (1994), Brian Finnegan notes that cottaging was 'a strong tradition in Ireland . . . often the only guaranteed sexual outlet for gay men in rural areas and small towns to meet other men'. See Finnegan, *Quare Fellas: New Irish Gay Writing* (Dublin: Basement Press, 1994), p. 9. Public toilets played an important role in developing sexual subcultures, as documented by Tim Edwards, who calls the 'cottage' or washroom 'probably the most established and oldest male homosexual information institution', because it was accessible, exclusively male, and 'a legitimate means for meeting others'. See Edwards, *Erotics and Politics: Gay Male Sexuality, Masculinity and Feminism* (London: Routledge, 1994), p. 100. Indeed, one might argue that the washroom evokes a kind of ground zero of resistant sexual subcultures in hostile places.

45 Ó Laoire, 'Introduction: A Yellow Spot in the Snow / Réamhrá: Ball Buí ar an tSneachta', in Cathal Ó Searcaigh, Gabriel Fitzmaurice (ed.), *Homecoming: Selected Poems / An Bealach 'na Bhaile: Rogha Dánta* (Indreabhán, Conamara: Cló Iar-Chonnachta, 1993), 13-40; see p. 38.

46 Eithne Luibhéid, 'Introduction: Queering Migration and Citizenship', in Eithne Luibhéid and Lionel Cantú Jr. (eds.), *Queer Migrations: Sexuality, U.S. Citizenship, and Border Crossings* (Minneapolis: University of Minnesota Press, 2005), ix–xlvi; see p. xxv.

47 Kennedy, pp. 113–114.

48 Jon Binnie, *The Globalization of Sexuality* (Thousand Oaks CA: Sage, 2004), p. 1.

49 Neasa Ní Chianáin, *Fairytale of Kathmandu* (Vinegar Hill Productions, 2007).

50 Padraig Rooney, 'The Carpet', *The Fever Wards* (London: Salt, 2010), p. 28.

51 Ramazani, p. 52.

52 Rooney, 'Ash', *The Escape Artist* (Westgate, Huddersfield: Smith/Doorstop, 2006), p. 13. All subsequent references to this text will be given in parenthetical, in-text references. See also Ted Hughes, 'Crow's Account of the Battle', *Crow: From the Life and Songs of the Crow* (London: Faber and Faber, 1972), pp. 15–17.

53 The line itself comes at the end of the second stanza of Hughes' poem and the apocalyptic end of the battle—the third stanza beginning, 'Then everybody wept,/ Or sat too exhausted to weep./Or lay, too hurt, to weep'. See Hughes, p. 16.

54 Madden, pp. 188–189.

55 The phrase 'of his own' may imply the youth of his sexual companions abroad, again invoking the homophobic discourses Binnie describes of sexual tourism and paedophilia.

56 James Liddy, *I Only Know That I Love Strength in My Friends and Greatness* (Galway: Arlen House, 2003), p. 66.

'HOME WITH A QUEASY NUDGE': TRANSNATIONALISM AND THE PERSISTENCE OF IRISH IDENTITY IN JULIA O'FAOLAIN'S *THREE LOVERS*

1 Title and date refer to the American publication; the novel was originally published in 1970 as *Godded and Codded*.

2 Jed Esty, 'Virgins of Empire: *The Last September* and the Antidevelopmental Plot', *Modern Fiction Studies*, vol. 53, no. 2, 2007, p. 258.

3 See, for example, Susan Cahill's *Irish Literature in the Celtic Tiger Years 1990 to 2008: Gender, Bodies, Memory*; Moira Casey's work on Emma Donoghue; Charlotte McIvor's study of post-Celtic Tiger Irish theatre; and Sarah Townsend's treatment of the playboy figure.

4 Stephen Clingman, *The Grammar of Identity: Transnational Fiction and the Nature of the Boundary* (Oxford University Press, 2009), p. 3.

5 Ulrich Beck, *What Is Globalization?* (Polity, 2000), p. 25.

6 Ulf Hannerz, *Transnational Connections: Culture, People, Places* (Routledge, 1996), p. 103.

7 Julia O'Faolain, *Three Lovers* (Coward, McCann & Geoghegan, 1971), p. 25. All subsequent references to this text will be given in parenthetical, in-text references.

8 Victor Roudometof, 'Transnationalism, Cosmopolitanism, and Glocalization', *Current Sociology*, vol. 53, 113, 2005, p. 119.

9 James M. Smith, 'The Politics of Sexual Knowledge: The Origins of Ireland's Containment Culture and the Carrigan Report (1931)', *Journal of the History of Sexuality*, vol. 13, no. 2, 2004, p. 212.

10 Smith, p. 232.

11 Smith, p. 212.

12 Smith, p. 227.

13 Edward W. Said, *Orientalism* (Vintage, 1979), p. 7.

14 Sally regards Mesli as an antidote to the emasculated Irish man; similarly, Mesli replaces 'shy' Algerian women with a European sexual partner. In projecting onto her the sexual experience and expectation implied by Europeanness but negated by Irishness, he wonders initially if she might be a prostitute.

15 Daniel Roux, 'Hybridity, Othello and the Postcolonial Critics', *Shakespeare in Southern Africa*, vol. 21, 2009, p. 28.

16 Carmen Kuhling and Kieran Keohane, *Cosmopolitan Ireland: Globalisation and Quality of Life* (Pluto, 2007), p. 70.

17 Like Kathleen, Sally seeks independence from paternalistic oppression. However, she leaves the 'four green fields' and resists a role in which she would produce and sacrifice a son in the name of Irish nationalism.

18 Pico Iyer, *The Global Soul: Jet Lag, Shopping Malls, and the Search for Home* (Knopf, 2000), p. 210.

19 Edward W. Said, *Reflections on Exile and Other Essays* (Harvard, 2000), p. 181.

20 Said, p. 177.

21 Antoinette M. Mastin, 'Stephen Dedalus in Paris?: Joycean Elements in Julia O'Faolain's *Three Lovers*', *Colby Quarterly*, vol. 30, no. 4, 1994, p. 244.

22 Mastin, p. 245.

23 Lorna Rooks-Hughes, 'The Family and the Female Body in the Novels of Edna O'Brien and Julia O'Faolain', *Canadian Journal of Irish Studies*, vol. 22.2, 1996, p. 90.

24 James Goodman, 'The Republic of Ireland: Towards a Cosmopolitan Nationalism?', in James Anderson and James Goodman (eds.), *Dis/Agreeing Ireland: Contexts, Obstacles, Hopes* (Pluto, 1998), p. 90.

25 Gerardine Meaney, *Gender, Ireland, and Cultural Change: Race, Sex, and Nation* (Routledge, 2010), p. 6.

26 Meaney, p. 5.

27 Timothy Brennan, *At Home in the World: Cosmopolitanism Now* (Harvard University Press, 1997), p. 39.

28 Raymond Williams, *Marxism and Literature* (Oxford University Press, 1977), p. 126.

29 Sarah Townsend, 'Belated Development and the Irish *Bildungsroman*', American Conference for Irish Studies, 2012.

BECOMING *CONTRAHECHO*: AN IRISH-IRELANDER IN ARGENTINA

1 Bulfin counted Arthur Griffith, Douglas Hyde, and Maude Gonne as his friends and admirers; his daughter married Gonne's son, Seán McBride.

2 In his travel book *Rambles in Eirinn*, Bulfin describes various individuals and communities—Anglo-Irish Protestants, Travellers, 'West Britons', Jewish immigrants, etc.—as undesirable elements within Ireland. See *Rambles in Eirinn* (Dublin: M. H. Gill & Son, Ltd, 1917).

3 Steve Garner, *Racism in the Irish Experience* (London: Pluto Press, 2004), p. 93.

4 See Palko, 'Triangulating Identity: The Afro-Irish Caribbean Act of Union in *Testimony of an Irish Slave Girl*', pp. 65–88.

5 Garner, p. 136.

6 Domingo Faustino Sarmiento, *Conflictos y armonías de las razas en América* (1883), quoted in Janet Burke and Ted Humphrey, 'Sarmiento on Barbarism, Race, and Nation Building,' Jorge J. E. Garcia (ed.), *Forging People: Race, Ethnicity, and Nationality in Hispanic American and Latino/a Thought* (Notre Dame, IN: University of Notre Dame Press, 2011), pp. 140–1.

7 Juan Corradi, *The Fitful Republic: Economy, Society, and Politics in Argentina* (Boulder, CO: Westview Press, 1985), p. 21.

8 Edmundo Murray, *How the Irish Became Gauchos Ingleses: Diasporic Models in Irish-Argentine Literature*, (Palo Alto, CA: Academica Press, 2009), p. 10, original italics.

9 Amy K. Kaminsky, *Argentina: Stories for a Nation* (Minneapolis: University of Minnesota Press, 2008), p. 105.

10 Corradi, p. 29.

11 Rock, p. 132.

12 Nicolas Shumway, *The Invention of Argentina* (Berkeley and Los Angeles, CA: University of California Press, 1991), p. 255.

13 As Klaminsky remarks, 'Sarmiento's racial purification rhetoric-turned social policy, the genocidal wars against the Patagonian Indians, the attempt to push the native peoples out for the desirable grazing lands of the pampas … and the consequent fabrication of the idea of Argentina as a purely immigrant society all participate in the crafting of Argentine whiteness' (p. 108).

14 Shumway, p. 255.

15 Shumway, p. 292.

16 Shumway, p. 77.

17 Quoted from Shumway, p. 265.

18 Kaminsky, p. 23.

19 Lack of marriage prospects back home was a common motivation for Irish women to immigrate to Argentina. Kathleen Nevin's novel, *You'll Never Go Back*, based on the author's mother's immigration to Argentina, offers a female immigrant's perspective. For a discussion of Nevin, see Edmundo Murray, *How the Irish Became Gauchos Ingleses: Diasporic Models in Irish-Argentine Literature.*

20 R. F. Foster, *Modern Ireland, 1600–1972* (London: Penguin Press, 1988).

21 Peadar Kirby, *Ireland and Latin America: Links and Lessons* (Dublin: Gill and MacMillan, 1992), p. 99.

22 McKenna provides the most in-depth account of Irish emigration to Argentina in 'Nineteenth Century Irish Emigration to, and Settlement in, Argentina,' M.Phil, National University of Ireland, Maynooth, 1994. Another still important source is Thomas Murray's *The Story of the Irish in Argentina* (New York: P.J. Kennedy & Sons, 1919).

23 Patrick McKenna remarks that many second-generation Irish-Argentine males were able to avoid the mandatory service in the armed forces by convincing army officers, with their atrocious Spanish language skills, that they were Irish-born and therefore exempt from service. See McKenna, 'Irish Migration to Argentina' in Patrick O'Sullivan (ed.), *Patterns of Migration* (Leicester: Leicester University Press, 1995), pp. 63–83.

24 William Bulfin, *Tales of the Pampas*, edited by Susan Wilkinson (Buenos Aires: L.O.L.A., 1997), p. 110. All subsequent references to this text will be given in parenthetical, in-text references.

25 As the nineteenth-century progressed, not all European immigrants were viewed equally, and some faced discrimination and violence. See Aline Helg, 'Race in Argentina and Cuba, 1880–1930', in Richard Graham (ed.), *The Idea of Race in Latin America, 1870–1940* (Austin: University of Texas Press, 1990), pp. 37–70.

26 As Murray reminds us, the Irish-Argentine community itself was far from homogeneous. He divides the Irish-Argentine community into three groups: the Standard group, composed of mostly upper-class Protestants; the middle-class Catholic *Southern Cross* group; and the labourer group, who were mostly working class. See Murray, pp. 6–9.

27 Mary Louise Pratt, *Imperial Eyes: Travel Writing and Transculturation* (New York: Routledge, 1992), p. 4.

28 *Pulpería* was a term used in Argentina and Uruguay to denote a general store that sold everything a person would need on the Pampas—clothing, food, tools, alcohol, etc. A *pulpería* is different from the *pulquerías* found in Mexico, which sold the alcoholic beverage, *pulque*.

29 The former song was written by the popular English composer Charles Dibdin and idealises the death of a sailor; the latter likely refers to 'The Death of Nelson', a rousing celebration of England's victory at the Battle of Trafalgar.

30 Murray, p. 53.

31 Murray, p. 52. Murray compares *Tales of the Pampas* to Kathleen Nevin's fictionalised memoir, *You'll Never Go Back* (1947), based on her mother's experiences as an Irish immigrant in Buenos Aires.

32 The narrator's characterisation of Castro as good-looking despite his swarthy skin also calls to mind the countless other British writers who describe marginalised individuals as attractive because they in some way match with European standards of beauty. Perhaps most famously, Robinson Crusoe writes admiringly of Friday's having 'all the Sweetness and Softness of a *European* in his Countenance'.

33 The proverb roughly translates to 'bulls don't gore each other'; that is, people in the same situation should work together.

34 The characterisation of the Irish as feckless and lazy can be found in the nineteenth century (especially post-Famine) in as disparate texts as Matthew Arnold, *On the Study of Celtic Literature* (1867) and T. Crofton Coker's *Fairy Legends and Traditions in the South of Ireland* (1834).

35 Murray, p. 49.

THE POLITICS OF COMPARISON: ROMANCE AT THE EDGES OF EUROPE

1 Joe Cleary, *Outrageous Fortune: Culture and Capital in Modern Ireland* (Dublin: Field Day, 2007), p. 48.

2 David Lloyd, 'Afterword: Hardress Cregan's Dream,' in Jacqueline Belanger (ed.), *The Irish Novel in the Nineteenth Century: Facts and Fictions* (Dublin: Four Courts Press, 2005,) p. 230.

3 For a wealth of eighteenth-century examples of this kind of argument, see Cheryl L. Nixon (ed.), *Novel Definitions: an Anthology of Commentary on the Novel* (London: Broadview Press, 2009).

4 The standard version of this account is to be found in Ian Watt, *The Rise of the Novel: Studies in Richardson, Defoe, and Fielding* (Oakland, CA: University of California Press, 1957).

5 Cited in Joep Leerssen, *Remembrance and Imagination: Patterns in the Historical and Literary Representations of Ireland in the Nineteenth Century*. (Cork: Cork University Press, 1997), p. 39.

6 See Srinivas Aravamudan, *Enlightenment Orientalism* (Chicago, IL: University of Chicago Press, 2012) and Nicholas Paige, *Before Fiction: the Ancien Regime of the Novel* (Philadelphia, PA: University of Pennsylvania Press, 2011).

7 Catherine Gallagher, 'The Rise of Fictionality', in Franco Moretti (ed.), *The Novel, Volume 1: History, Geography, and Culture* (Princeton, NJ: Princeton University Press, 2006), pp. 336–363, 339.

8 Gallagher, p. 345.

9 See Franco Moretti, 'Conjectures on World Literature'. The essay was first published in the *New Left Review* vol. 1, 2000, pp. 54–68 and was recently reprinted, with some degree of retraction, in Franco Moretti, *Distant Reading* (London: Verso, 2013).

10 Margaret Cohen has compellingly demonstrated the way that many writers who were considered forefathers of realism continued to rely on strategies associated with romance, even as they seemed to distance themselves from them. Margaret Cohen, *The Sentimental Education of the Novel* (Princeton, NJ: Princeton University Press, 1999). Michael McKeon also describes the continual links between romance and the novel in *Origins of the English Novel, 1600–1740* (Baltimore, MD: Johns Hopkins University Press, 2002).

11 Leerssen, p. 39.

12 One sees a similar idea in Terry Eagleton's account of the Anglo-Irish novel: '[t]he realist novel is the form *par excellence* of settlement and stability, gathering individual lives into an integrated whole, and social conditions in Ireland hardly lent themselves to any such sanguine reconciliation' (p. 147). See Terry Eagleton, *Heathcliff and the Great Hunger* (London: Verso, 1995).

13 Leerssen, p. 51.

14 Murphy focuses specifically on scholarship pertaining to later nineteenth-century works, writing that 'It is as if novels which do not overtly deal with Irish identity must be read as dealing with it in a covert fashion or not read at all. The approach betrays a secret anxiety about Irish fiction written during the Victorian age, that much of it was not truly Irish at all, but merely the product of an assimilation to British culture' (p. 5). Jacqueline Belanger points out that works that *do* fit the criteria of realism are dismissed as 'English' (pp. 11–33, 15). See James Murphy, *Irish Novelists in the Victorian Age* (Oxford: Oxford University Press, 2011) and Jacqueline Belanger, 'Introduction', *The Irish Novel in the Nineteenth Century: Facts and Fictions* (Dublin: Four Courts Press, 2005).

15 Cleary, p. 58.

16 Peter Baldwin, 'Comparing and Generalizing: Why All History is Comparative, Yet No History is Sociology' in Deborah Cohen and Maura O'Connor (eds.), *Comparison and History: Europe in Cross-National Perspective* (New York, NY: Routledge, 2004), pp. 1–22, 18.

17 The strongest candidate, Bolesław Prus' *Lalka, The Doll* (1890) does not fit uncontroversially into the category of realism. Fredric Jameson, in an essay that opens with a reference to 'the heroic stereotype of the Poles as the Irish of the East', argues that historical conditions leave a void in the text, 'an open wound left by Poland's subalternity' (p. 439). See Fredric Jameson, 'A Businessman in Love' in Franco Moretti (ed.), *The Novel, Volume 2: Forms and Themes* (Princeton, NJ: Princeton University Press, 2006), pp. 436–446, 436, 439.

18 Murphy, pp. 1–2. See also Brian Earls, '"By Reason of Past History": Poland Through Irish Eyes', *Dublin Review of Books* 8, 2008, p. 9.

19 Leerssen, p. 55.

20 Sydney Owenson (Lady Morgan), *The Wild Irish Girl: A National Tale* (Hartford: Silas Andrus & Son, 1855), Vol. 2, pp. 81–82. All subsequent references to this text will be given in parenthetical, in-text references.

21 Ina Ferris, *The Romantic National Tale and the Question of Ireland* (Cambridge: Cambridge University Press, 2002), p. 52.

22 Leerssen, p. 55.

23 Ferris, p. 51.

24 Claire Connolly, *A Cultural History of the Irish Novel, 1790–1829* (Cambridge: Cambridge University Press, 2011), p. 96.

25 Elsewhere I have also discussed the tensions inherent in the novel's seemingly simplistic efforts to resolve cross-cultural tensions with a marriage plot. See Katarzyna Bartoszyńska, 'Adam Smith's Problems: Sympathy in Owenson's *Wild Irish Girl* and Edgeworth's *Ennui*', *New Hibernia Review*, vol. 17.3, 2013, pp. 127–144.

26 Maria Wirtemberska, *Malwina, czyli domy lność serca* (Wirtualna Biblioteka Literatura Polskiej: Instytut Filologii Polskiej Uniwersytetu Gda skiego), p. 3. All subsequent references to this text will be given in parenthetical, in-text references, followed by a reference to the English translation.

27 Maria Wirtemberska and Ursula Phillips (trans.,), *Malvina, or the Heart's Intuition* (Clark, NJ: Polish Cultural Foundation, 2001), p. 3. All subsequent references to this text will be given in parenthetical, in-text references, following a reference to the Polish edition.

28 Clara Reeve, *The Progress of Romance Through Times, Countries and Manners; with Remarks on the Good and Bad Effects of it, On them Respectively, in a Course of Evening Conversations,* Vol. 1 (New York: Fascimile Text Society, 1930), p. 7. Reproduction of the Colchester edition of 1785.

29 Johann Wolfgang von Goethe, *Die Leiden des Jungen Werther* (Weygandsche Buchhandlung, 1825), p. 10.

30 Johann Wolfgang von Goethe and Michael Hulse (trans.), *The Sorrows of Young Werther* (New York: Penguin Classics, 1989), p. 28.

31 Goethe, p. 76.

32 Goethe and Hulse, p. 130.

33 Murphy, p. 3.

IMPERIAL INTERRELATIONS IN MARIA EDGEWORTH'S *ESSAY ON IRISH BULLS* (1802)

1 Emily Lawless, *Maria Edgeworth* (London: Macmillan,1904), p. 1.

2 Clíona Ó Gallchoir, 'Gender, Nation and Revolution: Maria Edgeworth and Stéphanie-Félicité de Genlis'. in Elizabeth Eger et al (eds.), *Women, Writing and the Public Sphere, 1700–1830*, (Cambridge: Cambridge UP, 2001), p. 202.

3 Ó' Gallchoir, p. 202.

4 See Miranda Burgess, 'The National Tale and Allied Genres, 1770s–1840s' in John Wilson Foster (ed.), *The Cambridge Companion to the Irish Novel* (Cambridge: Cambridge UP, 2006) and Katie Brundan, 'Cosmopolitan Complexities in Maria Edgeworth's Ennui', *Studies in the Novel*, vol. 37.2, 2005, pp. 123–140.

5 Kathryn J. Kirkpatrick, 'Gentlemen Have Horrors upon This Subject': West Indian Suitors in Maria Edgeworth's *Belinda*', *Eighteenth-Century Fiction*, vol. 5.4, 1993, p. 348.

6 George Eleftherios Boulukos, 'Maria Edgeworth's "Grateful Negro" and the Sentimental Argument for Slavery', *Eighteenth-Century Life*, vol. 23.1, 1999, 21. Somewhat ironically, Boulokos' statement curiously echoes that of an Irish

peasant in *The Absentee* regarding the squire Lord Clonbrony: 'He might as well be a West India planter, and we negroes, for anything he knows to the contrary – has no more care, nor thought about us, than if we were in Jamaica, or the other world'. Maria Edgeworth, *The Absentee*, 1812, W.J. McCormack and Kim Walker (eds.) (Oxford: Oxford UP, 1988), p. 130.

7 Michael Pakenham Edgeworth (1812–1881) was born to Richard Lovell's fourth wife, Frances Anne Beaufort (d. 1865) in 1812 and was thus almost 44 years younger than his eldest sister Maria. Appointed 'writer' to the East India Company in 1831, he became an esteemed botanist, publishing a number of papers in the *Journal of the Asiatic Society of Bengal*, as well as authoring a scholarly monograph on Pollen (1877). Known as 'Pakenham' within the family circle, he maintained a lively correspondence with his sister, Maria, until her death in 1849.

8 Augustus J.C. Hare (ed.) in Maria Edgeworth, *The Life and Letters of Maria Edgeworth* (London: Edward Arnold, 1894), Vol. II, p. 202. The original of this letter is held at the National Library of Ireland in the *Edgeworth Family Papers* collection (ms 8145).

9 Mary Jean Corbett, *Allegories of Union in Irish and English Writing, 1790–1870: Politics, History and the Family from Edgeworth to Arnold* (Cambridge: Cambridge UP, 2000), p. 81.

10 Seamus Deane, *Strange Country: Modernity and Nationhood in Irish Writing since 1790* (Oxford: Clarendon P, 1997), p. 30. See also Terry Eagleton, *Heathcliff and the Great Hunger: Studies in Irish Culture* (London: Verso, 1995).

11 Hare, p. 202.

12 Hare, p. 203.

12 Hare, p. 202.

14 Hare, p. 202.

15 Although originally published under the authorship of both Maria and her father Richard Lovell Edgeworth, in the introduction to her recent edition of the 1832 version of this text, Jane Desmarais states that 'the essay is understood to be a collaborative effort, with Maria as the principal author'. See Jane Desmarais and Marilyn Butler (eds.), 'Introduction', in Maria Edgeworth, *An Essay on Irish Bulls* (Dublin: University College Dublin Press, 2006), n. p. Subsequent references to this work will be given parenthet-ically in the text.

16 Françoise Lionnet and Shu-mei Shih, 'Introduction. Thinking through the Minor, Transnationally', in Françoise Linnet and Shu-mei Shih (eds.), *Minor Transnationalism* (Duke University Press, 2005), p. 8.

17 Maria Edgeworth and Richard Lovell Edgeworth, *An Essay on Irish Bulls*, 2nd ed. (London, 1802). All subsequent references to this text will be given in parenthetical, in-text references.

18 Jacqueline Belanger, 'Educating the Reading Public: British Critical Reception of Maria Edgeworth's Early Irish Writing', *Irish University Review* vol. 28.2, 1998, p. 245.

19 C.J. Woods (ed.), *Journals and memoirs of Thomas Russell, 1791–5* (Dublin, 1991), p. 35.

20 *The Speech of Lord Minto in the House of Peers, 11 April 1799 . . . respecting an Union* (London, 1799), pp. 109.

21 See Thomas Bartlett, 'Ireland, Empire and Union, 1690–1801', Kevin Kenny (ed.), *Ireland and the British Empire* (Oxford: Oxford UP, 2006), 61–89.

22 Bartlett, p. 84.

23 The Seven Years War of 1756–1763 involved many of the great European powers of the period, but was largely driven by British and French rivalry over their overlapping territorial and trade empires. Widely regarded as the first truly global conflict and Britain's greatest military success in over a century, the war also witnessed the start of regular enlistings of Irish Catholics into British imperial forces. See Barrie Crosbie, *Irish Imperial Networks: Migration, Social Communication and Exchange in Nineteenth-Century India* (Cambridge: Cambridge UP, 2011).

24 Peter Karsten, 'Irish Soldiers in the British Army, 1792–1922: Suborned or Subordinate?', *Journal of Social History*, vol. 17.1, 1983, pp. 31–64.

25 Bartlett, p. 88.

26 Barbara Daly Metcalf and Thomas R. Metcalf assert that, 'For the British, Tipu was the model of an "Oriental despot," and his defeat in 1799 provoked great rejoicing in Britain.' Barbara Daly Metcalf and Thomas R. Metcalf, *A Concise History of Modern India* (Cambridge: Cambridge UP, 2006), p. 69.

27 Julia M. Wright, *Ireland, India and Nationalism in Nineteenth-Century Literature* (Cambridge: Cambridge UP, 2007), pp. 36, 74.

28 See Marilyn Butler's aforementioned 'Edgeworth's Ireland', as well as her 'Edgeworth, the United Irishmen, and "More Intelligent Treason"' in Heidi Kaufmann and Chris Fauske (eds.), *An Uncomfortable Authority: Maria Edgeworth and Her Contexts* (Newark: University of Delaware Press, 2004), pp. 33–61.

29 Edmund Burke, *India: The Launching of the Hastings Impeachment 1786–1788*. Vol. VI of Paul Langford (ed.), *The Writings and Speeches of Edmund Burke* (Oxford: Oxford UP, 1981–2000), pp. 108–9.

30 Marilyn Butler, 'Edgeworth's Ireland: History, Popular Culture and Secret Codes', *Novel*, vol. 34.2, 2001, p. 270.

31 The song 'There's Nae Luck About the House' has been attributed to both William Mickle (1734/5–1788) and Jean Adams (1704–1765). Although a popular ballad across the British Isles, it was nonetheless widely regarded as a Jacobite tune throughout the eighteenth century.

32 As Edgeworth was well aware, the Jacobite War of 1745 was of crucial significance to subsequent Irish politics, with both Irish Catholics and Protestants anticipating a Catholic resurgence in the event of the restoration of Charles Edward Stuart (1720–1788). For a more detailed consideration of the enduring impact of Stuart's 1745 defeat on Irish politics and society see Frank McLynn, 'Ireland and the Jacobite rising of 1745', *Irish Sword*, vol. 13, 1979, pp. 339–52; Seán Connolly, *Political Ideas in Eighteenth-Century Ireland* (Dublin: Four Courts Press, 2000); Éamonn Ó Ciardha, *Ireland and the Jacobite Cause* (Dublin: Four Courts Press, 2002); and Murray Pittock, 'Jacobite Literature and National Identities' in David J. Baker and Willy Maley (eds.), *British Identities and English Renaissance Literature* (Cambridge: Cambridge University Press, 2002), pp. 226–42.

33 Homi K. Bhabha, 'Of Mimicry and Man: The Ambivalence of Colonial Discourse' in Philip Rice and Patricia Waugh (eds.), *Modern Literary Theory: A Reader* (London: Edward Arnold, 1987) p. 237.

34 In this way, Edgeworth inflects her father's account of his return to the Edgeworthstown estate with an added political dimension. See Richard Lovell Edgeworth and Maria Edgeworth, *Memoirs of Richard Lovell Edgeworth*, Vol. 1 (London: Hunter, 1820), p. 360.

35 For a number of recent postcolonial theorists, such questions are as much a reflection of specific flaws in Bhabha's formulation as any textual ambivalence. Most notably, Anne McClintock has repeatedly questioned 'the politics of agency implicit in the mimetic schema', querying 'if mimicry always betrays a slippage between identity and difference, doesn't one need to elaborate how colonial mimicry differs from anti-colonial mimicry?' (p. 64). Despite the evident validity of McClintock's reservations, it is worth remembering that although 'critics come to very different decisions about whether [Edgeworth's] "subversive" elements eventually succumb to a pervading 'domestic ideology"' (Toal, p. 213), such equivocality has long been regarded as a hallmark of her fiction. Moreover, as Julie Nash notes, whilst 'each of these critics advances different theses … they share the perspective that Edgeworth's life and work … resist easy categorization' (p. xv). See Anne McClintock, *Imperial Leather: Race, Gender, and Sexuality in the Colonial Conquest* (London: Routledge, 1995); Catherine Toal, 'Control Experiment: Edgeworth's Critique of Rousseau's Educational Theory' in Heidi Kaufmann and Chris Fauske (eds.), *An Uncomfortable Authority: Maria Edgeworth and Her Contexts* (Newark: University of Delaware Press, 2004), pp. 212–231; and Julie Nash, *Servants and Paternalism in the Works of Maria Edgeworth and Elizabeth Gaskell* (Aldershot, England: Ashgate, 2007). For alternative perspectives on the application of Bhabha's postcolonial critique to Edgeworth's fiction, see Sara L. Maurer 'Disowning to Own: Maria Edgeworth and the Illegitimacy of National Ownership', *Criticism* vol. 44, 2002, pp. 363–388.

36 Lionnet and Shih, p. 9.

37 Of course, as Susan Bayly remarks in *Caste, Society and Politics in India from the Eighteenth Century to the Modern Age* (1999), the supposedly 'ancient' caste system of India was 'largely a creation of [the eighteenth century]' (p. 65). However, from the early nineteenth century onwards, British Orientalists (and thus the British public) increasingly 'saw Hindus as the prisoners of an invariably hierarchical and Brahman-centred value system' (p. 97). Somewhat ironically, 'their insistence on this point played a significant part in the making of a more caste-conscious social order' (p. 97). See Susan Bayly, *Caste, Society and Politics in India from the Eighteenth-Century to the Modern Age* (Cambridge: Cambridge UP, 1999).

38 As previously noted, the tendency to view Edgeworth in this way largely derives from the late-twentieth-century critical works of critics such as Tom Dunne, Terry Eagleton, Seamus Deane and David Lloyd. See Dunne, 'Maria Edgeworth and the Colonial Mind', *The 26th O'Donnell Lecture* (Dublin: National University of Ireland, 1984); David Lloyd, *Anomalous States: Irish Writing and the Post-colonial Moment* (Dublin: Lilliput Press, 1993), p. 141; Seamus Deane, *Strange Country: Modernity and Nationhood in Irish Writing Since 1790* (Oxford: Clarendon Press, 1997), pp. 48–49; and Eagelton, p. 167. For a succinct summary and response to this stance, see Cliona Ó Gallchoir, *Maria Edgeworth* (Dublin: University College Dublin Press, 2005), in which she contends that 'Edgeworth is a very unlikely madwoman in the Irish attic' (p. 16).

39 Importantly, Sharon Murphy has revealed the vital role of both lending libraries and book imports within the cultural life of the East Indian Company's various ranks. Most significantly for our discussion here, Murphy has thoroughly established the fact that Edgeworth's *Popular Tales* were exceedingly sought after throughout the first half of the nineteenth century. Given Edgeworth's eager interest in the reading habits of the colonial soldier (p. 76), it is very likely that she was both aware of and gratified by the popularity of her fiction amongst the British and Irish soldiers of the East India Company. However, the question of whether her popularity extended to an indigenous Indian readership, as well as the matter of her own potential cognisance of this possibility remains unanswered. Given the enduring popularity of Edgeworth's works in the Indian colonies, it is fair to assume that members of the later nineteenth-century anglicised Indian elite would have had opportunities to read her fictions. See Sharon Murphy, 'Imperial Reading? The East India Company's Lending Libraries for Soldiers, c.1819–1834', *Book History*, vol. 12, 2009, pp. 74–99.

SUBVERTING THE WAVES OF GLOBAL CAPITAL: PIRACY AND FICTION IN THE WAKE OF UNION

1 An account of this frightful episode can be found in the *Journal of the Royal Society of Antiquaries of Ireland, Vol. VIII, Fourth Series* (Dublin: University Press, 1888), p. 210. A popular version is recounted in Frank Hopkins, *Hidden Dublin: Deadbeats, Dossers and Decent Skins* (Dublin: Mercier Press, 2007), pp. 36–37.

2 The fascinating story of Luke Ryan's employment by Ben Franklin is told fully in Ben Franklin's *Privateers: A Naval Epic of the American Revolution* (Baton Rouge: Louisiana State University Press, 1956).

3 Quoted from John de Courcy Ireland, *Ireland and the Irish in Maritime History* (Dun Laoghaire: The Glendale Press, 1986).

4 G. E Manwaring and Bonamy Dobree, *The Floating Republic: An Account of the Mutinies at Spithead and Nore in 1797* (Pen and Sword Military Classics, 1935).

5 Article Sixth, Act of Union (1800), www.legislation.gov.uk/aip/Geo3/40/38

6 Liz Curtis, *The Cause of Ireland: From the United Irishmen to Partition* (Belfast: Beyond the Pale Publications, 1994), p. 13.

7 Thomas Bartlett, *A Military History of Ireland* (Cambridge University Press, 1996) p. 253.

8 Brian D. Behnken and Simon Wendt, *Crossing Boundaries: Ethnicity, Race and National Belonging in a Transnational World* (New York: Lexington Books, 2013) p. 5.

9 Vegso, Robert, 'The Mother Tongues of Modernity: Modernism, Transnationalism, Translation,' *Journal of Modern Literature*, vol. 33, 2010, p. 29.

10 Tucker and Casey, 'National and Transnational Irish Literatures', p. 7.

11 Edmund Burke, *On Taste, On the Sublime and the Beautiful, Reflections on the French Revolution, A Letter to a Noble Lord* (London: Collier and Son, 1937).

12 Sigmund Freud, *Civilization and its Discontents* (New York: Dover Thrift, 1994).

13 Michel Foucault, 'Of Other Spaces', *diacritics*, vol. 16.1, 1986, p. 27.

14 Email exchange with the author.

15 Hester Blum, 'The Prospect of Oceanic Studies', *PMLA*, vol. 125.3, 2010, p. 671.

16 For a systematic treatment of stages of piracy, see Rodolphe Durand and Jean-Philippe Vergne, *The Pirate Organization: Lessons from the Fringes of Capitalism* (Harvard Business Review Press, 2013).

17 Marcus Rediker, *Villains of All Nations* (Boston: Beacon Press, 2004).

18 Michael J. Carroll, *Irish Pirates and Privateers* (Michael P. Carroll, 2007).

19 For an accounting of pirates in early modern literature, see Claire Jowitt, *Pirates? The Politics of Plunder, 1550–1650* (London: Palgrave Macmillan, 2007).

20 Rolf and Magda Loeber, *A Guide to Irish Fiction, 1650–1900* (Dublin: Four Courts Press, 2006).

21 A Friend, *The Life and Adventures of John Connor, commonly called Jack the Bachelor. The famous Irish bucker* (Dublin: William Jones, 1785 and 1821). All subsequent references to this text will be given in parenthetical, in-text references.

22 The Skerries Historical Society, 'Some Interesting Characters', <http://www.oldskerries.ie/lochist/30chars.html>

23 Eneas MacDonnell, *The Hermit of Glenconella* (London: G. Cowie and Co., 1820). All subsequent references to this text will be given in parenthetical, in-text references.

24 See, for example, William Maxwell, *The Dark Lady of Doona* (London: Smith and Elder and Co., 1834) and Mary Grace Crumpe, *The Death Flag* (London: William Shoberl, 1852).

Bibliography

Adams, Jean, 'There's Nae Luck About the House', in Catherine Kerrigan, ed., *An Anthology of Scottish Women Poets*, Edinburgh: Edinburgh University Press, 1991, pp. 160–1.

Adigun, Olabisi, 'An Irish Joke, A Nigerian Laughter' in Eric Weitz, ed. *The Power of Laughter*, Dublin: Carysfort Press, 2005, pp. 76–94.

—, 'Arambe Productions: An African's Response to the Recent Portrayal of the *Fear Gorm* in Irish Drama', in Karen Fricker and Ronit Lentin, eds, *Performing Global Networks*, Cambridge: Cambridge Scholars Publishing, 2007, pp. 52–66.

—, 'Why + how = Wow', *Irish Times Magazine*, 1 Nov. 2008.

Adigun, Bisi, and Roddy Doyle, *The Playboy of the Western World in a New Version*, Unpublished script for the Premiere production 2007.

Aljoe, Nicole N, *Creole Testimonies: Slave Narratives from the British West Indies, 1709–1838*, New York: Palgrave Macmillan, 2012.

'Animals and Adaptations', http://www.learninghaven.com/science/articles/animals_and_adaptation.htm Access date 22 Mar 2014.

Anthias, Floya, 'Evaluating "Diaspora": Beyond Ethnicity?', *Sociology*, vol. 32.3, 1998, pp. 557–80.

Appadurai, Arjun, *Modernity at Large: Cultural Dimensions of Globalization*, Minneapolis: University of Minnesota, 1996.

—, 'Putting Hierarchy in its Place', *Cultural Anthropology*, vol. 3.1, 1988, pp. 36–49.

Appiah, Kwame Anthony, *Cosmopolitanism: Ethics in a World of Strangers*, New York: WW Norton, 2006.

Aravamudan, Srinivas, *Enlightenment Orientalism*, Chicago, IL: University of Chicago Press, 2012.

Arnold, Matthew *On the Study of Celtic Literature*, London: Smith, Elder, and Co., 1867.

Article Sixth, Act of Union (1800), http://www.legislation.gov.uk/aip/Geo3/40/38

Arulkumaran, Sabaratnam, 'Final Report: Investigation of Incident 50278 from time of patient's self referral to hospital on the 21st of October 2012 to the patient's death on the 28th of October, 2012', Dublin: Health Service Executive, June 2013.

Bahaloo, Ali, 'Are We Still Evolving?' http://alibahaloo.com/blog/are-we-still-evolving/Access date 22 Mar 2014.

Baldwin, Peter, 'Comparing and Generalizing: Why All History is Comparative, Yet No History is Sociology' in Deborah Cohen and Maura O'Connor, eds., *Comparison and History: Europe in Cross-National Perspective*, New York, NY: Routledge, 2004, pp. 1–22.

Bartlett, Thomas, *A Military History of Ireland*, Cambridge University Press, 1996.

Bartoszyńska, Katarzyna, 'Adam Smith's Problems: Sympathy in Owenson's *Wild Irish Girl* and Edgeworth's *Ennui*', *New Hibernia Review*, vol. 17.3, 2013, pp. 127–144.

Battista, Anna. 'An interview with Emer Martin', *Go Barcelona*. Rptd at http://www.erasingclouds.com/04emer.html, access date 23 Mar. 2014.

Bayly, Susan, *Caste, Society and Politics in India from the Eighteenth-Century to the Modern Age*, Cambridge: Cambridge University Press, 1999.

Beck, Ulrich, *What Is Globalization?* London: Polity, 2000.

Beckles, Hilary McD., 'Historicizing Slavery in Western Indian Feminisms', *Feminist Review* 59, 1998, pp. 34–56.

—, 'A "riotous and unruly lot": Irish Indentured Servants and Freemen in the English West Indies, 1644–1713', *The William and Mary Quarterly* 3rd Ser. vol. 47.4, 1990, pp. 503–22.

—, *White Servitude and Black Slavery in Barbados, 1627–1715*, Knoxville: U of Tennessee P, 1989.

Behnken, Brian D. and Wendt, Simon, *Crossing Boundaries: Ethnicity, Race and National Belonging in a Transnational World*, New York: Lexington Books, 2013.

Belanger, Jacqueline, 'Educating the Reading Public: British Critical Reception of Maria Edgeworth's Early Irish Writing', *Irish University Review* vol. 28.2, 1998, pp. 240–255.

—, 'Introduction', *The Irish Novel in the Nineteenth Century: Facts and Fictions*, Dublin: Four Courts Press, 2005.

Bhabha, Homi, *The Location of Culture*, London: Routledge, 2004.

Binnie, Jon, *The Globalization of Sexuality*, Thousand Oaks CA: Sage, 2004.

Block, Kristen and Shaw, Jenny, 'Subjects without an Empire: The Irish in the Early Modern Caribbean', *Past and Present* 210, Feb. 2011, pp. 33–60.

Blum Hester, 'The Prospect of Oceanic Studies', *PMLA*, vol. 125.3, 2010, pp. 670–677.

Boal, Augusto, *Theatre of the Oppressed*, London: Pluto Press, 1979.

Boulukos, George Eleftherios, 'Maria Edgeworth's "Grateful Negro" and the Sentimental Argument for Slavery', *Eighteenth-Century Life*, vol. 23.1, 1999, pp. 12–29.

Boyd, Clodagh, et. al. (Dublin Lesbian and Gay Men's Collective), *Out for Ourselves: The Lives of Irish Lesbians and Gay Men*, Dublin: Dublin Lesbian and Gay Men's Collective and Women's Community Press, 1986.

Bracken, Claire, and Susan Cahill. 'Interview with Anne Enright, August 2009,' in Bracken and Cahill, eds, *Anne Enright*, Dublin: Irish Academic Press, 2011, pp. 13–32.

Bradley, Anthony and Valiulis, eds., *Gender and Sexuality in Modern Ireland*, Amherst: University of Massachusetts Press, 1997.

Brannigan, John, *Race in Modern Irish Literature and Culture*, Edinburgh: Edinburgh University Press, 2010.

Brennan, Timothy, *At Home in the World: Cosmopolitanism Now*, Cambridge: Harvard University Press, 1997.

Brook, Peter, *The Shifting Point*, London: Methuen Drama, 1994.

Brundan, Katie, 'Cosmopolitan Complexities in Maria Edgeworth's *Ennui*', *Studies in the Novel*, vol. 37.2, 2005, pp. 123–140.

Bulfin, William, *Rambles in Eirinn*, Dublin: M. H. Gill & Son, Ltd, 1917.

—. *Tales of the Pampas*, edited by Susan Wilkinson, Buenos Aires: L.O.L.A., 1997.

Burgess Miranda, 'Edgeworth, the United Irishmen, and "More Intelligent Treason"' in Heidi Kaufmann and Chris Fauske, eds), *An Uncomfortable Authority: Maria Edgeworth and Her Contexts*, Newark: University of Delaware Press, 2004, pp. 33–61.

—, 'The National Tale and Allied Genres, 1770s–1840s' in John Wilson Foster, ed., *The Cambridge Companion to the Irish Novel*, Cambridge: Cambridge UP, 2006, pp. 39–59.

Burke, Edmund. *India: The Launching of the Hastings Impeachment 1786–1788*. Vol. 6 of *The Writings and Speeches of Edmund Burke*. 9 vols. Gen. ed. Paul Langford. Oxford: Oxford University Press, 1981–2000.

—, *On Taste, On the Sublime and the Beautiful, Reflections on the French Revolution, A Letter to a Noble Lord*, London: Collier and Son, 1937.

Burke, Janet and Humphrey, Ted, 'Sarmiento on Barbarism, Race, and Nation Building' in Jorge J. E. Garcia, ed., *Forging People: Race, Ethnicity, and Nationality in Hispanic American and Latino/a Thought*, Notre Dame, IN: University of Notre Dame Press, 2011, pp. 127–151.

Butler, Marilyn, 'Edgeworth's Ireland: History, Popular Culture and Secret Codes', *Novel*, vol. 34.2, 2001, pp. 267–292.

—, 'Edgeworth, the United Irishmen, and "More Intelligent Treason" in Heidi Kaufmann and Chris Fauske, eds., *An Uncomfortable Authority*, Newark: University of Delaware Press, 2004, pp. 33–61.

Bryson, Bill, *Shakespeare: The Illustrated Edition*, London: Harper Press, 2009.

Carroll, Michael J., *Irish Pirates and Privateers*, Michael P. Carroll, 2007.

Casey, Moira, '"If Love's a Country": Transnationalism and the Celtic Tiger in Emma Donoghue's Landing', *New Hibernia Review*, vol. 15. 2, 2011, pp. 64–79.

Central Statistics Office, 'Profile 6: Migration and Diversity in Ireland' 2011 Census Report, October 2012. <http://www.cso.ie/en/census/census2011reports/census2011profile6migrationanddiversity-aprofileofdiversityinireland/>

Chan, Suzanna. '"Kiss My Royal Irish Ass" Contesting Identity: Visual Culture, Gender, Whiteness and Diaspora', *Journal Of Gender Studies*, vol. 15.1, 2006, pp. 1–17.

Clark, William Bell, *Ben Franklin's Privateers: A Naval Epic of the American Revolution*, Baton Rouge: Louisiana State University Press, 1956.

Cleary, Joe, *Literature, Partition and the Nation-State: Culture and Conflict in Ireland, Israel and Palestine*, Cambridge: Cambridge University Press, 2002.

—, *Outrageous Fortune: Culture and Capital in Modern Ireland*, Dublin: Field Day, 2007.

Clingman, Stephen, *The Grammar of Identity: Transnational Fiction and the Nature of the Boundary*, Oxford University Press, 2009.

Cohen, Margaret, *The Sentimental Education of the Novel*, Princeton, NJ: Princeton University Press, 1999.

Connolly, Claire, *A Cultural History of the Irish Novel, 1790–1829*, Cambridge, Cambridge University Press, 2011.

Connolly, Seán, *Political Ideas in Eighteenth-Century Ireland*, Dublin: Four Courts Press, 2000.

Conrad, Kathryn, *Locked in the Family Cell: Gender, Sexuality, and Political Agency in Irish National Discourse*, University of Wisconsin Press, 2004.

Corbett, Mary Jean, *Allegories of Union in Irish and English Writing, 1790–1870: Politics, History and the Family from Edgeworth to Arnold*, Cambridge: Cambridge University Press, 2000.

Corradi, Juan, *The Fitful Republic: Economy, Society, and Politics in Argentina*, Boulder, CO: Westview Press, 1985.

Correspondence of Sir Walter Scott, with related material. Archival Material. Leeds University Library, Leeds.

Coughlan, Patricia, '"Without a blink of her lovely eye": *The Pleasure of Eliza Lynch* and visionary skepticism', *Irish University Review: A Journal of Irish Studies*, vol. 35.2, Autumn-Winter 2005, pp. 349–373.

Croker, T. Crofton, *Fairy Legends and Traditions in the South of Ireland*, London: J. Murray, 1834.

Cronin, Michael, 'Inside Out: Time and Place in Global Ireland,' *New Hibernia Review*, vol. 13.3, 2009, pp. 74–88.

Cronin, Michael G. '"He's My Country": Liberalism, Nationalism, and Sexuality in Contemporary Irish Gay Fiction', *Éire-Ireland*, vol. 39:3&4, 2004, pp. 250–267.

Crosbie, Barrie, *Irish Imperial Networks: Migration, Social Communication and Exchange in Nineteenth-Century India*, Cambridge: Cambridge University Press, 2011.

Crumpe, Mary Grace, *The Death Flag*, London: William Shoberl, 1852.

Cullingford, Eliabeth Butler. *Ireland's Others: Ethnicity and Gender in Irish Literature and Popular Culture*, University of Notre Dame Press, 1992.

Curtis, Liz, *The Cause of Ireland: From the United Irishmen to Partition*, Belfast: Beyond the Pale Publications, 1994.

Daly, Mary E., *The Slow Failure: Population Decline and Independent Ireland, 1920–1973*, Madison: University of Wisconsin Press, 2006.

Deane, Seamus, *Strange Country: Modernity and Nationhood in Irish Writing since 1790*, Oxford: Clarendon Press, 1997.

de Courcy Ireland, John, *Ireland and the Irish in Maritime History*, Dun Laoghaire: The Glendale Press, 1986.

Defoe, Daniel. *Robinson Crusoe*, London: W. Taylor, 1719.

Denny, Kenny and Cormac Ó Gráda, 'Irish Attitudes to Immigration During and After the Boom', Working Papers 201322, Geary Institute, University College Dublin, 2013.

Deparle, Jason, 'Born Irish, But with Illegal Parents', *The New York Times*, 25 Feb 2008.

Derrida, Jacques, *Specters of Marx: The State of the Debt, the Work of Mourning, and the New International*, Peggy Kamuf, trans., New York: Routledge, 1994.

Desmarais, Jane, 'Introduction', *An Essay on Irish Bulls*, Maria Edgeworth, author; Jane Desmarais and Marilyn Butler, eds. Dublin: University College Dublin Press, 2006, n. p.

Diner, Hasia R., *Erin's Daughters in America: Irish Immigrant Women in the Nineteenth Century*, Baltimore: Johns Hopkins University Press, 1983.

Doan, James and Frank Sewell, eds., *'On the Side of Light': The Poetry of Cathal Ó Searcaigh*, Galway: Arlen House, 2002.

Doyle, Roddy, *The Barrytown Trilogy*, New York: Penguin, 1995.

—, *The Deportees*, New York: Viking, 2007.

Draper, Nicholas, '"Dependent on precarious subsistences": Ireland's slave-owners at the Time of Emancipation', *Britain and the World*, vol. 6.2, 2013, pp. 220–242.

Du Bois, W. E., *The Souls of Black Folk*, New York: Penguin Books, 1996.

Dudgeon, Jeff, 'Gays and the Phoney War in Northern Ireland', *Gay Left*, Winter 1978.

Dunne, Tom, 'Maria Edgeworth and the Colonial Mind', The 26th O'Donnell Lecture. University College Cork. 27 June 1984. *O' Donnell Lectures* 26. Dublin: National University of Ireland, 1984.

Durand, Rodolphe and Vergne, Jean-Philippe, *The Pirate Organization: Lessons from the Fringes of Capitalism*, Harvard Business Review Press, 2013.

Eagleton, Terry, *Heathcliff and the Great Hunger: Studies in Irish Culture*, London: Verso, 1995.

Earls, Brian, '"By Reason of Past History": Poland Through Irish Eyes', *Dublin Review of Books*, nr 8, 2008.

Ebest, Sally Barr, 'These Traits Also Endure: Contemporary Irish and Irish-American Women Writers', *New Hibernia Review*, vol. 7.2, 2003, pp. 55–72.

Edgeworth, Maria. *The Absentee*, 1812, W.J. McCormack and Kim Walker, eds., Oxford: Oxford UP, 1988.

—, *Belinda*, 1801, Kathryn Kirkpatrick, ed., Oxford: Oxford University Press, 1999.

—, *Castle Rackrent* and *Ennui*, 1800 and 1809, Marilyn Butler, ed., London: Penguin, 1992.

—, *An Essay on Irish Bulls*. 2nd ed., London, 1802.

—, *Memoirs of Richard Lovell Edgeworth*. 2 vols. London: Hunter, 1820.

—, 'Murad The Unlucky', 1804, *Oriental Tales*, Robert L. Mack, ed., Cambridge: Cambridge University Press, 1992.

—, *Ormond*, 1817, Claire Connolly, ed., London: Penguin, 2000.

—, *Popular Tales*, 1804. London: Macmillan, 1895.

Edgeworth Family Papers. National Library of Ireland, Dublin.

Edgeworth, Michael Pakenham, *Pollen*, London: Hardwicke and Bogue, 1877.

Edgeworth, Michael Packenham, *India in the Age of Empire: The Journals of Michael Pakenham Edgeworth* (1812–1881). Bodleian Library, University of Oxford, Oxford.

Edwards, Tim, *Erotics and Politics: Gay Male Sexuality, Masculinity and Feminism*, London: Routledge, 1994.

Enright, Anne, *The Pleasure of Eliza Lynch*, New York: Grove, 2002.

Esty, Jed, 'Virgins of Empire: *The Last September* and the Antidevelopmental Plot', *Modern Fiction Studies*, vol. 53. 2, 2007, pp. 257–75.

Fanning, Bryan. *Racism and Social Change in Ireland*, Manchester: Manchester University Press, 2002.

—, *Taking Racism Seriously: Migrants' Experiences of Violence, Harassment and Anti-social Behaviour in the Dublin Area*, Immigrant Council of Ireland, 2011. <http://www.immigrantcouncil.ie/images/stories/191680_Immigrant_council_report_Final_with_cover.pdf>

Ferris, Ina, *The Romantic National Tale and the Question of Ireland*, Cambridge: Cambridge University Press, 2002.

Finnegan, Brian, ed., *Quare Fellas: New Irish Gay Writing*, Dublin: Basement Press, 1994.

Fortier, Anne-Marie, 'Making home: queer migrations and motions of attachment', published by the Department of Sociology, Lancaster University, Lancaster LA1 4YL, UK at <http://www.lancs.ac.uk/fass/sociology/papers/fortier-making-home.pdf>. Access date 13 May 2013.

—, 'Queer Diaspora', in Diane Richardson and Steven Seidman, eds., *Handbook of Lesbian and Gay Studies*, Thousand Oaks CA: Sage, 2002, pp. 183–197.

Foster, John Wilson, *Fictions of the Irish Literary Revival: A Changeling Art*, Syracuse: Syracuse University Press, 1987.

Foster, R. F., *Modern Ireland, 1600–1972*, London: Penguin Press, 1988.

Foucault, Michael, 'Of Other Spaces,' *diacritics*, vol 16.1, 1986, pp. 22–27.

Freud, Sigmund, *Civilization and its Discontents*, New York: Dover Thrift, 1994.

Fricker, Karen, 'Review of *Mixing it on the Mountains*', *Irish Theatre Magazine*, 3, 15, 2003, pp. 74–76.

Gallagher, Catherine, 'The Rise of Fictionality' in Franco Moretti, ed., *The Novel, Volume 1: History, Geography, and Culture*, Princeton, NJ: Princeton University Press, 2006, pp. 336–363.

Gates Jr., Henry Louis, *The Signifying Monkey*, New York: Oxford University Press, 1988.

Garner, Steve, *Racism in the Irish Experience*, London: Pluto Press, 2003.

Gibbons, Luke, 'Ireland, Immigration, and the Ethics of Memory', in Julieann Veronica Ulin, Heather Edwards, and Sean T. O'Brien, eds., *Race and Immigration in the New Ireland*, Notre Dame: University of Notre Dame Press, 2013, pp. 205–20.

—, '"We Knew Their Plight Well": Race and Immigration in Some Recent Irish Films', *Third Text*, vol. 19.5, 2005, pp. 557–568.

Gilroy, Paul, *Between Camps: Nations, Cultures and the Allure of Race*, London: Allen Lane, 2000.

Goethe, Johann Wolfgang von, *Die Leiden des Jungen Werther*, Weygandsche Buchhandlung, 1825.

Goldsmith, Oliver, *The Citizen of the World*, University Press of the Pacific, 2002.

Goodman, James, 'The Republic of Ireland: Towards a Cosmopolitan Nationalism?' in James Anderson and James Goodman, eds., *Dis/Agreeing Ireland: Contexts, Obstacles, Hopes*, London: Pluto, 1998, pp. 89–107.

Gordon, Avery, *Ghostly Matters: Haunting and the Sociological Imagination*, 2nd edition with new introduction, Minneapolis: U of Minnesota P, 2008.

Gray, Breda, 'The Irish Diaspora: Globalized Belonging(s)', *Irish Journal of Sociology*, vol. 11.2, 2002, pp. 123–144.

Grewal, Inderpal, *Transnational America*, Durham: Duke University Press, 2005.

Grewal, Inderpal and Caren Kaplan, 'Global Identities, Theorizing Transnational Studies of Sexuality', *GLQ: A Journal of Lesbian & Gay Studies*, vol. 7.4, 2001, pp. 663–680.

—, 'Postcolonial Studies and Transnational Feminist Practices', *Jouvert: A Journal of Postcolonial Studies*, 5.1, 2000, n. p.

Gupta, Suman, *Globalization and Literature*, Cambridge: Polity Press, 2009.

Haberstroh, Patricia Boyle and Christine St. Peter, eds., *Opening the Field: Irish Women, Texts and Contexts*, Cork: Cork University Press, 2007.

Hannerz, Ulf, *Transnational Connections: Culture, People, Places*, New York: Routledge, 1996.

Hare, Augustus J.C. ed., *The Life and Letters of Maria Edgeworth*, 2 vols. London: Edward Arnold, 1894.

Harvey, Alison, 'West Indian Obeah and English "Obee"': Race, Femininity and Questions of Colonial Consolidation in Maria Edgeworth's *Belinda*' in Julie Nash, ed., *New Essays on Maria Edgeworth*, Aldershot: Ashgate, 2006, pp. 1–29.

Healy, Alison, 'Citizenship "denied for penalty points"', *The Irish Times*, 4 November 2010.

Held, David, *Global Covenant*, Cambridge: Polity, 2004.

Helg, Aline, 'Race in Argentina and Cuba, 1880–1930', in Richard Graham, ed., *The Idea of Race in Latin America, 1870–1940*, Austin: University of Texas Press, 1990, pp. 37–70.

Herr, Cheryl, '"Re-Imagining Ireland": Rethinking Irish Studies', *New Hibernia Review*, vol. 7.4, 2003, pp. 123–135.

Hitchcock, Peter, *Imaginary States: Studies in Cultural Transnationalism*, Champaign: University of Illinois Press, 2003.

Hopkins, Frank, *Hidden Dublin: Deadbeats, Dossers and Decent Skins*, Dublin: Mercier Press, 2007.

Hulse, Michael, trans., *The Sorrows of Young Werther*, Johann Wolfgang von Goethe, auth., New York: Penguin Classics, 1989.

Immigration Control Platform, 'About Us', *Immigration Control Platform*, n.d. Web. Access date 23 June 2014.

Inglis, Tom, 'Origins and Legacies of Irish Prudery: Sexuality and Social Control in Modern Ireland', *Éire-Ireland*, vol. 40.3–4, 2005, pp. 9–37.

Iyer, Pico, *The Global Soul: Jet Lag, Shopping Malls, and the Search for Home*, Knopf, 2000.

Jameson, Fredric, 'A Businessman in Love' in Franco Moretti, ed., *The Novel, Volume 2: Forms and Themes*, Princeton, NJ: Princeton University Press, 2006, pp. 436–446.

Jay, Paul, *Global Matters: The Transnational Turn in Literary Studies*, Ithaca, New York, 2010.

Jenks, Chris, 'Watching Your Step: The History and Practice of the *Flâneur*' in Chris Jenks, ed., *Visual Culture*, London: Routledge, 1995, pp. 142–160.

Jones, Darryl, '"Distorted Nature in a Fever": *Irish Bulls*, Irish Novels, the 1798 Rebellion and their Gothic Contexts', in Heidi Kaufman and Christopher J. Fauske, eds., *An Uncomfortable Authority: Maria Edgeworth and Her Contexts*, Newark: University of Delaware Press, 2004, pp. 127–45.

Jordan, Don and Michael Walsh, *White Cargo: The Forgotten History of Britain's White Slaves in America*, New York: New York University Press, 2008.

Journal of the Royal Society of Antiquaries of Ireland, Vol. VIII, Fourth Series, Dublin: University Press, 1888.

Jowitt, Claire, *Pirates? The Politics of Plunder, 1550–1650*, London: Palgrave Macmillan, 2007.

Kaminsky, Amy K., *Argentina: Stories for a Nation*, Minneapolis: University of Minnesota Press, 2008.

Karsten, Peter, 'Irish Soldiers in the British Army, 1792–1922: Suborned or Subordinate?', *Journal of Social History*, vol. 17.1, 1983, pp. 31–64.

Kay, Sean, *Celtic Revival? The Rise, Fall, and Renewal of Global Ireland*, New York: Rowman & Littlefield, 2011.

Keating-Miller, Jennifer, 'Explorations of affiliation: Irish indentured servitude in the English West Indies', *Working Papers in Irish Studies*, Dept. of English, Winthrop University. 8.3, 2008, pp. 3–25.

Kennedy, Kieran. '"Oirféas as gach *orifice*": The Irish Language Question, Globalization and Homosexuality', in Doan and Sewell (eds., *'On the Side of Light': The Poetry of Cathal Ó Searcaigh*, Galway: Arlen House, 2002, pp. 107–132.

Kiberd, Declan, *The Irish Writer and the World*, Cambridge: Cambridge University Press, 2005.

Kilroy, Thomas, 'Adaptation: a privileged conversation with a dead author', *The Irish Times*, 13 Feb. 2010, p. 9.

Kim, Young Yun, *Becoming Intercultural*, London: Sage Publications, 2001.

Kirby, Peadar, *Ireland and Latin America: Links and Lessons*, Dublin: Gill and MacMillan, 1992.

Kirkpatrick, Kathryn J., '"Gentlemen Have Horrors upon This Subject": West Indian Suitors in Maria Edgeworth's *Belinda*', *Eighteenth-Century Fiction*, vol. 5.4, 1993, pp. 331–348.

Kuhling, Carmen and Kieran Keohane, *Cosmopolitan Ireland: Globalisation and Quality of Life*, London: Pluto Press, 2007.

Lanters, Jose, 'Cobwebs on your walls: The State of the Debate about Globalisation and Irish Drama' in Ondrej Pilny and Clare Wallace, eds, *Global Ireland*, Prague: Literaria Pragensia, 2005, pp. 33–44.

Lawless, Emily, *Maria Edgeworth*, 1904, Honolulu, HI: University Press of the Pacific, 2004.

Leerssen, Joep, *Remembrance and Imagination: Patterns in the Historical and Literary Representations of Ireland in the Nineteenth Century*, Cork: Cork University Press, 1997.

Lennon, Joseph, *Irish Orientalism: A Literary and Intellectual History*, Syracuse: Syracuse University Press, 2004.

Lentin, Ronit and Robbie McVeigh, *After Optimism?: Ireland, Anti-Racist Responses*, Dublin: Metro Éireann Publications, 2006.

—, 'Anti-Racist Responses to the Racialisation of Irishness: Disavowed Multiculturalism and its Discontent' in Ronit Lentin and Robbie McVeigh, eds, *Racism and Anti-Racism*, Belfast: Beyond the Pale Publications, 2002, pp 226–238.

—, *Migrant Activism and Integration from Below in Ireland*, New York: Palgrave McMillan, 2012.

Liddy, James, *I Only Know That I Love Strength in My Friends and Greatness*, Galway: Arlen House, 2003.

The Life and Adventures of John Connor, commonly called Jack the Bachelor, the famous Irish bucker, Anonymous, Dublin: William Jones, 1785 and 1821.

Lionnet, Françoise and Shu-mei Shih, 'Introduction. Thinking through the Minor, Transnationally', in Françoise Lionnet and Shu-mei Shih, eds., *Minor Transnationalism*, London: Duke University Press, 2005.

Lloyd, David, *Anomalous States: Irish Writing and the Post-colonial Moment*, Dublin: Lilliput, 1993, pp. 229–237.

—, 'Afterword: Hardress Cregan's Dream', in Jacqueline Belanger, ed., *The Irish Novel in the Nineteenth Century: Facts and Fictions*, Dublin: Four Courts Press, 2005, pp. 229–237.

Loeber, Rolf and Magda, *A Guide to Irish Fiction, 1650–1900*, Dublin: Four Courts Press, 2006.

Lonergan, Patrick, Review of *The Cambria*, *Irish Theatre Magazine*, vol. 5.23, 2005, p. 63.

Loyal, Steve, 'Welcome to the Celtic Tiger: racism, immigration and the state' in Colin Coulter and Steve Coleman, eds., *The end of Irish history? Critical reflections on the Celtic Tiger*, Manchester University Press, 2003, pp. 74–94.

Luibhéid, Eithne, 'Introduction: Queering Migration and Citizenship', in Eithne Luibhéid and Lionel Cantú Jr., eds., *Queer Migrations: Sexuality, U.S. Citizenship, and Border Crossings*, Minneapolis: University of Minnesota, 2005, pp. ix–xlvi.

Lyons, F.S.L., *Ireland Since the Famine*, New York: Scribner, 1973.

Mac an Ghaill, Martin, 'Beyond a black-white dualism: racialization and racism in the Republic of Ireland and the Irish diaspora experience', *Irish Journal of Sociology*, 3.2, 2002, pp. 99–122.

MacDonnell, Eneas, *The Hermit of Glenconella*, London: G. Cowie and Co., 1820.

Madden, Ed, 'Queering the Irish Diaspora: David Rees and Padraig Rooney', *Éire-Ireland* vol. 47.1–2, 2012, pp. 172–200.

Malouf, Michael, 'Feeling Éire(y)': On Irish-Caribbean Popular Culture', in Diane Negra, ed., *The Irish in Us: Irishness, Performativity, and Popular Culture*, Durham: Duke University Press, 2006, pp. 318–53.

—, *Transatlantic Solidarities: Irish Nationalism and Caribbean Poetics*, Charlottesville: University of Virginia Press, 2009.

Manwaring, G. E. and Dobree, Bonamy, *The Floating Republic: An Account of the Mutinies at Spithead and Nore in 1797*, Pen and Sword Military Classics, 1935.

Martin, Emer, *More Bread or I'll Appear*, London: Allison and Busby Limited, 2000.

Mastin, Antoinette M., 'Stephen Dedalus in Paris?: Joycean Elements in Julia O'Faolain's *Three Lovers*', *Colby Quarterly*, 1994, pp. 244–51.

Maurer, Sara L., 'Disowning to Own: Maria Edgeworth and the Illegitimacy of National Ownership', *Criticism*, 44, 2002, pp. 363–388.

Maxwell, William, *The Dark Lady of Doona*, London: Smith and Elder and Co., 1834.

McCafferty, Kate, *Testimony of an Irish Slave Girl*, New York: Penguin, 2003.

McCann, Colum, *Let the Great World Spin*, New York: Random House, 2009.

—, *Songdogs*, New York: Picador, 1995.

McCracken, Donald, *Forgotten Protest: Ireland and the Anglo-Boer Wars*, Belfast: Ulster Historical Foundation, 2003.

McGuinness, Frank, *Booterstown*, Loughcrew, Oldcastle, County Meath: Gallery Books, 1994.

McIvor, Charlotte, 'Staging the "New Irish": Interculturalism and the Future of the Post-Celtic Tiger Irish Theatre', *Modern Drama*, 54.3, 2011, pp. 310–332.

McKenna, Patrick, 'Irish Migration to Argentina' in Patrick O'Sullivan, ed., *Patterns of Migration*, Leicester: Leicester University Press, 1995, pp. 63–83.

—, 'Nineteenth Century Irish Emigration to, and Settlement in, Argentina,' M.Phil, National University of Ireland, Maynooth, 1994.

McKeon, Michael, *Origins of the English Novel*, 1600–1740, Baltimore, MD: Johns Hopkins University Press, 2002.

McLynn, Frank. 'Ireland and the Jacobite Rising of 1745', *Irish Sword*, 13 (1979), pp. 339–52.

Meaney, Gerardine, *Gender, Ireland and Cultural Change: Race, Sex and Nation*, New York: Routledge, 2010.

Metcalf, Barbara Daly and Metcalf, Thomas R., *A Concise History of Modern India*, 2nd ed. Cambridge: Cambridge UP, 2006.

Mickle, William, 'There's Nae Luck About the House', in Roger Lonsdale, ed., *The New Oxford Book of Eighteenth-Century Verse*, Oxford: Oxford UP, 1984, pp. 551–52.

Migration Policy Institute, http://migrationpolicy.org Access date 13 Mar. 2013

Moretti, Franco, *Atlas of the European Novel*, New York: Verso, 1999.

—, 'Conjectures on World Literature', *New Left Review*, vol. 1, 2000, pp. 54–68.

—, *Distant Reading*, London: Verso, 2013.

Mulhall, Anne, 'Forms of Exile: Reading *Cyphers*', *Irish University Review* vol. 37.1, 2007, pp. 206–229.

Murphy, James, *Irish Novelists in the Victorian Age*, Oxford: Oxford University Press, 2011.

Murphy, Sharon, 'Imperial Reading? The East India Company's Lending Libraries for Soldiers, c.1819–1834', *Book History* 12, 2009, pp. 74–99.

Murray, Edmundo, *How the Irish Became Gauchos Ingleses: Diasporic Models in Irish-Argentine Literature*, Palo Alto, CA: Academica Press, 2009.

Murray, Patrick, 'Introduction', *The Playboy of the Western World*, Dublin: Criterion Press Limited, 1986.

Murray, Thomas, *The Story of the Irish in Argentina*, New York: P.J. Kennedy & Sons, 1919.

Myers, Mitzi, 'Goring John Bull: Maria Edgeworth's Hibernian Jinks Versus the Imperialist Imaginary', in James E. Gill, ed., *Cutting Edges: Postmodern Critical Essays on Eighteenth-Century Satire*, Knoxville, TN: University of Tennessee Press, 1995, pp. 367–394.

Negra, Diane, 'Irishness, Innocence, and American Identity Politics before and after September 11', in Diane Negra, ed., *The Irish in Us: Irishness, Performativity, and Popular Culture*, Durham: Duke University Press, 2006, pp. 354–71.

Nevin, Kathleen, *You'll Never Go Back*, Maynooth: Cardinal Press, 1999.

Nixon, Cheryl L., ed., *Novel Definitions: an Anthology of Commentary on the Novel*, London: Broadview Press, 2009.

O'Brien, Eugene, '"*What Ish My Nation?*": Towards a Negative Definition of Identity', *Minerva: An Internet Journal of Philosophy*, vol. 2, 1998, <http://www.ul.ie/~philos/vol2/negation.html> Access date 18 May 2013.

—, 'Introduction: A Yellow Spot on the Snow / Réamhrá: Ball Buí ar an tSneachta' in Cathal Ó Searcaigh, *Homecoming: Selected Poems / An Bealach 'na Bhaile: Rogha Dánta*, Gabriel Fitzmaurice, ed., Indreabhán, Conamara: Cló Iar-Chonnachta, 1993, pp. 13–40.

O'Callaghan, Evelyn, 'Re-working the Slave Narrative? Fictions of White Indentured Servitude in the Caribbean', in Judith Misrahi-Barak, ed., *Revisiting Slave Narratives / Les avatars contemporains des récits d'esclaves*, Montpellier: Presses universitaires de la Méditerranée, 2005, pp. 397–424.

O'Callaghan, Seán, *To Hell or Barbados: The Ethnic Cleansing of Ireland*, Dingle: Brandon, 2000.

Ó Ciardha, Éamonn, *Ireland and the Jacobite Cause*. Dublin: Four Courts Press, 2002.

Ó Conchubhair, Brian, 'Cathal Ó Searcaigh: Teip Agus Téagar na Teanga / Falling Down and Falling Back on Language', in Doan and Sewell, eds., *'On the Side of Light': The Poetry of Cathal Ó Searcaigh*, Galway: Arlen House, 2002, pp. 167–204.

O'Connor, Joseph, *Desperadoes*, London: Flamingo, 1995.

—, *Redemption Falls*, New York: Free Press, 2007.

O'Faolain, Julia, *Three Lovers*, New York: Coward, McCann & Geoghegan, 1971.

Ó Gallchoir, Clíona, 'Gender, Nation and Revolution: Maria Edgeworth and Stéphanie-Félicité de Genlis' in Elizabeth Eger, Charlotte Grant, Clíona Ó Gallchoir, Penny Warburton, eds., *Women, Writing and the Public Sphere, 1700–1830*, Cambridge: Cambridge University Press, 2001, pp. 200–217.

—, *Maria Edgeworth: Women, Enlightenment and Nation*, Dublin: University College Dublin Press, 2005.

Ó Gráda, Cormac, *Jewish Ireland in the Age of Joyce: A Socioeconomic History*, Princeton, New Jersey: Princeton University Press, 2006.

O'Hare, Shawn, 'Joseph O'Connor', in Robert Hogan, ed., *Dictionary of Irish Literature*, vol II, Westport: Greenwood Press, p. 947.

Ó Laoire, Lillis, 'Dearg Dobhogtha Cháin / The Indelible Mark of Cain: Sexual Dissidence in the Poetry of Cathal Ó Searcaigh', in Éibhear Walshe, ed., *Sex, Nation, and Dissent in Irish Writing*, New York: St Martin's Press, 1997, pp. 221–234.

O'Malley, Kate, *Ireland, India, and Empire: Indo-Irish Radical Connections, 1919–1964*, Manchester University Press, 2010.

Ó Searcaigh, Cathal, *Homecoming: Selected Poems / An Bealach 'na Bhaile: Rogha Dánta*, Gabriel Fitzmaurice, ed., Indreabhán, Conamara: Cló Iar-Chonnachta, 1993.

—, *Light on Distant Hills: A Memoir*, London: Simon and Schuster, 2009.

—, *Out in the Open*, Frank Sewell, trans., Indreabhán, Conamara: Cló Iar-Chonnachta, 1997.

Ó Siochrú, Micheál, *God's Executioner: Oliver Cromwell and the Conquest of Ireland*, London: Faber and Faber Limited, 2008.

O'Toole, Fintan, 'A Gallous Story and a Dirty Deed: Druid's Synge' in Colm Tóibín, ed, *Synge: A Celebration*, Dublin: Carysfort Press, 2006, pp. 33–47.

Owenson, Sydney, (Lady Morgan), *The Wild Irish Girl: A National Tale*, Hartford: Silas Andrus & Son, 1855.

Paige, Nicholas, *Before Fiction: the Ancien Regime of the Novel*, Philadelphia, PA: University of Pennsylvania Press, 2011.

Papademetriou, Demetrios G., 'Rethinking National Identity in the Age of Migration', Council Statement, Migration Policy Institute, February 2012. Washington DC: MPI, pp. 1–10.

Pavis, Patrice, *Theatre and Crossroads of Cultures*, Routledge: London, 1992.

Pethica, James L. and James C. Roy, 'Introduction', '*To the Land of the Free from this Island of Slaves': Henry Stratford Persse's Letters from Galway to America, 1821–1832*, Cork: Cork University Press, 1998.

Phillips, Ursula, trans., *Malvina, or the Heart's Intuition*, Maria Wirtemberska, auth., Clark, NJ: Polish Cultural Foundation, 2001.

Pittock, Murray, 'Jacobite Literature and National Identities' in David J. Baker and Willy Maley, eds., *British Identities and English Renaissance Literature*, Cambridge: Cambridge University Press, 2002, pp. 226–42.

Pratt, Mary Louise, *Imperial Eyes: Travel Writing and Transculturation*, New York: Routledge, 1992.

Ramazani, Jahan, *A Transnational Poetics*, Chicago and London: University of Chicago Press, 2009.

Reddy, Maureen, 'Talking the Talk: Codes of Racialization', in Borbála Faragó and Moynagh Sullivan, eds., *Facing the Other*, Newcastle: Cambridge Scholars Publishing, 2008, pp. 220–31.

Rediker, Marcus, *Villains of All Nations*, Boston: Beacon Press, 2004.

Reeve, Clara, *The Progress of Romance Through Times, Countries and Manners; with Remarks on the Good and Bad Effects of it, On them Respectively, in a Course of Evening Conversations*, Vol. 1, New York: Fascimile Text Society, 1930. Reproduction of the Colchester edition of 1785.

Robertson, Roland, *Globalization: Social Theory and Global Culture*, London: Sage Publications, 1992.

Rock, David, *Argentina, 1516–1987: From Spanish Colonization to Alfonsín*, Berkeley: University of California Press, 1987.

Rodgers, Nini, *Ireland, Slavery and Anti-Slavery: 1612–1865*, New York: Palgrave Macmillan, 2007.

Rolston, Bill and Michael Shannon, *Encounters: How Racism Came to Ireland*, Belfast: Beyond the Pale Publications, 2002.

Rooks-Hughes, Lorna, 'The Family and the Female Body in the Novels of Edna O'Brien and Julia O'Faolain', *Canadian Journal of Irish Studies*, 22.2, 1996, pp. 83–97.

Rooney, Padraig, *The Escape Artist*, Westgate, Huddersfield: Smith/Doorstop, 2006.
—, *The Fever Wards*, London: Salt, 2010.

Roudometof, Victor, 'Transnationalism, Cosmopolitanism, and Glocalization', *Current Sociology*, vol. 53.113, 2005, pp. 113–135.

Roux, Daniel, 'Hybridity, Othello and the Postcolonial Critics', *Shakespeare in Southern Africa*, vol. 21, 2009, pp. 23–29.

Rushdy, Ashraf H., 'The Politics of the Neo-Slave Narratives', in Judith Misrahi-Barak, ed., *Revisiting Slave Narratives / Les avatars contemporains des récits d'esclaves*, Montpellier: Presses universitaires de la Méditerranée, 2005, pp. 91–102.

Said, Edward W., *Orientalism*, New York: Vintage, 1979.

—, *Reflections on Exile and Other Essays*, Cambridge, MA: Harvard, 2000.

Schiller, Nina Glick; Basch, Linda; Szanton-Blanc, Cristina, 'From Immigrant to Transmigrant: Theorizing Transnational Migration', *Anthropological Quarterly*, 68.1, 1995, pp. 48–63.

Sewell, Frank, 'Preface' in Ó Searcaigh, *Out in the Open*. Frank Sewell, trans., Indreabhán, Conamara: Cló Iar-Chonnachta, 1997, pp. 13–15.

—, 'Between Staisiún Chaiseal na gCorr and Stantzia Zimá: the poetry of Cathal Ó Searcaigh', in Doan and Sewell, eds., *'On the Side of Light': The Poetry of Cathal Ó Searcaigh*, Galway: Arlen House, 2002, pp. 57–86.

Shapiro, Rebecca, 'Educating the English: Maria Edgeworth's *Castle Rackrent* and "Essay on Irish Bulls"', *Women's Writing*, vol. 10.1, 2003, pp. 73–92.

Shumway, Nicolas, *The Invention of Argentina*, Berkeley and Los Angeles, CA: University of California Press, 1991.

Sihra, Melissa, 'Re-location and Re-locution: Adapting Synge' in Patrick Lonergan, ed., *Synge and His Influences*, Dublin: Carysfort Press, 2011, pp. 225–243.

Singleton, Brian, 'Performing Conflict Migration and Testimony' in Karen Fricker and Ronit Lentin, eds, *Performing Global Networks*, Cambridge: Cambridge Scholars Publishing, 2007, pp. 25–37.

Skerries Historical Society, 'Some Interesting Characters', <http://www.oldskerries.ie/lochist/30chars.html> Access date 23 June, 2014.

Smith, James M., 'The Politics of Sexual Knowledge: The Origins of Ireland's Containment Culture and the Carrigan Report (1931)', *Journal of the History of Sexuality*, vol. 13.2, 2004, pp. 208–33.

Smyth, Jaime, 'Refugee Recognition Rate Draws Concern', *The Irish Times*, 25 May 2011.

Sorenson, Ninna Nyberg, ed., *Living Across Worlds: Diaspora, Development and Transnational Engagement*, International Organization for Migration, 2007.

Soyinka, Wole, *Conversations with Soyinka*, ed. Jeyifo Biodun, Jackson: University Press of Mississippi, 2001.

Spangler, Matthew, 'The New Irish in Irish Theatre: Arambe Productions and Irish/West African Performance', *SIAR: The Journal of the Western Institute of Irish Studies*, vol. 2.1, 2008, n. p.

Sundquist, Eric, *To Wake the Nations: Race in the Making of American Literature*, Cambridge, Massachusetts: Harvard University Press, 1993.

Sweeney, Fionnghuala, *Frederick Douglass and the Atlantic World*, Liverpool: Liverpool University Press, 2007.

Synge, J.M., *The Aran Islands*, London: Serif, 2008.

—, Preface in *The Playboy of the Western World*, Bloomsbury: Methuen Drama, 1983.

Talbott, William J., *Which Rights Should Be Universal?*, New York: Oxford UP, 2005.

Toporek, Rebecca L., 'Violence against Individuals and Communities: Reflecting on the Trayvon Martin Case – An Introduction to the Special Issue', *Journal For Social Action In Counseling & Psychology*, vol. 5.1, 2013, pp. 1–10.

Townsend, Sarah, 'Belated Development and the Irish *Bildungsroman*', American Conference for Irish Studies, 17 Mar. 2012. Conference presentation.

Tucker, Amanda, 'Strangers in a Strange Land: The New Irish Multicultural Fiction' in Pilar Villa-Argáiz, *Celtic Others: Irish Literary Representations of the Migrant*, Manchester: Manchester University Press, 2014, pp. 50–62.

Urry, John, *Consuming Places*, London: Routledge, 1995.

Vegso, Robert, 'The Mother Tongues of Modernity: Modernism, Transnationalism, Translation' *Journal of Modern Literature*, vol. 33, 2010, pp. 24–46.

Villar Argaiz, Pilar, ed., *Celtic Others: Irish Literary Representations of the Migrant*, Manchester: Manchester University Press, 2014.

Walkowitz, Judith, *City of Dreadful Delight: Narratives of Sexual Danger in Late-Victorian London*, Chicago: University of Chicago Press, 1992.

Watt, Ian, *The Rise of the Novel: Studies in Richardson, Defoe, and Fielding*, Oakland, CA: University of California Press, 1957.

Williams, Eric, *From Columbus to Castro: The History of the Caribbean 1492–1969*, 1970, New York: Vintage, 1984.

Williams, Raymond, *Marxism and Literature*, Oxford: Oxford University Press, 1977.

Wirtemberska, Maria, *Malwina, czyli domyślność serca* (Wirtualna Biblioteka Literatura Polskiej: Instytut Filologii Polskiej Uniwersytetu Gdańskiego).

Wright, Julia M., *Ireland, India and Nationalism in Nineteenth-Century Literature*, Cambridge: Cambridge UP, 2007.

Woods, C.J., ed., *Journals and memoirs of Thomas Russell*, 1791–5, Dublin: Irish Academic Press, 1991.

Yeoh, Brenda S. A.; Karen P. Y. Lai; Charney, Michael W; and Kiong, Tong Chee, 'Approaching Transnationalisms' in *Approaching Transnationalisms: Studies on Transnational Societies, Multicultural Contacts, and Imaginings of Home*, Boston: Kluwer, 2003, pp. 1–12.

Yerima, Ahmed, *Basic Techniques in Playwriting*, Nigeria: Kraft Books Limited, 2003.

Index